Unfettered Expression

The University of Michigan Senate's
Davis, Markert, Nickerson Lecture
on Academic and Intellectual Freedom

February 18, 1991	Robert M. O'Neil
April 20, 1992	Lee C. Bollinger
February 18, 1993	Catharine R. Stimpson
March 21, 1994	Walter P. Metzger
March 20, 1995	Linda Ray Pratt
October 21, 1996	Avern Cohn
March 17, 1997	Roger Wood Wilkins
March 16, 1998	Eugene L. Roberts Jr.
March 15, 1999	David A. Hollinger

Unfettered Expression

Freedom in American Intellectual Life

Edited by *Peggie J. Hollingsworth*

With a foreword
by *David Halberstam*

Ann Arbor

The University of Michigan Press

Copyright © by the University of Michigan 2000
All rights reserved
Published in the United States of America by
The University of Michigan Press
Manufactured in the United States of America
⊗ Printed on acid-free paper

2003   2002   2001   2000   4   3   2   1

*A CIP catalog record for this book is available
from the British Library.*

Library of Congress Cataloging-in-Publication Data

Unfettered expression : freedom in American intellectual life / edited by
Peggie J. Hollingsworth ; with a foreword by David Halberstam.
p.   cm.
Lectures given at the University of Michigan from 1991 to 1999.
ISBN 0-472-11179-5 (alk. paper)
1. Academic freedom—United States.   2. Freedom of speech—
United States.   I. Hollingsworth, Peggie J.

LC72.2 .U64   2000
378.1'21—dc21   00-060199

Contents

Foreword
David Halberstam
vii

Acknowledgments
xvii

Lecture Honorees
xix

Introduction
Peggie J. Hollingsworth
1

Academic Freedom in Retrospect and in Prospect
Robert M. O'Neil
19

The Open-Minded Soldier and the University
Lee C. Bollinger
31

Dirty Minds, Dirty Bodies, Clean Speech
Catharine R. Stimpson
51

A Stroll along the New Frontiers of Academic Freedom
Walter P. Metzger
73

Academic Freedom and the Merits of Uncertainty
Linda Ray Pratt
99

Contents

A Federal Trial Judge Looks at Academic Freedom
Avern Cohn
117

Opportunity and Academic Integrity
Roger W. Wilkins
137

Free Speech, Free Press, Free Society
Eugene L. Roberts Jr.
151

Money and Academic Freedom
a Half-Century after McCarthyism:
Universities amid the Force Fields of Capital
David A. Hollinger
161

Contributors
185

Foreword

As I write this foreword a crude baseball pitcher named John Rocker has become something of a celebrity in Sports America by dint of saying some truly appalling things about the citizens of New York—the color of their hair (mostly purple, it would seem), their sexual orientation, whether they are HIV positive, and, of course, the places of their birth. He seems to think of himself as a real American and others, whom he dislikes and chooses not to understand, as foreigners. His statements, coarse and ugly, turned him almost immediately into a cause célèbre (which I suspect he wanted) and something of an embarrassment to the owners of his team, the Atlanta Braves, and his teammates (which I suspect he did not). The future of his career, despite the fact that he is young and talented and left handed (which makes him a potential gem in the world of relief pitchers), is somewhat in doubt.

I cite the Rocker case, unlikely though it may seem, in connection with this exceptional collection of essays on much the same subject for two reasons. The first is the obvious one, for one of the things at the heart of the Rocker controversy is the issue of free speech. After all, we know there are all kinds of people out there, nativists at heart, who feel similarly about New York and other large, socially diverse cities. So the question arises: Does a crude, irritating, and not very bright young man have the right to say deeply offensive things about other Americans—to do something so odiously un-American in our national pastime? The answer, I think, is yes, there is an inalienable right in this society to be dumb and crude. Freedom of speech belongs to louts as well as to saints. Nor should he be sent to some psychological reeducation camp, as others have suggested—exactly the kind of thing the Soviets used to do with their dissenters.

But because this is a market-driven society, the limits on Rocker's words are probably set by a number of things, most critically performance. Baseball fans being who they are (civil liberties issues are secondary to issues of ability), they will probably not boycott a favored, successful team just because one player says dopey things. And indeed because this is a large, diverse society undergoing major social and economic change at an ever-accelerating rate, all kinds of fellow Americas covertly and sometimes overtly agree with Rocker.

Well, then, is there any kind of limit on someone like Rocker and what he says? I would suggest that there is, and it is not just the general public's essential good taste and decency, no small thing on its own. I would suggest that there is another very important and subtle check on Rocker, and that is the good opinion and well wishes of his teammates, who are, given the nature of our ever more pluralistic society, likely to be what he condemns. Many of them are what he calls foreigners, born in foreign lands, and some who are native sons come from groups that have long been shunned and are uncommonly sensitive to the kind of ethnic slurs that seem to emanate so readily from Rocker's mouth. John Rocker's problem in the long run is not as likely to be political correctness as it is to be the goodwill of his teammates, who are considered to be among the most thoughtful and attractive players in Major League Baseball. If he doesn't straighten up and fly right, he may soon find himself out of Atlanta, a favored team of quality people that always contends for the championship, and instead on his way to one of those teams that are the baseball equivalent of Siberia. This is probably, in a society like ours, as it should be; or, as the words of the Gilbert and Sullivan song suggest, let the punishment fit the crime.

There is a second thing that is important about Rocker's case and that is the fact that it is of concern at all, because in another era, one that I remember all too well, almost everyone in baseball used all kinds of what are now considered ethnic slurs. It was simply a part of the contemporary vernacular; the older, more settled ethnic groups felt free to describe those more newly arrived with words that had a certain cruelty to them. On the Yankees team of the 1940s, baseball's best and most elegant team, the great Joe DiMaggio was known as Big Dago and his teammate Phil Rizzuto was known as Little Dago to their teammates. Other players were known as and called kikes and guineas, niggers and polacks. You would not want to know the slurs that came out of the Philadelphia Phillies dugout when Jackie Robinson first came up. It got a little better for Robinson when Don Newcombe, the great black fastball pitcher, joined him in Brooklyn. There was an old coach on the Phillies team named McDonald who was noted for his vituperative bench jockeying against the black Dodgers. Finally after a few seasons Robinson, by then a good deal more sure of his place in the game, ordered his teammate Newcombe to drill one of the Philly hitters. Newk did just that, throwing at Del Ennis, then their best hitter, and just missing his head. Ennis immediately called time-out, walked over to the bench, and told McDonald to shut the hell up because Ennis was the guy who had to pay for McDonald's big mouth. If he did not shut up, Ennis said, he would tear McDonald's tongue out. That is how things got sorted out in the old days.

Even in the early 1970s, Leo Durocher, a man whose roots were in a very different and less sensitized America and who did not know better (and had little intention of learning better) referred to Ken Holtzman, one of his star pitchers, as the Kike. When someone mentioned the insensitivity of his nomenclature, Durocher said, in his own defense, that that was what they had called Jews when he was young and that was what he was going to keep on calling them. Durocher was on the last leg of a long and volatile career, and his attitudes in almost every way were about to make him ineligible to handle the new, more sensitive, more outspoken athletes of the 1970s and 1980s, many of them black and Hispanic and unwilling to tolerate ethnic slurs. Clearly we have all come a long way, baby.

I think the preceding is germane to the topic under discussion. We are, in matters such as this, talking about historical evolution. The subject of academic freedom became a heated one in the postwar years when it came under assault from the right, principally Senator Joseph McCarthy and the lesser McCarthys of the time, who in a time of national anxiety often seemed to take some pleasure in confusing ideas that challenged contemporary political orthodoxy with issues of espionage, something very different. These men made a brief name for themselves by pursuing academics who were different, were presumed to be on the far left, had on occasion been fellow travelers, or had refused to sign loyalty oaths. It was, for a brief time, that most anxious moment of the post–World War II years when the two new superpowers were sorting out their relationships, the hot button issue in academia.

We would do well to remember the historical context. America had been catapulted almost overnight from sleepy isolationist nation to superpower status. That status was, I think, and is an important part of the equation; largely unwanted, only very slowly did it become a comfortable fit. A recent ally, the Soviet Union quickly became a sworn adversary in the postwar tensions, and we entered a long, difficult struggle with the Soviets—the cold war. Worse, the combination of modern technology—nuclear warheads and bombs carried by rockets and jet bombers—had deprived us of our two longtime security blankets, the Atlantic and the Pacific. Our two great oceans had been shrunk to the size of ponds by the new weaponry. Suddenly we felt vulnerable, consigned to a formidable new historical role we were not entirely sure we wanted to accept. This, by the way, was particularly true in the Midwest, where isolationism was unusually powerful and where the *Chicago Tribune* was the dominating paper, one that seemed to send out steady signals that in World War II we might have been fighting on the wrong side against the wrong enemy.

The political equation of the late 1940s and early 1950s was very painful. Mao had come to power on the mainland of China, and many Americans did not lightly accept the vagaries of history; they believed that if beloved China had gone communist, then there must be a conspiracy at work that had caused it. To them we had lost China, which was unthinkable, as if China with its then 600 million people had ever been ours. An ever-escalating arms race with the Soviets was in full flight. In addition, the Democrats had held the presidency in five straight elections, the elemental economic issues of the time in a blue-collar economy greatly favored them, and as such the Republicans, even men like Bob Taft who knew better, were delighted to use the issue of subversion and loyalty against the Democrats. McCarthy became the accidental demagogue who lent his name to a difficult, edgy time, even though in the words of George Reedy, who covered him, he would not have been able to tell the difference between Karl Marx and Groucho Marx and probably could not have found a communist in Red Square.

From that flowed the McCarthy period. Much of the activity focused on college campuses, which were for a variety of obvious reasons unusually vulnerable to witch-hunts. Some universities stood tall, some bent a little, and some bent a lot. In time, over the ensuing decade, the nation made its accommodation to its new and anxious status, the fears receded, ordinary people adjusted to living in a nuclear age, and the political rationale for much of McCarthyism died down (in no small part because Dwight Eisenhower, a Republican, soon replaced Truman in the White House, and so there was less political capital to be made from the exploitation of security as an issue). From the experiences of those who bent in that period when they should not have, there is much to be learned. Why, after all, was there such a loss of faith in freedom and elemental fair play? How could a cartoon figure such as McCarthy cause such trembling on the part of those who should have known better? Those questions are celebrated and honored in this lecture series; as we deal with them now we must be aware not merely of the failures of the past but that questions of honor and decency and belief in the Bill of Rights cast themselves up again and again, often in new disguise, often with the forces of free speech now necessarily aligned behind people who are odious and pitted against people who are in some ways more politically sympathetic. We have met the would-be hero of this new era, and he is likely to be, regrettably, John Rocker and others like him.

For now, as it becomes clear from reading these varying essays, there is a new kind of freedom of speech controversy on campus, this one infinitely more complicated and painful because more often than not it places those who believe most passionately in the rights of free speech in a difficult situation—one in which groups that have been historically vulnerable within the society and are properly and naturally sensitive about any kind of ethnic slurs are protesting not only casual (and not so casual) slurs against them but books that they do not like, and on occasion ideas that they do not like, and professors and courses with which they disagree. It is not just David Duke who becomes the enemy but Mark Twain with *Huckleberry Finn* as well. Inevitably it places free speech advocates in conflict with groups whose backgrounds and histories and purposes they have reason to be sympathetic with, those who in the past have been the most vulnerable of the society but who now in their newly asserted anger and their sensitivity to slights of the past seem ready to sweep safeguards of free speech away.

I think there is a certain historical inevitability as to why this is happening now, and some of that can be readily gleaned from Roger Wilkins's excellent essay in this collection. After all, in the fifty-one years since Wilkins arrived here as the loneliest young black man imaginable, America has become an infinitely more inclusive society. If anyone were to try and categorize the second half of the twentieth century in the United States it would be, I think, to describe it as the coming of a more inclusive society, starting with the arrival of Jackie Robinson in Major League Baseball in 1947 and *Brown v. Board of Education* in 1954. Those who had long been suppressed historically have now begun to find their place in America and are no longer scorned, and they are finding their place first and foremost at our great universities. The invisible have become the visible. At the same time, some of those who once assumed a kind of natural position of superiority, white native sons, often feel more vulnerable than ever; they find it harder to get into certain colleges that now accept students from an ever broader base. Collisions occur. All kinds of groups—blacks, Hispanics, Asian Americans, women, gays—once suppressed, silent, or invisible, have become not only more visible but also more confident, more outspoken, and more politicized. Many have formed their own caucuses. They are quick to protest, eager to strike back in honor of those who were never given such a chance.

In the old days, at the Michigan of the early 1950s, as on most campuses back then, blacks were not only virtually invisible but also unlikely to protest any affront other than the burning of a cross. Gays were by and large incognito, anxious to pass as straight, and unlikely to call attention to themselves. Women were just beginning what would be a long, historic process to break out of existing gender stereotypes—driven in part in the ensuing years by political changes, technological changes (in contraception), and economic changes (i.e., a workplace that depended less and less on muscularity and more and more on brains).

Not surprisingly, these political changes—profound as they are—have had considerable impact on the campuses, not just as different groups want to assert their rights but as they demand retribution for historic wrongs, slights, and injustices. In addition they often demand changes in the curriculum. As in a different way the university was vulnerable during the McCarthy era when a certain kind of politician wanted to make an easy name for himself, it is vulnerable again; it is a great deal easier to make an assault at a university than at a Fortune 500 company. For much more than most places in the private sector, the university is now a place in which newly minted social and ethnic forces find themselves in conflict with older ones; it is in many ways the battlefield on which the new America challenges the old one. All of this, the unleashing of new social force, creates the possibility for all kinds of confrontation between the traditionalists, those who want academe to remain exactly as it was in the 1950s, a place where no one but white men studied the works of other white men, and those newly arrived and newly empowered. And to some degree the new voices are right about the curriculum of the 1950s—it was too white and European oriented, and there was too little about the colonial conquest of the Third World and the price paid by those conquered and too little about the pain of slavery and race. The faculties of the 1950s, lest we forget, were largely without Jews and almost completely devoid of nonwhites and women.

To the new forces now surfacing in the society, that older academe was nothing less than the stronghold of the enemy. In addition, in the new era, as can be gleaned from any one of the essays in this book, there is a new sensitivity not just to racial or gender slur but also to ideas that many consider outdated or ideas that have been used in the past to oppress. Thus a new dimension of struggle ensues over issues of free speech, with the center under attack not just from the right (as in the past) but seemingly on many occasions from forces aligned with the left. It seems to me that in this ongoing debate it should not be too hard to find a just and thoughtful accord between the best of that which existed in the past and that which is being proposed by the newer voices on campus.

I suspect there is a historic inevitability to this clash and this debate. I believe that they are as well a reflection of the strength and pluralism of our society, not its weaknesses. I do not think you can change as dramatically in so short a time as America has in this past half century, that you can have so many different groups once spurned now welcomed, without some degree of accompanying tension and conflict, and much of that tension is playing itself out in academe over issues of free speech.

Whether I am in a minority in the way I feel about this does not matter, but I think of these recent clashes and incidents, painful though they must be to those immediately involved and difficult as they must be for those on campus to resolve them, as a sign of strength. Our tolerance for intolerance is, I think, in considerable decline, an important index of a healthy society. I believe as an article of faith that the more inclusive we are and the more we use the fullest talents of all our people, the stronger we are. Every bit of evidence of the last fifty years seems to show that.

Some seventeen years ago when we had developed a number of bad habits in the auto industry, principally from enjoying a de facto monopoly auto business for too long, the Japanese briefly surged ahead of us in the quality of their cars. I spent more than a year in Japan working on a book, and late at night when Japanese auto executives were relaxed, one theme emerged in their conversation again and again— America, in their opinion, was weak because of the women's movement. I disagreed; I saw the women's movement being produced by a number of historical forces, and I saw it changing us rather than weakening us. I did not think we were weak, in fact, just momentarily vulnerable in certain economic areas for a number of rather predictable reasons. Now, seventeen years later, the American economy is booming, the Japanese economy is sluggish, and in a new high-tech economy—one that replaces muscularity with brains—the fact that we handle gender equity better than any other developed country seems to me a great strength. As Bill Polk, the headmaster of one of America's great boarding schools, said to me when I congratulated him on the skillful and just way he had helped carry out the gender changes at Groton, once an all-male bastion, "Yes, and how could you ignore that great gene pool?"

I think of the new America as infinitely stronger and more vibrant than the old, the one I remember, when, like Mr. Wilkins, I was in college. We of my generation in America are often nostalgic for the period of the 1950s, a simpler time when things, for white men at least, seemed easier and more orderly. In truth, I doubt in fact that many people today want to go back to the 1950s, a much narrower, much more prejudiced time; what they want is for all their neighbors to live as they did in the 1950s while they themselves continue to enjoy the far greater fruits and possibilities of the late twentieth and early twenty-first centuries. The Dow, lest we forget, in the summer of 1951 when I graduated from high school, stood at 250. Yes, 250.

I think we as a nation are therefore more vital, stronger, more inclusive, and not surprisingly more volatile than ever. The pace of social change, driven as it is by the speed of modern communications, overwhelms many of us—it is simply harder to keep up with. That which was once understood to be the social and economic baseline keeps changing—almost daily. Our universities are more broadly based than ever, but we do not all arrive there at the same moment in our respective ethnic and cultural histories. Some arrive infinitely edgier, bearing far more grievance; for them the pain from the past remains quite immediate. The decision of black students at one school to destroy the pressrun of a student newspaper because they took exception to the work of a columnist becomes something new—understandable, perhaps, but still completely unacceptable. Nothing will make an idea more powerful than the brute suppression of it. We do not do that in this country, good idea or bad idea.

I think it is a good idea to think back to the McCarthy era, when all too many people, quavering before this sad little alcoholic demagogue, forgot the strengths of the country, its innate resilience, its great reservoirs of common sense and decency. Today, again, I also think it is important not to underestimate the common sense of ordinary people, nor their innate wisdom and sense of fairness, nor the immense amount of elasticity that our society, by the nature of its diversity, enjoys. We need to remember that such issues are produced by a process of ever greater inclusion, which is a strength, and we need to remember to deal with such issues, which are often painful, with common sense and with a respect for the rights of all. But we also need an awareness that it is always dangerous to subtract any degree of freedom of speech from even the most unlikable of people, because if you do, you will soon start subtracting it from others.

Acknowledgments

All of the lectures were cosponsored by the Academic Freedom Lecture Fund, the University of Michigan Chapter of the American Association of University Professors, and the Senate Advisory Committee on University Affairs. In 1999 the University of Michigan Office of the President became a cosponsor of the lectures.

In addition, four of the lectures were cosponsored by other university groups:

Avern Cohn: Law School
Roger W. Wilkins: Martin Luther King, Jr.,
    César Chávez, Rosa Parks Visiting Professor Program
Eugene L. Roberts Jr.: Michigan Journalism Fellows
David A. Hollinger: Department of History

Support for the publication of the book has been made possible through the generosity of the Academic Freedom Lecture Fund, the American Association of University Professors (Committee on Academic Freedom and Tenure), the Herbert H. and Grace A. Dow Foundation, the W. K Kellogg Foundation, and the University of Michigan Office of the President.

The publication of the book would not have been possible without the extraordinary dedication of the authors and of Colin Day, director of the University of Michigan Press, and his staff. Impressions Book and Journal Services, and copyeditor, Susan Brehm, took our disparate parts and created a book worthy of the individuals for whom the lecture is named.

H. Chandler Davis

H. Chandler Davis, a preeminent mathematician, is a professor emeritus at the University of Toronto. He was vice president of the American Mathematical Society (1991–94). He was long an advisory editor and is now distinguished editor of *Linear Algebra and Its Applications*. He is now editor in chief of *The Mathematical Intelligencer*.

Professor Davis earned his academic credentials, B.S., M.A., and Ph.D. degrees, at Harvard University. He began his professional career as an instructor at the University of Michigan from 1950 to 1954.

In addition to publishing research articles in mathematics, Davis has published science fiction, poetry, and several hortative essays, including "From an Exile," in *The New Professors*, edited by R. O. Bowen (1960); "The Purge," in *A Century of Mathematics in America* (1989); and "Science for Good or Ill," in *Waging Peace II* (1992).

While an instructor at the University of Michigan in 1954, Chandler Davis chose to test the constitutionality of the House Un-American Activities Committee by refusing to testify before the committee without invoking protection from self-incrimination under the Fifth Amendment. As a result of his actions, Davis was suspended from the university. His reinstatement was supported by his department and college but not by the Faculty Senate, and he was subsequently dismissed from the university. He was also cited for contempt of Congress, indicted in 1954, and convicted in 1957. His appeals to the courts were exhausted in 1959, and he served a sentence in federal prison in 1960.

Clement L. Markert

Clement L. Markert was professor of biology at Johns Hopkins University (1957–65), the Henry Ford II Professor of Biology and chair of the Department of Biology at Yale University (1965–86), and Distinguished University Research Professor of Animal Science and Genetics at North Carolina State University (1986–93). His research interests were focused on developmental genetics, reproductive biology, and biotechnology. He was a member of the National Academy of Sciences and served as cochair of the Developmental Biology Interdisciplinary Cluster for President Ford's Biomedical Research Panel in 1975. Markert was elected to the presidency of the American Institute of Biological Sciences, the American Society of Zoologists, the Society for Developmental Biology, and the American Genetics Association.

He began his academic career as an assistant professor of zoology at the University of Michigan in 1950 after earning his bachelor's degree from the University of Colorado, his M.A. from the University of California at Los Angeles, and his doctorate from Johns Hopkins University. He died on October 1, 1999, in Colorado Springs, Colorado.

In 1954 Clement Markert was called to testify before the House Un-American Activities Committee. He invoked constitutional rights according to the Fifth Amendment and refused to answer the committee's questions concerning his political associations. Consequently, he was suspended from the University of Michigan. He was later reinstated with the support of the Faculty Senate, his department, and his college, and he eventually achieved tenure.

Mark Nickerson

Mark Nickerson, perhaps the most eminent pharmacologist of the twentieth century, was professor of pharmacology and therapeutics at McGill University. He joined the faculty at McGill in 1967, where he chaired his department from 1967 to 1975. He also held academic positions at the University of Manitoba, the University of Michigan, and the University of Utah. Professor Nickerson died on March 12, 1998, in Ottawa, Canada, where he had moved after his retirement.

Professor Nickerson made major contributions to the field of pharmacology, in part through his seminal research on the adrenergic blocking drugs that are used to treat high blood pressure and other major medical disorders. He was awarded the John Jacob Abel Award in Pharmacology in 1949 and served as president both of the Pharmacological Society of Canada and of the American Society for Pharmacology and Experimental Therapeutics. He chaired the Canadian Federation of Biological Sciences and was the author of more than 250 scientific publications.

Mark Nickerson was born on October 22, 1916, in Montevideo, Minnesota, the eldest child of Mark Nickerson and Ada Honey. Professor Nickerson graduated *summa cum laude* from Linfield College, earned his Sc.M. from Brown University, his Ph.D. from Johns Hopkins University, and an M.D. from the University of Utah.

In 1954, Mark Nickerson was an associate professor of pharmacology at the University of Michigan, with tenure. He was called to testify before the House Un-American Activities Committee and chose to invoke the Fifth Amendment in response to the committee's questions. He was immediately suspended by the university as a result. Professor Nickerson's reinstatement was supported by the Faculty Senate but not by his departmental chairman or by the dean and the executive committee of the Medical School. He was subsequently dismissed from the university despite his tenured appointment.

Introduction
Peggie J. Hollingsworth

Unfettered Expression: Freedom in American Intellectual Life is a compilation of lectures given at the University of Michigan from 1991 through 1999 in honor of three professors who were faculty members at the university when the House Un-American Activities Committee (HUAC) visited Michigan in 1954. The following is an account of the events that led up to the establishment of the lecture series.

Congressman Kit Clardy along with several colleagues from the HUAC held hearings in early 1954 in the Michigan state capitol at Lansing, where they summoned before them three faculty members from the University of Michigan. All three faculty members refused to testify before Clardy's committee, citing their First Amendment "right of the people peaceably to assemble." Two, who later said that they were concerned for their families and their future careers and consequently did not wish to be sent to prison and hoped not to lose their jobs, followed legal advice and exercised their Fifth Amendment right against self-incrimination, but the third, as a matter of principle, based his refusal only on his First Amendment right.[1] Immediately following the hearings, University of Michigan President Harlan Hatcher suspended the faculty appointments of Chandler Davis, an instructor in the Department of Mathematics, Clement Markert, an assistant professor in the Department of Biology, both in the College of Literature, Science, and the Arts (LS&A), and Mark Nickerson, a tenured associate professor in the Department of Pharmacology of the Medical School. Hatcher fired both Davis and Nickerson in August 1954, and they eventually left the country for faculty positions and distinguished careers in Canada. Although Hatcher lifted Markert's suspension and only censured him, within a few years Markert received tenure and left Michigan shortly thereafter.[2]

Faculty Approve a Resolution. The University of Michigan Senate Assembly, at its monthly meeting on November 19, 1990, expressed its concern that free expression be promoted and protected on the campuses of the University of Michigan when it approved a resolution that established a lecture series to be known as the University of Michigan Senate's Davis, Markert, Nickerson Lecture on Academic and Intellectual Freedom. The Senate Assembly is the governing body of the Faculty Senate and is composed of elected representatives from the schools, colleges, and other academic units of the university, and its executive committee, the Senate Advisory Committee on University Affairs (SACUA), is made up of nine members elected from the Senate Assembly. Sociology professor Gayl D. Ness, who until May 1990 had served as chair of SACUA, presented to those assembled on that bright November day a resolution that, after several minor modifications, was approved in the following form:

> The faculty of the University of Michigan affirms that academic and intellectual freedom are fundamental values for a university in a free society. They form the foundation of the rights of free enquiry, free expression, and free dissent that are necessary for the life of the university.
>
> The faculty recognizes that such rights are human creations, the product of both the reasoned actions and the deep seated commitments of women and men. When such actions and commitments are set in human institutions, people may secure for themselves and for others, in the present and the future, the enjoyment of those rights.
>
> We also recognize that these values and the rights they imply are vulnerable to the fads, fashions, social movements, and mass fears that threaten to still dissent and to censure carriers of unpopular ideas. Such was the case in 1954 when the University of Michigan suspended three faculty members and subsequently dismissed two of them. We deeply regret the failure of the University Community to protect the fundamental values of intellectual freedom at that time. It is to guard against a repetition of those events, and to protect the fundamental freedoms of those who come after us that we make this resolution today.

Introduction

The protection of academic and intellectual freedoms requires a constant reminder of their value and vulnerability. To provide for that reminder, the Faculty of the University of Michigan hereby resolves to establish an Annual Senate Lecture on Academic and on Intellectual Freedom, to be named:

THE UNIVERSITY OF MICHIGAN SENATE'S
DAVIS, MARKERT, NICKERSON LECTURE
ON ACADEMIC AND INTELLECTUAL FREEDOM

In the debate that preceded the affirmative vote, members of the Senate Assembly raised several questions. Was it appropriate that the lecture be named after the three former faculty members, Chandler Davis, Clement Markert, and Mark Nickerson? Why did the regents of the university fail to make some gesture of reconciliation to the three when asked to do so in a resolution passed the preceding February by the Senate Assembly? What effect might adoption of the resolution have on Harlan Hatcher, the ninety-year-old former university president who had suspended the three and then fired Davis and Nickerson from their university positions? Some had been upset when Alan Wald, a professor of English, had written letters several years earlier to the *University Record* and the *Detroit Free Press* in which he proposed that Hatcher's name be removed from the university's graduate library because of the former president's act of firing the two professors thirty-five years earlier.

I had been elected in March 1990 to succeed Ness as chair of SACUA and the Senate Assembly, and in response to several questions I indicated that SACUA planned to hold the lecture each year after the annual meeting of the Faculty Senate and that a special committee appointed by SACUA would choose the speaker. The minutes of the November 19 Senate Assembly meeting do not record the actual number of votes cast in favor of the resolution, but those present recollect that support was overwhelming. Ness next offered a motion that the Senate Assembly establish a fund to support the annual program and lecture, and the motion passed unanimously. What follows is my reconstruction of the events that led up to the adoption by the Senate Assembly of the resolution that established the Davis, Markert, Nickerson Lecture on Academic and Intellectual Freedom.

The University Commemorates the Fiftieth Anniversary of the Construction of a Building and an Undergraduate English Major Produces a Video Honors Thesis. To celebrate the fiftieth anniversary of the construction of the Rackham Building, the University of Michigan held a two-day symposium on September 30 and October 1, 1988. One featured speaker, David A. Hollinger, a history professor, covered the period in the university's history from 1938 to 1988 and focused on two sets of events—the establishment of the Institute for Social Research (ISR) and its influence on the study of social and political sciences and psychology at Michigan and the manner in which the university dealt with those in its ranks who were accused of being communists during the late 1940s and early 1950s. Hollinger cited Ellen Schrecker's extensive survey of and commentary on the impact of McCarthyism on American universities in her book *No Ivory Tower: McCarthyism and the Universities* (1986). Schrecker repeatedly referenced the University of Michigan in her book. Hollinger, in his exceptionally thorough presentation, *Academic Culture at Michigan, 1938–1988: The Apotheosis of Pluralism* (1989), explored in considerable depth the manner in which the university administration, the regents, the Medical School, and the LS&A elected and appointed representatives of the faculty, including the Senate Assembly, and others who handled the individual cases of Davis, Markert, and Nickerson. He noted that one key committee, appointed by SACUA and headed by ISR scholar Angus Campbell, applied an "integrity" test to Davis, Markert, and Nickerson. As Hollinger (1989, 71) writes "integrity meant, above all, a willingness to tell one's colleagues exactly what one's politics were, and academic freedom did not extend to the right to refuse to do so." Markert and Nickerson passed but Davis failed the integrity test. Despite the recommendations of the Campbell Committee that Markert and Nickerson be retained with censure, Hatcher fired not only Davis but Nickerson as well. Hollinger's account persuades the reader that at least in Nickerson's case personalities and personal interactions rather than principles might have been the dominant factors that guided Hatcher's decision and that questions of loyalty and "integrity" provided convenient excuses to rid the university of a faculty member who was disliked by his departmental chairman and perhaps by some faculty colleagues as well.[3]

In the fall of 1988 Adam Kulakow, a senior undergraduate English major, knew of the Hollinger lecture, had been exposed to publicity that stemmed from it, and read in the *Michigan Daily*, the student newspaper, that some in the university community had asked that former university president Harlan Hatcher's name be removed from the graduate library because of his role in the cases of Davis, Markert, and Nickerson. He was enrolled in Professor William (Buzz) Alexander's documentary film senior seminar in the Department of English. An enterprising student, Kulakow chose for his class project the production of a forty-minute documentary film on the circumstances that surrounded the suspension of the three faculty members and the subsequent firing of two thirty-five years earlier. He proceeded to interview Hollinger and people who were knowledgeable about the McCarthy era, who were at the University of Michigan during the 1950s, and who recalled the events that surrounded the firings of the three professors or who were personally acquainted with the professors. When he completed his project in December, he decided to begin a more extensive audio-video documentary project for an undergraduate honors thesis that would feature interviews with the three professors themselves. In seeking permission to pursue a documentary film for his honors thesis, Kulakow writes, "I also recall making a case that this 'thesis' should take the form of a film because of the need to record and capture the voices of the aging principals in this story and to reach a broad and younger audience through the audio-visual medium—and I argued that researching and 'writing' the story for this film was just as legitimate a form of writing as doing the same thing in book form."[4] Kulakow notes that he received major support from Professors Alexander, Hollinger, and Edmund Creeth, who at the time was heading an alternative honors program in the Department of English.

Kulakow assembled a "production team" of fellow students and raised funds for the project from sources such as the LS&A, the Horace Rackham School of Graduate Studies, the Leo Burnett Film and Video Scholarship Fund, the Bentley Historical Library (which paid for all of the film), and the University of Michigan–Ann Arbor Chapter of the American Association of University Professors (AAUP). He then proceeded to assemble an impressive group of interviewees for his documentary that included Davis, Markert, Nickerson, Schrecker, Hatcher, and others who had something to contribute to the documentary. He asked Wilfred Kaplan, mathematics professor and executive secretary of the local AAUP chapter, to arrange for a meeting with Chandler Davis, who was well-known to Kaplan. For that meeting he took his production team to

Toronto, where Davis was a professor of mathematics. After that interview he and his team traveled to Montreal to interview Nickerson and to Raleigh, North Carolina, to interview Markert. Ellen Schrecker was invited to do a reading of her book and traveled to Ann Arbor, where she was interviewed for the video. Kulakow recalls that the most difficult interview to arrange was that with Harlan Hatcher, and the manner in which he carried out that interview, as well as the other interviews in the documentary, attest to this former student's remarkable talents.[5]

Once the documentary was completed, the Department of English and the local AAUP chapter arranged for a public showing of the film at a special program on the evening of April 19, 1989. To enable Professors Davis, Markert, and Nickerson to return to Ann Arbor to participate in a panel discussion the AAUP secured funds from the Academic Freedom Fund managed by the national AAUP's Committee A on Academic Freedom and Tenure. More than four hundred spectators crowded into Auditorium 3 of the Modern Languages Building that night for the special program "The McCarthy Era at the University of Michigan," to view Kulakow's film documentary "Keeping in Mind," and to hear the panel discussion with the three professors. The event received wide media coverage, and in response to popular demand two more showings of the documentary, followed by extensive debate, were held in October of that year. I was nearly six months into my year as chair of SACUA when I attended one of those fall showings with my husband, a professor of pharmacology. My husband felt that Nickerson was one of the leading biomedical scientists of the century, but he was unaware of Nickerson's history at the University of Michigan. We were both surprised and impressed by the intensity of the feelings that came forth from members of the audience.

The AAUP Drafts a Resolution. The showing of the Kulakow documentary was only one of a long series of occasions on which the AAUP and its local chapter expressed dissatisfaction with the University of Michigan's handling of the cases of Davis, Markert, and Nickerson. In 1958, nearly four years after the firings of Davis and Nickerson, the national AAUP censured the University of Michigan for procedural improprieties in the manner in which the cases were handled. But merely a year later in 1959 the AAUP lifted the censure when the university's board of regents passed Bylaw 5.09, which established a procedure that must be used before a tenured faculty member's appointment could be terminated.

6

In October 1987, Historica Critica, an organization devoted to the encouragement of study and publication of historical work on the university's past, joined the local AAUP chapter in sponsoring a program on the history of the AAUP at the University of Michigan. Wilburt J. McKeachie, a psychology professor, was clearly still upset when he spoke of the treatment that had been meted out to Davis and Nickerson. He told the audience, "When I started working out my remarks, I discovered that I'm not going to get past the House Un-American Activities Committee and the firing of Professors Davis and Nickerson. As I began thinking about it, my blood began boiling again." He then reviewed the reasons that the national AAUP censured the University of Michigan in 1958 and then removed the censure the following year. He concluded by saying, "In my career here, this is probably the period when I felt most upset, angry, frustrated, and, thus, most committed to a strong AAUP and strong faculty action in opposition to the administration."[6]

After the first showing of the Kulakow documentary, in May 1989 James L. Miller, professor of education and president of the AAUP chapter, and Wilfred Kaplan wrote a letter to Harlan Hatcher in which they asked the former university president to support a "gesture of reconciliation towards the three professors who left the University directly or indirectly because of the hearings in 1954." They further wrote to Hatcher, "Would you be willing to encourage such an action by a letter to President Duderstadt? We have discussed the matter with him. He is very supportive of the idea and would be happy to hear from you." As he was leaving for his vacation home in Leland, Michigan, Hatcher sent a letter to Duderstadt (who had just begun his appointment as university president) in which he said, "Having had a long career as a professor and having been an active member of the AAUP in many troubled times, I am sensitive to their concerns. Also as a long time administrator, I learned that there is another and wider focus to issues of this kind. What I still find troubling in this one is the prevailing premise that the conduct of these three involved was wholly exemplary, and that of the Regents, Administration, and Faculty Committees censurable." Hatcher concluded his letter as follows: "My personal belief is that the way to 'close the books' is to consider them closed. I am truly sorry that you should have this added to all your other burdens." There is no record that the new president responded to the AAUP chapter, but Wilfred Kaplan (in a note to me in 1993) recalls that Duderstadt did send a message to the chapter saying that the matter was closed.

But the AAUP chapter clearly did not feel that the matter was closed. During the summer months of 1989 the newly elected chapter president, Mary Crichton, a professor of German, and the outgoing chapter treasurer, Marsha Dutton, an editor with the Middle English Dictionary project, worked with Wilfred Kaplan on a statement about the events of 1954 and a request for the administration to make that gesture of reconciliation addressed in the earlier letter to former president Hatcher. Frustrated in its attempt to work with the administration directly, the chapter now decided on a different approach. At a meeting on October 25, 1989, the chapter endorsed the Crichton-Dutton statement, and Crichton sent the statement to SACUA with the following request. "On behalf of the Chapter, I now request that SACUA consider our proposal that the University make a significant gesture of reconciliation to the three professors and that the matter be brought before Senate Assembly. We hope that SACUA and Senate Assembly will endorse the statement and authorize its presentation to President Duderstadt with a recommendation that he implement the action proposed." The statement concluded with the following: "Therefore, in recognition of the unfortunate University action against faculty members taken in 1954, in awareness of the inadequate procedures used at that time as recognized by the enactment of Bylaw 5.09 in 1959, and in a desire to show respect for former colleagues of that date as well as to reaffirm the University commitment to the highest standards of academic freedom, the University of Michigan Chapter of AAUP urges the university at this time to make a significant gesture of reconciliation to the three professors."[7] In other words, any initiative that might occur with respect to reconciliation was now squarely in the hands of the elected representatives of the faculty, the Senate Assembly, and SACUA.

The Senate Assembly and SACUA Ask for a Regental Action. SACUA received the AAUP reconciliation proposal at its meeting of November 6, 1989, and discussed the most appropriate manner in which to bring it to resolution at subsequent meetings. At its first January meeting after the winter break, SACUA decided to present the AAUP reconciliation proposal to the Senate Assembly at the assembly's February meeting and discussed the covering statement that would accompany the proposal. SACUA Chair Ness drafted a resolution and a statement on behalf of SACUA in support of the resolution that he presented at the SACUA meeting of January 27, 1989.[8]

When the SACUA resolution was presented to the assembly on February 19, 1989, only two faculty members commented. One expressed concern that "there seemed to be too many qualifying statements and it seemed too apologist in tone." The other said that she agreed with her colleague and that she "would like to see an endorsement of the sentiment without all of the explanations." The resolution in support of the reconciliation gesture passed with thirty-three in favor, one against, and two abstentions. Ness told the assembly that SACUA would send the resolution to President Duderstadt, that SACUA would present it to the board of regents, and that he would report back on any action that either the administration or the board might take. SACUA proceeded to prepare an action request for consideration at the March meeting in Ann Arbor of the board of regents.

The Regents Defer Action Indefinitely. At its March 1990 meeting the board of regents received a "Regents Communication" on the subject "recommendation for faculty members Davis, Nickerson, and Markert" with a request for action, namely "that a significant gesture of reconciliation be made to faculty members H. Chandler Davis and Mark Nickerson for dismissal and to Clement Markert for temporary suspension and subsequent censure in 1954." Meetings of the regents are often taken up with issues related to the financial affairs of the university. On the preceding day the regents had dealt with a proposal to lease university-owned land in the Northern Peninsula to two mining companies. And, as soon as they finished with the SACUA proposal, they were to receive a report on the financial status of the university hospitals, a matter that is always of great interest and concern for them.

President Duderstadt introduced SACUA Chair Ness to those present, and Ness proceeded to explain the reasons for the request for the gesture of reconciliation. Regent Deane Baker (R–Ann Arbor) said that he needed more information but had a conviction that "people had acted in good faith at that time, and that it is difficult to make judgments now about what should have or could have been done differently then." Regent Thomas Roach (D–Ann Arbor), who spoke at some length, said that he had read Ellen Schrecker's book *No Ivory Tower* and that he understood from that book that faculty committees had recommended the dismissals and that the Supreme Court had upheld a case of conviction that was parallel to that of Davis's case. He challenged the faculty to correct any errors in Schrecker's book and expressed the opinion that to be a Communist in 1954 was "to advocate the violent overthrow of the United States government." Regent Nellie Varner (D–Detroit) said that although she was very much in favor of academic freedom, she "was concerned about any possible liabilities, damage claims, or other legal obligations the university might incur were it to act on SACUA's request." Regent Philip Power (D–Ann Arbor) was concerned that the board of regents might set a dangerous precedent and asked Ness what was meant by "a gesture of reconciliation." Ness mentioned severance pay in 1990 dollars for the two professors who had been dismissed, granting emeritus status to the three professors, or establishing a lecture "to remind the community of the university's commitment to protecting its cherished values of academic freedom." Regent Paul Brown (D–Mackinac Island) agreed with Regent Baker that a gesture of reconciliation could not be extended "without admitting that the decision that had been made in the 1950s was wrong." The regents and President Duderstadt asked for further information.

Immediately after the March meeting, SACUA sent a letter to the regents thanking them for their attention and attaching additional materials. Ness met again with the regents at their April 1990 meeting. Regent Baker again advised that to take the requested action "would pose a danger to the university by bringing up old issues that had since been laid to rest." Regent Veronica Latta Smith (R–Grosse Ile) shared a view, often expressed when one does not want to take an unpleasant action, that "this was not the first time that someone had been dismissed from the university because of his beliefs." She read to her colleagues a newspaper article about a German faculty member who had been removed in 1917 because of his "pro-German attitude." Only one regent seemed to have some understanding of the motivation behind the request for action. According to the minutes of the April meeting, "Regent Power disagreed (with Regent Baker), noting that the real issue is not to look backward and examine all of the events of the past, but rather to look forward to discover what the university can do to prevent hindering academic freedom and freedom of inquiry in the future." President Duderstadt thanked Ness and explained to the regents that this was the last time that Ness would meet with them as chair of the Senate and SACUA. The SACUA minutes of April 30, 1990, Ness's last meeting as chair, stated, "The next step in the continuing issue of reconciliation was considered. It was decided that Ness would draft a proposal for an annual lecture on academic and intellectual freedom named for the three faculty members that would be presented at each future Senate meeting. We will stress that our sense of the faculty is that there is a strong desire to make a gesture of reconciliation. In that spirit, we will invite the regents to join the faculty in making this gesture in remembrance of a time of great anxiety and as a symbol for looking forward."

On May 1, 1990, I became chair of SACUA and the Senate Assembly and inherited the task of dealing with the university administration and with the regents. On several occasions over the course of the summer I discussed the proposal for an annual lecture with the president and with various regents, but mainly with Regent Roach, who indicated that he would pursue our cause with his colleagues. By the beginning of the fall term, however, it was clear to all that neither the administration nor the regents were interested in pursuing the matter. Thus, SACUA drafted the proposal for the annual lecture and prepared to present it to the Senate Assembly at its November 1990 meeting. I notified the regents one week before that Senate Assembly meeting as to the action that we were prepared to take.

The Resolution Establishes the Annual Davis, Markert, Nickerson Lecture. The resolution the Senate Assembly adopted on November 19, 1990, carried with it a clear message to the university's administration and the board of regents that if they would not act in a righteous way on behalf of the university to right a wrong, the faculty would at least act for itself. This action might seem surprising and even remarkable to some. In his 1989 history of the university Hollinger had written about faculty governance in the following manner: "The Senate and the Senate Assembly have engaged the rank-and-file faculty when the interests of the faculty are felt to be at stake in an issue that cuts across the lines of the schools and colleges. This was clearly the case during the McCarthy era, and again in the late 1960s when faculties debated the relationship of universities to the Vietnam War. Although Senate veterans of the 1930s and 1940s insist that a genuine, almost familial sense of community was once a reality at Michigan, during the last forty years the faculty seems not to have functioned very actively as a *polity* in the absence of crisis" (88).

On November 19, 1990, at the monthly meeting of the Senate Assembly in the Rackham Amphitheater, certainly no more than two of those present had been affiliated with the university in 1954. Most had given little if any thought to the events of the McCarthy era. Why, then, was the faculty so united in its support for the resolution to establish the Davis, Markert, Nickerson Lecture on Academic and Intellectual Freedom? It is hard to believe that many were concerned with the well-being of Davis, Markert, and Nickerson or saw any reason to extend to these unfortunate gentlemen a significant gesture of reconciliation. It seems highly unlikely that many knew or understood much about the events that surrounded their suspensions and subsequent departure from the university. Was there a crisis or the perception of an impending crisis? One can only speculate as to what might have been in the minds of faculty members who voted that day for the resolution that established the lecture series.

Some faculty might have been concerned and unhappy with increasing signs that the university was following a corporate model. The number of administrators was growing exponentially, and although most of the highest-ranking administrators had faculty appointments, the number of faculty, who viewed these administrators as their peers, was diminishing rapidly. Soon there would be one administrator for each faculty member. These administrators did not seem to understand that the rules of the business world might not apply comfortably to the academy, and the administrators often did not find it necessary to consult the faculty when making important policy decisions.

The role of the tenure-track faculty member now was to function as a scholar whose scholarship brought significant revenues into the university. Graduate student teaching assistants and a growing cadre of non-tenure-track lecturers were entrusted to an increased degree with that other revered mission of the university, the education of undergraduate students.

The administration had recently terminated the world-famous geography department for cost-saving reasons. Some felt that the faculty had not been given adequate opportunity for discussion and debate before the administration had taken its action. Some also believed that the administrators had not given sufficient attention to the effect that closing the department would have on tenured faculty members.

Some faculty might have been uneasy with the changing nature of the university community. Protests of the 1960s and 1970s had brought new faces to the campus. Asian and African-American students had become a visible presence in the classroom, and the small but perceptible increase in the number of women and persons of color who now were members of the tenure-track faculty created new tensions and new problems. There were discussions about an erosion of the quality of scholarship.

As the first woman to serve as chair of the faculty whose ancestors had been brought to America from Africa as slaves and the first member of my family to receive a college education, I was acutely aware of those tensions.[9] The possibility of hate speech and other noxious acts engendered by the presence of these new members of the university community led administrators to propose codes that were designed to regulate the speech and behavior of students, faculty, and staff. Such codes presented a clear challenge to the freedom of expression so dear to the professoriat.[10] Whatever the reason or reasons that any individual member of the Senate Assembly voted for the resolution to establish the lecture series, many of those issues before that faculty group were to become subjects covered in the lectures that follow.[11]

The first lecture in the series addressed some of the issues noted earlier. Robert O'Neil, founding director of the Thomas Jefferson Center for the Protection of Free Expression and a former president of the University of Virginia, delivered the first Davis, Markert, Nickerson Lecture on February 18, 1991, in the Rackham Amphitheater at the time of the annual Senate meeting. In his lecture he addressed hate speech and codes of conduct that had been proposed for various groups within the university community. The three professors after whom the lecture is named were present for that lecture and for many of the subsequent lectures. In a panel discussion that followed the lecture, the three professors in various ways related their experiences of the 1950s to current times. As the reader will learn, O'Neil's lecture and the panel discussion set the high standards of quality, scholarship, and relevance that typify the University of Michigan Senate's Davis, Markert, Nickerson Lecture on Academic and Intellectual Freedom.

NOTES

1. Clement Markert and Mark Nickerson based their refusal to testify on both the First and the Fifth Amendments. Chandler Davis based his refusal on the First Amendment only and entered into prolonged litigation that ended when he served a six-month sentence in a federal penitentiary for contempt of Congress.

2. Clement Markert first became a professor at Johns Hopkins University, then was appointed professor and chairman of the Department of Biology at Yale University, and ended his academic career as a distinguished professor at North Carolina State University. He received many honors including election to the National Academy of Sciences. Mark Nickerson eventually became professor of pharmacology and chairman of the Department of Pharmacology at McGill University in Montreal. Among his many honors was election as president of the American Society for Pharmacology and Experimental Therapeutics. Chandler Davis became a professor of mathematics at the University of Toronto and also achieved a considerable reputation as a minor poet.

3. Davis did not endear himself to the Campbell Committee when he told members in essence that whether he was a communist was or should be irrelevant to them. Many faculty found it difficult to rally behind a fellow faculty member who was so uncooperative, irrespective of whatever principles might be involved. As Hollinger points out, Nickerson was actively disliked by Maurice Seevers, his departmental chairman, who told one investigating committee that "Nickerson is antiauthority, and that is something that I am personally unable to put up with." Seevers commented that Nickerson's talk around the luncheon table in the department was "a leftish type of conversation . . . basically following the communist line without saying so." Seevers claimed that his department was engaged in classified research and that Nickerson potentially threatened the security of that research. Years later when the nature of the research was made public, it was found to consist of fairly low-level studies on the pharmacology of marijuana, studies that could not possibly have been of any military significance or, indeed, of more than minor scientific significance. In an interview shortly before his death in 1998, Nickerson commented that the environment of the Department of Pharmacology and the Medical School at Michigan was the most "despotic" he had ever encountered in his lifetime.

4. Adam Kulakow is currently a screen writer living in southern California who wrote these comments in an e-mail message sent on April 5, 2000.

5. In his e-mail message to me Adam Kulakow wrote the following about some of the major interviews that he conducted:

> So, one by one, I met the professors with my production team, traveling to meet Chan Davis at his home near the University of Toronto and then later going over to Montreal—to McGill—to meet Nickerson for a couple of frigid February days . . . and lastly, we went down to Raleigh—to NC State—and stayed at the Markert house, chopped wood with Clem and dined with his wife and him while conducting a weekend's worth of interviews. In each case, I felt a close personal bond to the professors, enjoying their incredible life histories (Chan's being a "red diaper baby." . . . We met his wife, Natalie Davis, and Hollie Davis, Chan's radical father who had also been hauled up before McCarthy committees . . . ; There were Nick-

erson's terrible stories of family strife and real political persecution as he became an MD just to make a living and fled to Canada to find a job as his department chair tracked his movements through a mole at his travel agency, telling everyone not to hire Nickerson because he's a red; and then there was Markert's incredible story of fighting in Spain with the Abe Lincoln Brigade, his deep appreciation for the support of his colleagues in the bio department, his utter clarity in saying that "they could've hauled me up against a wall and shot me before I'd have named names"). My team and I were so well received by these three men, and I was crushed to hear of the deaths of Markert and Nickerson this year. These were vigorous thinkers, scholars, people with values and humor and a deep sense of right and wrong. Nickerson was also a wealth of dirty limericks, and Markert was a mountain man who could dive for fish in a frozen Colorado lake with a knife in his mouth. Even at seventy-two, he could split a log in one blow. Davis is a poet and a math prodigy . . . and a bona fide political prisoner who went to jail for the First Amendment. This made a big impression on a twenty-one-year-old documentary filmmaker.

The hardest interview to get was Harlan Hatcher. He was very friendly and collegial on the phone, but also very guarded and not at all happy with even the minor controversy about the renaming of the Hatcher library. We went to at least three lunches at the Michigan League . . . which I remember being a dyed in the wool old school Michigan place. He actually took me to lunch on each occasion (paid for it on his University of Michigan American Express Corporate Card) and we would talk about the progress of the film and the issues at stake and the people I was meeting with . . . but we'd also talk about his life history, his writing, his time in Paris in the 1920s, his memories of Hemingway and Gertrude Stein and the whole famous scene there among the "Lost Generation." I recall him saying how wonderful it was in Paris, and I was so struck by how young and vigorous he looked at ninety, and here I was having lunch with a veteran of that very different and much more distant era to the one I already saw him as an old veteran of—the 1950s. By the time he agreed to the interview, I knew pretty well what he'd say in terms of seeing the "uncooperative" professors as disloyal to the university, of putting him and the school in a bad position and playing into the idea that they had something to hide by not being "forthright." I didn't feel that I needed to editorialize or manipulate the footage I had of him saying these things to make him look particularly bad or wrongheaded. What I liked is that the issues as they came out of his mouth and really out of all the principal figures seemed pretty clearly framed and the positions accessible to an audience's ability to make its own analysis and retrospective judgment. I didn't have to do that for anyone—and that's one huge advantage of the documentary format that allows people to tell their stories in their own words. I invited Hatcher to the big screening and symposium we held that April in 1989, but I don't think he came. I would have wanted him to be there and I hope he saw the film before he died. I'm curious what he would have said about it, and I believe that I represented his views fairly and importantly for the historical record. I felt very, very lucky to have him included in the documentary.

6. *AAUP Newsletter*, March 1988. In 1945 McKeachie had come to the University of Michigan, fresh out of the Navy. He became involved in "liberal" movements and spoke about efforts to keep Communists out of liberal organizations. His presentation is not as rigorously researched and documented as was the subsequent Hollinger history, being composed mainly of McKeachie's recollections, but it clearly reflects the feelings of many faculty members who were in Ann Arbor in 1954.

7. Memorandum to Gayl Ness, chair of SACUA, from Mary C. Crichton, president of the University of Michigan Chapter of the AAUP, dated November 1, 1989. In her memorandum Crichton writes: "The phrase 'significant gesture' can be interpreted in various ways. Such gestures have been made at Temple University, Reed College, and the University of Vermont. . . . Our University might choose, for instance, to award emeritus status to the three professors. The two who were terminated received no severance pay and the gesture could include some financial compensation."

8. The draft resolution that Ness distributed to SACUA at its meeting on January 22, 1990, read as follows: "The Senate Assembly endorses the October 25, 1989 Statement of the American Association of University Professors calling for a gesture of reconciliation to Professors H. Chandler Davis and Mark Nickerson, dismissed from their positions, and to Professor Clement Markert, temporarily suspended from his position at the University of Michigan in 1954." The resolution was accompanied by the following endorsement:

We find the statement compelling in its support of the fundamental values of academic freedom and of justice. We note that other universities have made similar gestures and believe it would be most appropriate for the University of Michigan to do so as well. This is especially fitting given the stature of the University of Michigan as one of the world's preeminent public universities. Finally, we note that this is a request for a gesture of reconciliation by an institution, rather than an attempt to assign blame to individuals for past action. (A parallel decision can be found in the recent U.S. federal government's decision to compensate Japanese Americans for their internment during the second world war.) We recognize that political and public pressures during that time reached excessive proportions and did damage to individuals and institutions throughout the nation. A gesture of reconciliation can remind us that such times and pressures are a constant threat to free societies and can help us to strengthen our resolve to defend the values of justice and academic freedom that we cherish.

9. On December 3, 1990, in a letter that I wrote to Mark Nickerson, inviting him to attend the first annual Davis, Markert, Nickerson Lecture, the following paragraph appeared that represents my thoughts at that time:

The impetus for these actions (establishment of the lecture and of the fund to support the lecture) came from a recommendation last year by the University of Michigan Chapter of the American Association of University Professors (AAUP) that some form of compensation be provided for individuals such as yourself who during the era of the 1950s suffered as a result of discrimination and persecution for their political beliefs and prior political activities. That such concerns should be rekindled at this time is not mere coincidence but is the result of a growing awareness and uneasiness among members of our community that those attitudes and behaviors which led to the persecutions of that earlier era are still very much with us today, although they might manifest themselves in subtler but potentially more dangerous ways. Whereas in the 1950s, attention focused upon political beliefs and affiliations, issues of gender and ethnicity, which existed then, have today come to the forefront. As our society becomes more diverse and as the social and economic structure of society changes, considerations of gender and ethnicity as a basis for discrimination and persecution within our universities are increasingly prevalent. As the first African American woman to be elected Chair of the University of Michigan Senate Assembly and Chair of the Senate Advisory Committee on University Affairs (SACUA), and only the second woman to hold this position in the history of the University, I am acutely aware of these issues.

10. The first such code of student behavior was rejected in August 1989 by Federal District Judge Avern Cohn, a judge who, although dedicated to the University of Michigan, is more dedicated to the Constitution. At the time of the Senate Assembly vote, the university administration had revised its student code and had sent to the Senate Assembly a faculty "discriminatory harassment code" for consideration.

11. In September 1991 nine faculty members elected to the Senate Assembly from the University of Michigan Medical School sent a memorandum to the Medical School Executive Committee that stated, "As Dr. Robert A. Green of the Department of Internal Medicine has brought to SACUA's attention, the Medical School, at the level of the Executive Committee, has done nothing. This seems particularly unfortunate since in 1954 Dr. Nickerson

was dismissed on the recommendation of the Medical School Executive Committee. As Senate Assembly members from the Medical School we believe it would be appropriate for the Medical School Executive committee to extend an apology or to give some indication of regret. An apology or gesture is even more important today in view of the 'Fundamental Tenets of Membership in the University Community,' recently endorsed by all the University of Michigan Faculties. Such an action would reaffirm in a very real way the importance to the Medical School of the right 'to free expression, free inquiry, intellectual honesty, and respect for the rights and dignity of others' and 'the importance of reasoned dissent . . . (and) the right to express unpopular views.'" Dean Giles Bole responded in February 1992 as follows: "As I indicated to you in my letter of October 4, 1991, the Medical School Executive Committee, in response to your request of September 23, asked for a review of the minutes of the Executive Committee during the period (1950–1955) pertinent to the University's dismissal of Dr. Mark Nickerson. Such a review has now been completed. After thoughtful discussion, the Executive Committee has declined to take further action. The Executive Committee respects your interest in this matter, but feels that the university's Regents and Officers have expressed the University's final word on this event of over forty years ago."

WORKS CITED

Hollinger, David A. *Academic Culture at Michigan, 1938–1988: The Apotheosis of Pluralism.* Ann Arbor, Mich.: Rackham Reports, 1989.
Schrecker, Ellen. *No Ivory Tower: McCarthyism and the Universities.* New York: Oxford University Press, 1986.

Academic Freedom in Retrospect and in Prospect
Robert M. O'Neil

I accepted with deep appreciation your invitation for this event. It would be hard to imagine auspices more fitting than these. Anyone familiar with the American academic community and with faculty governance knows the fine traditions and the high standards of this body. One does not need to be a summer Michigan resident (as I have been for twenty years) to appreciate the honor of being called upon for this purpose.

The Senate deserves high praise for establishing such a lecture. All of us across the country who care deeply about academic and intellectual freedom applaud your commitment and your vision. I would also commend Professors Davis, Markert, and Nickerson, and I am delighted they could be here to inaugurate the lecture. They are fighters, and survivors, in the very best sense. We have perilously few colleagues who did—or would have done—what they did. Their courage has inspired us all. They deserved to be honored much sooner, though it is never too late to make amends.

The institutional setting is also especially fitting. The University of Michigan is unique among American public universities—not in its constitutional status (for that it shares with a good many others) but in the persistence of its regents in using that status for good causes, including the protection of academic freedom. Since the adoption of the constitution in 1850, the regents have on half a dozen occasions gone to court to protect their own autonomy and the interests of faculty and students on this campus. That, I regret to say, few other constitutional governing boards have done.

The Michigan suits have almost always been effective. They have served to shield from legislative control such varied and vital matters as faculty appointments in the 1850s, the location of academic departments in the 1890s, and in recent years faculty teaching loads, discipline of student protestors, and out-of-state enrollments.

In California, by contrast, the major victory for constitutional autonomy had an ironic twist: The university board of regents convinced the state courts of their primacy in matters of loyalty and security. But the net effect of the suit was to leave in place a regents' loyalty oath even more onerous than the statutory oath it preempted. More will be said of loyalty oaths a bit later. At the start I wanted to give proper credit to the Michigan constitution and to the university's regents. However deeply one laments what happened here in 1954—as surely we do—one should view the University of Michigan's long record with a sense of pride.

The reasons for acclaiming an event such as this are quite varied. I suspect each of us would define its value differently. But there is one goal that seems to me to transcend all others: Bringing back to mind—and to public attention—what happened so long ago, especially in the presence of our three courageous colleagues, ought to be the best possible antidote for the future. Periodic commemoration should, if nothing else, greatly lessen the risk of recurrence.

Even for professors who lived through those traumatic times, there is much value in such recollections. But for this faculty as for most others, the risk is less one of forgetting than one of never knowing. Fewer than half the Michigan faculty are likely to recall those years from their own experience, since they were born after 1945. Even among those who are older—my age-mates now entering the senior quarter of the professoriat—the memories are dim and hazy since we were mostly students at the time. We could not possibly have understood the gravity of harm inflicted on academic and intellectual freedoms.

For me, the recollection has one deeply personal if vicarious quality. My father-in-law, a Chicago attorney named Alex Elson who still practices actively at eighty-five, represented over a hundred persons—many of them Northwestern and University of Chicago faculty and staff—who faced internal security threats. I am told (though not by him) that he never lost such a case. For his courage and devotion, he was later honored by the Illinois chapter of the American Civil Liberties Union.

My own memories are less dramatic, though surprisingly durable. During my junior year in college, two brothers named Lubell were elected on the basis of their grades to the editorial board of the *Harvard Law Review*. Election was at that time automatic—except in this case. Some at the law school knew that, as Cornell undergraduates, the Lubells had joined a suspected Communist "front group." The law faculty found them unfit for the *Law Review*—not because of any doubt about their legal ability or their integrity but solely because they were presumed to be politically ineligible for admission to the New York Bar. Few voices of protest were raised, even within the Harvard community. The only outcry I recall, in fact, was an editorial in the *Harvard Crimson*, of which I was then photographic chairman.

I mention the Lubells because in two ways their plight typified what occurred in those fearsome years. As in so many cases, outstanding and deserving people were denied opportunities that were rightfully theirs, solely because of their political beliefs and their associations. And the judgments made about them, based on animus or cowardice or both, often turned out to be dead wrong. The Lubell brothers were eventually admitted to the bar and have for many years maintained an active practice in New York City.

This outcome suggests one of three themes I plan to develop this afternoon. My first point is that, partly because of the courage and determination of persons like our three honored colleagues, the nightmare of the McCarthy era will not recur in that form. Second, however, we have no cause to be complacent; today's threats to academic freedom are much subtler, but they demand continuing vigilance. Third, in a quite different way I wonder if we may not have come full circle—if we may not have won a series of battles only to risk losing the war.

Let me begin with a bit of history. The loyalty-security apparatus of the period Lillan Hellman so aptly called "Scoundrel Time" now seems almost the creation of a single U.S. Senator, or at least of a small group of red-baiters and witch-hunters whose spokesman he was. Yet we know there had been recurrent pressures of the same type since the end of World War I. Through the Depression, investigating committees chaired by Martin Dies, J. Parnell Thomas, and others fashioned the tools and techniques of postwar McCarthyism.

Those techniques might well have resurfaced in recent years, but mercifully they have not. If what provokes such hateful vendettas is a perceived threat to national security, we might well have expected a recurrence of red-baiting or witch-hunting in the 1960s; that was, after all, a time when protest against government policy reached as violent a level as at any time in our history. We might also have expected a revival of McCarthyism in the 1980s, amid revelations of actual espionage by real spies with names like Morrison and Pollard. And within the past few weeks, curiously little note was taken of the sentencing of the first Federal Bureau of Investigation (FBI) agent ever convicted of espionage.

To our great credit, we Americans have remained relatively rational since the 1950s. There has, to be sure, been what seems to me an unacceptably high level of FBI surveillance of peace and civil rights organizations, of groups opposed to U.S. policy in Latin America, and now of people who support certain causes in the Middle East. But we have on the whole avoided a resumption of hysteria. And there has been little threat of indiscriminate, mindless suspicion of disloyalty in government or in the academy.

In fact, we may have done even a bit better than that. Last winter Congress took a step almost unprecedented in the internal security area. Without waiting for a court order, it repealed the McCarran-Walter Act, under which visas had for forty years been denied to foreign visitors with uncongenial beliefs. (The last victim of the law seems to have been Farley Mowat, the Canadian naturalist and author of *Never Cry Wolf*, who was denied entry because he had been an outspoken critic of U.S. defense policy.)

The new law says that no one may be denied a visa "because of any past, current, or expected beliefs, statements, or associations which, if engaged in by a U.S. citizen, would be protected under the Constitution of the United States." That goes further than the courts would likely say Congress need go. Although the new law does create rule-making authority that rightly makes civil libertarians uneasy, this step still seems reassuring.

Would I be overly confident to say, "it can't happen again"? At least, that would be tempting fate, so I will not say it. But let me suggest how dramatic have been the changes that, taken together, minimize the risk of a recurrence of the McCarthy era and its abuses. These changes come mainly from a series of Supreme Court cases, especially the handiwork of Justice William Brennan.

The justice's impact in this area actually predates his first Supreme Court opinion. His was a recess appointment in the fall of 1956. Because the Senate was not then in session, he sat on the Court for some weeks until confirmation hearings began. During those hearings, Senator McCarthy repeatedly demanded the justice disclose his views—or even his votes—on several sensitive and complex loyalty-security cases, most of which had already been argued.

Brennan steadfastly refused to reveal his views, much less his votes, in conference. He explained patiently to McCarthy and others the need for confidentiality—and also gave a few lessons in separation of powers. Confirmation eventually followed. Before that term was over several tentative but valuable precedents had been created. During the next four years, the Court would make clear that only knowing and active membership in the Communist Party, with a specific intent to bring about an unlawful end, would justify criminal sanctions. And by then Senator McCarthy was gone.

The ending of legislative inquiry into political beliefs and associations took a bit longer. The liberal members of the Warren Court did not yet have a majority; in fact, they were not in control until 1962, when Justice Goldberg joined them. As late as 1959 the Court could still send a young psychologist named Lloyd Barenblatt to jail for refusing to answer questions about his political associations put to him by the House Un-American Activities Committee. Although he was by then teaching at Vassar, the events that intrigued the committee all took place on this campus when Barenblatt was a graduate student in the late 1940s.

Among the questions Barenblatt refused to answer were these: "Were you ever a member of the Haldane Club of the Communist Party while at the University of Michigan?" and "Were you a member of the University of Michigan Council of Arts, Sciences, and Professions?" These and other questions, said Barenblatt, called for information he had a First Amendment right to withhold. A bare majority of the justices disagreed, and he was sentenced to prison for six months.

Four years later a dramatic change occurred. The case dealt not with Congress but with a state legislative inquiry. An officer of the Florida chapter of the National Association for the Advancement of Colored People (NAACP) had refused to turn over to the committee the organization's membership lists. A majority of the Court now recognized a First Amendment interest strong enough to resist the committee's demand and protect the witness. Because the focus of the inquiry was not the witnesses' own politics, but suspected ties between the NAACP and the Communist Party, the nexus was too weak to justify compelling disclosure of such sensitive information.

Of course that judgment did not overrule the old cases; that is not the way of a Court that deeply respects stare decisis. But the change in philosophy was clear by 1963. Overruling the McCarthy-era decisions seemed almost unnecessary. Even today cases such as *Barenblatt* remain technically intact—though I doubt they would command much deference even from the Rehnquist Court.

I am even more confident of the permanence of constitutional change in the related area of loyalty oaths. As late as 1952, the Court could say of teachers who refused to disavow certain political ties (as New York law demanded): "If they do not choose to work on such terms, they are at liberty to retain their beliefs and associations and go elsewhere." Answering its own question—"has the State deprived them of any right to free speech or assembly?"—a confident majority said, "we think not."

By 1960 the Court was ready to reexamine the most sweeping of the disclaimer-type oaths. The next several years brought down several oaths that had proved intractable during the McCarthy era. By 1967 the Court was ready to modify its deference to the New York oath. Let me quote briefly from Justice Brennan's opinion in that case, holding the oath violative of freedoms of expression:

> Our Nation is deeply committed to safeguarding academic freedom, which is of transcendent value to all of us and not merely to the teachers concerned. That freedom is therefore a special concern of the First Amendment, which does not tolerate laws that cast a pall of orthodoxy over the classroom. . . . The classroom is peculiarly the "marketplace of ideas." The Nation's future depends upon leaders trained through wide exposure to that robust exchange of ideas which discovers truth "out of a multitude of tongues" [rather] than through any kind of authoritative selection.[1]

This case resolved any possible doubt that free expression would not tolerate disclaimer-type oaths. I might, however, share an anecdote about how slowly change sometimes occurs in practice despite change in principle. My role was to write the amicus curiae brief for the American Association of University Professors in the New York case. The decision came down in January. That summer I was moving from Berkeley to the State University of New York at Buffalo. When the mail brought the new faculty orientation packet, you can imagine what was atop the pile—a sheet explaining why I had to file a signed loyalty oath form before I could be paid. When I explained to the powers in Albany a more than casual concern about this lapse, I received a most apologetic reply. That was 1967; by now I assume the oath has been removed from faculty orientation materials.

What is true for legislative investigations and loyalty oaths is also true for two other McCarthy-era vestiges in higher education. Campus speaker bans were at one time commonplace. They were widely used to bar not only Communists but far less controversial visitors as well. Some administrators and boards, to their great credit, declared that such bans not only abridged academic freedom but in a potentially dangerous way implied that some speakers and their messages came with campus approval while others did not. A university, they insisted, must of all places be open to all viewpoints and ideas. Gradually that view prevailed. Though the Supreme Court never struck down a speaker ban, the lower courts used relevant precedents to consign these laws to the same fate as the disclaimer oath.

The Supreme Court later took one other important step. It held in 1972 that no student organization could be barred from a public campus because the administration or board disliked its views or because violence had occurred at other times and places. Despite its publications or pronouncements, any group that agreed to abide by the basic rules of the institution had a First Amendment right to campus recognition and privileges.

To summarize briefly here: It would, I fear, be tempting fate to say that the excesses of the McCarthy era could not return—so I will not incur that risk. I am also well aware that at some time after the Gulf crisis we will probably face a postwar period of the kind that has historically brought out the worst instincts in us as a people. So let me rest the case with the cautiously optimistic belief that the academic freedom concerns of the 1990s will not likely repeat those of the 1950s.

Let us turn then to a briefer view of the agenda of the 1990s. The current issues are, as I suggested, subtler and more complex. It is much harder to differentiate between the "good guys" and the "bad guys" than it used to be. I do not attribute to twenty years in administration my present sense that faculty and administration are as often allied as opposed on the new academic freedom issues. Perhaps for that reason we seem to lack the old capacity for indignation. There is little of the outrage or anguish of the McCarthy era.

Nor is there even agreement on what are the major governmental concerns of the day. For example, few of us seem to be deeply troubled about an issue that would in earlier times have been much more troublesome. This issue is in fact now before the Supreme Court. The Family Planning Guidelines adopted two years ago under the Public Health Service Act have two worrisome features: They forbid physicians and other persons in health facilities that receive federal funds from offering any abortion information or counseling. They also require that such health professionals provide to their clients information about alternatives such as adoption.

Although it is not primarily academic medicine that feels the brunt of these regulations, the potential effect on clinicians in certain fields is too obvious to overlook. And before we leave medical research, what of the constraints on research that involves the use of fetal tissue, valuable though such studies are, but increasingly difficult to pursue because of government policies that reflect extrinsic pressures and not scientific or medical merit?

There is another issue affecting the sciences, on which my concerns about academic freedom apparently put me in a minority. I have in mind the federal rules that apply to investigations of suspected fraud or misconduct by agencies such as the National Institutes of Health. The rules reflect a primary—and quite salutary—concern for the complainant. But in protecting the accuser, it seems to me they slight the interests of the accused. An established senior investigator may be charged with misconduct without any formal record and has no right to a hearing while the charges are being reviewed. There is no right of access to damaging information in agency files, nor any right to attend agency interviews with witnesses, to cross-examine those witnesses, or even to see transcripts of their statements.

Such safeguards would routinely be afforded in other proceedings where an adverse judgment could do far less harm than destroying a senior scientist's reputation. The validity of these policies remains to be tested; a suit brought by a senior University of Wisconsin scientist resulted in a judgment a few weeks ago that dealt the rules only a technical blow.

I would turn from science to the arts and humanities. Consider the new restrictions Congress imposed last fall on those who receive grant support from the National Endowment for the Arts (NEA). Maybe the indifference I sense is mainly a result of initial relief over the repeal of the Helms amendment, a law almost certainly violative of artists' First Amendment rights—as a federal judge in Los Angeles recently held in the first court test.

But I fear the euphoria over the new and more benign language may be premature. The compromise that replaced the Helms amendment is not without problems—a preamble that invokes "decency" as a criterion for grant making and a process that empowers the endowment to recover the grant from any person convicted on obscenity charges for any funded work. The new law shifts the locus of decision making from the agency to the courts, and that is welcome. But the key term *decency* is nowhere defined and could therefore be used as a random screen—even though the current NEA chairman disclaims any such prospect.

There is another concern: It is only federally funded artists who risk collateral sanctions for obscenity convictions, and among transgressions that might cause the loss of a grant, only this one—directly linked as it is to the content of a work of art—could bring such dire results. Although it may seem ungracious to fault these new and improved provisions on academic freedom grounds, the early euphoria of the arts community seems to me premature.

Of course these threats are a far cry from those of the 1950s. Most of our disputes with Congress and federal agencies these days relate to indirect cost rates and formulas, adequate support for graduate fellowships, and rules on such matters as student loan defaults and minority-specific scholarships. But I would still suggest that we keep a close eye on what government is doing in the 1990s, in Washington and in state capitals.

My final concern—one that marks this period as different from others—has nothing to do with government. I have an ominous feeling that we have met the enemy and (if I may paraphrase Pogo in the interest of syntax) it is we ourselves. I surely hope we have not come full circle—that we have not spent four decades winning major battles outside the academy only to forfeit the war within our own ranks. Yet there are warning signs.

Take the matter of so-called hate speech as one portent. Let us be very clear about what we are doing and why. No one who served two decades as a state university president or vice president is unaware how intense can be the desire to do something to redress the anguish of victims of epithets, slurs, and verbal assaults. Even where existing rules may well suffice, the appeal of a new racist-sexist speech code is powerful.

Yet I wonder whether by adopting rules on what may and may not be said on campus we may not make matters worse—raising false hopes among those we seek to help and stiffening resistance among those we seek to constrain.

Beyond practical concern, I wonder what we sacrifice by acceding to that pressure: Do we not mark certain thoughts as well as words—however abhorrent and unreasoned—as "politically incorrect," to use the new parlance? Do we not imply as an academic community that we have given up on those means of influence that distinguish universities from other institutions and have resorted instead to a form of censorship?

How does all this relate to academic freedom? At the very least, we ought to ask what sort of example a university sets by ever repressing *any* words or thoughts. There is an even deeper concern about the precedent we may unwittingly create for repressing different kinds of speech. Recall, if you will, the arguments that helped to pull the teeth of the speaker bans of the 1950s: We allow and even encourage on campus the presentation of all viewpoints, however hateful and unsettling, because that is the nature of a university. Can we make that claim with equal force these days? Or could we now be faulted for having done the very thing we faulted reactionary lawmakers in earlier times for doing to us?

There is one other risk that may seem fanciful or speculative to some but seems quite plausible to me. Most of the hate speech rules have been limited to student behavior. Yet I have wondered whether sanctions aimed at the dormitory or the locker room might eventually find their way into the classroom and the library.

Some critics of hate speech rules express just such a fear: that even if these rules do not apply to faculty, or do not seem to cover lectures and course assignments, it would not take much to turn them in that direction. Distinguishing between the student lounge and the classroom is easy for us but not so obvious to those outside the academy.

(If you find this fear fanciful, recall how very close we came in 1972 to having federal Title IX regulations that would have forbidden the use in college and university classes of materials vaguely labeled as "sexist." Only the personal intervention of then Secretary Casper Weinberger on final review kept that from happening.)

I do not suggest for a moment that the answer is clear—or that there may not be some language that could be curbed to preserve a tolerable climate for learning. But I do ask if we have not gone too far in our zeal to combat racism, sexism, and ethnic insult.

Discussion of hate speech brings me to my last area of concern— a growing fear that we may be imposing (or condoning) standards of political correctness or orthodoxy. Let me make my own view on the merits clear: When it comes to matters of curriculum, I am as strong an advocate of diversity as you will find. I have long felt we focus too much on traditional writings and histories and that the next generation of students needs to know much more about the thoughts and achievements of people who are not white or male or Western. I have also been deeply involved in efforts to increase the diversity of our faculties. For me the question is much less what we add to the curriculum, or who we add to the faculty, but more how we do so and what happens to those of our colleagues who differ.

There are several worrisome signs these days. The stridency of debate on both sides—even among groups of scholars known for impatience and intemperance—seems unusual. It has been charged by those who should know that some of the best departments at our best universities have imposed ideological "litmus tests" of a kind we abhor when it comes to cabinet members or Supreme Court justices. Trust and even collegiality seem to have abated in those parts of the academy where they are most essential.

When most of the potential signers of a statement challenging affirmative action in faculty hiring at Madison say they are fearful of revealing their names, I take that not as criticism of the administration—which has threatened no one—but as ominous evidence of a perceived loss of collegiality among members of a faculty to which I once belonged and that I know well.

If colleagues of a given political or intellectual persuasion feel inhibited from speaking out on issues from race to gender to curriculum to the war in the Gulf, those of us who hold views different from theirs should be no less alarmed—even if we believe the acceptance of their views would undo much that has happened in the academy in this last generation that is sound and healthy and promising. In short, I am no more comfortable about what I sense is developing these days just because my own views on most of the issues happen to be "politically correct."

The enemy is not so much PC, if you will, but how we respond to it. Let me leave with you the disquieting thought that the sanctity of the classroom and the laboratory seems to me threatened not so much by government, as often in the past, but much more these days by members of the academic community itself.

Indeed, this may be the clearest link between the events we recall this afternoon and the current condition of the academy. While I would be the last to suggest we need to create a common enemy beyond our walls, the fact is we do not really have one. Perhaps as a result, we have the luxury of doing battle more openly with one another. We may also feel the need for combat on campus at a time when there is relatively little of it in public life. The risks are profound at a time when higher education needs all the friends it can possibly claim. It is not only groups such as Accuracy in Academia and the *Dartmouth Review* that pose very real threats. To the extent that we show intolerance to fellow members of our own community, to that degree I fear we invite the return of alien forces from outside that community.

We come together this afternoon to recall the traumatic events of four decades ago. The best way we can show we have learned the lessons of that terrible time is by resolving to resist notions of what is politically correct or incorrect—to combat self-imposed orthodoxy as vigorously as we protested orthodoxy imposed on us from outside. Our commitment to treat colleagues and students in this way may turn out to be the most durable tribute we can pay to the three colleagues we honor today.

I thank you for inviting me to be with you and to help inaugurate this series. This is an honor I shall always treasure.

NOTE

1. *Keyishian v. Board of Regents*, 385 U.S. 589, 603 (1967).

The Open-Minded Soldier and the University
Lee C. Bollinger

I am honored to deliver the second Davis, Markert, Nickerson Lecture. This lecture series is a belated institutional apology to these three individuals who were deprived of their faculty positions because of their refusal to explain their political beliefs to a congressional committee, one so bent on uncovering subversive and seditious activities that fundamental principles of the society were cast aside. The lecture is, therefore, also a reminder to us of the injustices that can be inflicted on innocent individuals in times of fear, frustration and anger, and of the apparent difficulty even good-hearted colleagues and bystanders have both of seeing injustice when it occurs and of standing up to it when they do see it.

In my lecture today, I wish to explore the tensions of these dual errors—the injustices of the impulse to intolerance and the failure to confront those injustices; and to think about the role of institutions like freedom of speech and the university in a world continually at risk of being afflicted by these errors.

It is, of course, not an academic issue (or, to play the game of double-entendre, it *is* an academic issue) for our own time, for our ears are filled with cries of alarm that we are about to be swept away by a new flowing of the sea of intolerance. Comparisons are even being drawn to the McCarthy era. And as the problem has come to be characterized in the last few years, the present phenomenon of intolerance is possessed of a double irony. Where the McCarthy era involved the *right wing* of the American political spectrum victimizing the *university* (among others), now it is said to be the *university itself* in the thralls of the *left* devouring its own members. The charge is that a political orthodoxy has arisen, about issues that are reasonably debatable. There are, it is said, prescribed views about various subjects, but mostly about issues relating to certain groups—blacks, women, gay and lesbian individuals and so on. Indiscriminate charges of racism and sexism are said to be everywhere. Mere ideas are being equated with acts of discrimination. And an insistence on the dominance of a single ideological perspective is masquerading as protection of civil rights, just as the McCarthyites with willful blindness mistook political opinion for subversion and revolutionary action. The new orthodoxy is supposedly enforced, as before, through defamatory accusations—rather than assertions that an individual is a "sympathizer" or "fellow traveler," the person is now said to be "racist" or "sexist"—and, in recent years, through official sanctions under university speech codes, ranging from coerced courses in "right" thinking to expulsion from the university.

Last year's inaugural lecturer, Professor Robert O'Neil, former university president and now professor of law at Virginia, closed his lecture by saying he had an "ominous feeling" that the McCarthyism of the 1950s was now resurfacing in American universities. He worried about the "sort of example a university sets by ever repressing any words or thoughts," because it thereby creates a "precedent" for repressing different kinds of speech." This was, he said, inconsistent with the "nature of the university." While professing a personal commitment to "diversifying" our curriculum, he expressed alarm at the "stridency of debate" that surrounded discussion of these issues, he abhorred the imposition of an "ideological 'litmus test' " within academic departments, and he said he was concerned that people should feel, as he thought they do, "inhibited" from expressing certain views, such as opposition to affirmative action.

My own view is that there is, indeed, a problem of intolerance within the American university today, but it is not as simple as many believe. First, it is not, in my judgment, reasonable to view the adoption by universities of speech codes as automatically evidencing disrespect for freedom of speech. First Amendment jurisprudence has always left room for regulation of some offending speech. This is true even of the two most relevant cases from the liberal Warren Court, *Cohen v. California*[1] and *Tinker v. Des Moines Community School District*.[2] Cohen was arrested in a Los Angeles courthouse for wearing a jacket inscribed with the words "Fuck the Draft" across the back. This was protected speech, the Supreme Court said in 1968, but the Court allowed that states could restrict speech when "substantial privacy interests are being invaded in an essentially intolerable manner."[3]

Mary Beth Tinker was a thirteen-year-old junior high school student when she, along with several other teenagers, wore a black armband to school in protest against the war in Vietnam. The Supreme Court in 1969 held that this too was protected speech, but the Court allowed that schools could forbid speech that "would 'materially and substantially interfere with the requirements of appropriate discipline in the operation of the school.' "[4] The real problem, therefore, which the Supreme Court has done nothing since *Cohen* and *Tinker* to alleviate, is to figure out what these highly ambiguous qualifications mean or ought to mean. Yet the Court's qualifications are not the stuff out of which to fashion razorsharp statutes; and, while every reasonable person recognizes that there is a zone of speech that ought not to be encompassed by the principle of freedom of speech, we are having a very difficult time describing it in words, at least with sufficient clarity to overcome the First Amendment's concern with vagueness in the area of speech regulation.

Indeed, in more recent cases, the Court has only further clouded the area. In one case, *Bethel School District v. Fraser*[5] (1986), the Court permitted a high school to sanction a student who at a school assembly delivered a nominating speech with indecent innuendos, in the adolescent style. This was a "captive audience," the Court said, without explaining why the students in Mary Beth Tinker's classrooms were not equally a "captive audience." And in its most recent case, *Hazelwood School District v. Kuhlmeier*[6] (1988), the Court affirmed a high school's prerogative to refuse to publish a journalism class newspaper in which students had reported on teenage pregnancies and the effects of divorce on children. This, said the Court, was a "school sponsored" activity, without explaining why the classrooms in which Mary Beth Tinker sat wearing her armband were not also.

The point is simply that, at the very least, given the lack of guidance from the Supreme Court, one ought to have some sympathy for universities as they seek to locate the appropriate boundary of constitutional authority to regulate speech. (I could make this point even more forcefully, if I had time, by showing how in certain contexts—most notably, the workplace—the Court is developing different First Amendment rules.) The fact is that we are at a new frontier of the First Amendment, and it is important to bear in mind the inevitable uncertainties attendant on being at such a difficult spot.

On the other hand, I do not want to be taken as trying to excuse the first University of Michigan speech code, which was finally dealt a constitutionally devastating blow when a university office published the amazing "yellow booklet," which declared that "discriminatory harassment" included such actions as a "male student" remarking in class that "women just aren't as good in this field as men."[7] It is difficult, in the face of such interpretations, to maintain a belief that there has been progress over the past decades in the general understanding of the principle of freedom of speech.

But I do not wish today to talk about cases and law, at least not in this limited sense. I want instead to focus on the intellectual attitudes, among faculty and students and administrators, and the principle of academic freedom. I agree with Professor O'Neil that there is a serious problem of intolerance within the university community, though it is admittedly difficult to document. I do not think, however, that this is a problem, as many claim, that is exclusively, or even primarily, of the left. I see many intolerant people on the right and in the middle as well, perhaps especially among those who view themselves as preservers of the status quo. People more and more, it seems to me, view it as necessary and desirable to be committed to certain positions, to the point where discussion is virtually closed off or infected by hostility. Viewpoints are too quickly dismissed as nondiscussable. And positions are deliberately taken with a vehemence that augurs high costs for those who would disagree.

At the same time, it is too easy simply to criticize extreme examples of intolerant-mindedness. There are many issues of great importance to people within and without the academic world being debated today. I think many reasonable people within the university are deeply confused, or conflicted, about how to be an intellectual, or how to *conceive* of being an intellectual, in such an environment. More than anything, therefore, I want to try to understand the internal and external pressures we feel, or at least I feel, and, drawing particularly on the theoretical literature of freedom of speech, to offer some working assumptions about the human character that help us understand both the basis for the principle of academic freedom and why it is continuously at risk of being undermined.

Today, therefore, I am interested not in legal rules but in what legal thought can tell us about some of the tensions that govern our everyday lives. Beyond all else, what I have to say today is premised upon the belief that the daily acts of every one of us create an atmosphere far more powerful than the official acts we so often focus on. Every hiss in class when a student expresses an unpopular view, every opinion expressed (whether by professor or student) with unbending certitude, every mocking of opposing views, every unjust charge of bigotry, is another thread woven into the fabric that is our culture—the life we live.

What I have to say I have divided into four parts, each with its own theme and each qualifying the theme that preceded it—all leading up to what I hope will be an explanation of my title, "The Open-Minded Soldier and the University."

The Dangers of Belief

To begin to understand the underlying reasons and social function of academic freedom, or of intellectual values, we must begin with the problem of belief. We need to situate our inquiry in a broader theoretical context. The basic theme is this:

The impulse to intolerance arises out of the wish to believe, which is an ever present and powerful force in the human psyche. Never far from the surface in social interactions, it is a continual threat to democratic societies and to respecting fundamental principles of human decency. It attacks at every point of disagreement, insisting on conformity of every outward action, including speech, and frequently attempts to control the inner world of the mind as well. It is capable of producing the most vicious behavior human beings are capable of, the potential for which is detectable in its more modest manifestations. And the impulse to intolerance does not follow bad ideas only; some of the worst cruelty in human affairs has been committed in the pursuit of morally perfect utopian visions—leading to speculation that beliefs sometimes only provide a protective cover for other impulses, such as the wish to dominate and destroy.

This wary vision of the human personality is a profoundly important theme in the traditions of this country and of Western political and social theory. The literature of freedom of speech is steeped in it. The history of censorship of speech, and of persecution (or punishment) of those who hold and express those ideas, has produced some of the most eloquent and insightful observations about the human desire to have your way, to demand that others conform to your way of thinking and to rid the world of those who would not.[8] "Persecution for the expression of opinions is perfectly logical," Justice Oliver Wendell Holmes wrote in a famous judicial passage, "if you have no doubt of your premises or your power and want a certain result with all your heart, you naturally express your wishes in law and sweep away all opposition. To allow opposition by speech seems to indicate that you think the speech impotent . . . or that you do not care wholeheartedly for the result, or that you doubt either your power or your premises."[9] And this potential "logic" of belief impels people to very destructive ends. This is the central theme of Socrates, John Milton, John Stuart Mill, and great jurists like Louis Brandeis and Learned Hand. Indeed, the "logic" of belief is ultimately the annihilation of those who disagree: "Pleasures are ultimates," Holmes said in one of his many letters to Harold Laski, "and in cases of difference between ourself and another there is nothing to do except in unimportant matters to think ill of him and in important ones to kill him."[10] "[O]n their premises," Holmes continued, "it seems to me logical in the Catholic Church to kill heretics and [for] the Puritans to whip Quakers—and I see nothing more wrong in it from ultimate standards than I do in killing Germans when we are at war. When you are thoroughly convinced that you are right—wholeheartedly desire an end—and have no doubt of your power to accomplish it—I see nothing but municipal regulations to interfere with your using your power to accomplish it. The sacredness of human life is a formula that is good only inside a system of law."[11]

But belief and the impulse to intolerance lead us not only to throw speakers into the flames or to hang them by the stake but also to insist on having our way in every decision about ordering the society. Writers of social and political theory, therefore, often also express the same fears about the hegemonic tendencies of belief.

Take, as a recent example, a newly-published volume of essays by the political theorist and philosopher Isaiah Berlin, entitled *The Crooked Timber of Humanity*. In his opening essay ("The Pursuit of the Ideal") Berlin begins with the observation that two forces above all others have shaped human history in this century, the first being "advances in scientific and technological knowledge" and the second the "great ideological storms that have altered the lives of virtually all mankind."[12] Berlin's theme is the dangers of "ideology" or belief. "Happy are those," he says at one point, "who live under a discipline which they accept without question, who freely obey the orders of leaders, spiritual or temporal, whose word is fully accepted as unbreakable law; or those who have, by their own methods, arrived at clear and unshakeable convictions about what to do and what to be that brook no possible doubt." But, though perhaps happy, these people are also very dangerous: "[T]he possibility of a final solution," says Berlin, "—even if we forget the terrible sense that these words acquired in Hitler's day—turns out to be an illusion; and a very dangerous one." "For if one really believes that such a solution is possible, then surely no cost would be too high to obtain it: to make mankind just and happy and creative and harmonious forever—what could be too high a price to pay for that?" As with Holmes, and surprisingly echoing Holmes's very language, Berlin's mind follows the path of certitude about our beliefs to killing: "You declare that a given policy will make you happier, or freer, or give you room to breathe; but I know that you are mistaken, I know what you need, what all men need; and if there is resistance based on ignorance or malevolence, then it must be broken and hundreds of thousands may have to perish to make millions happy for all time."[13]

With this vision of such a dangerous propensity in the human character to intolerance, writers like Berlin and Holmes prescribe a heavy dosage of self-doubt and uncertainty. While their views differ to some extent, they tend to differ only in the degree to which they would commit themselves, and others, toward a posture of relativism in the world. "Tolerance is the twin of incredulity," Learned Hand once said to Holmes.[14] And Holmes himself wrote in a famous opinion that once we "have realized that time has upset many fighting faiths," we must "come to believe even more than [we] believe the very foundations of [our] own conduct that the ultimate good desired is better reached by free trade in ideas—that the best test of truth is the power of the thought to get itself accepted in the competition of the market. . . ."[15]

Berlin tells how he came to accept the position of "pluralism." For many years, he writes, his study of ideas proceeded on the notion that all questions "must have one true answer and one only," which could be reached by a "dependable path," and that all the truths so discovered would "necessarily be compatible." Then he read Machiavelli and was forever changed. Machiavelli wished to create a successful state capable of withstanding the inevitable attacks of a hostile world. To do this he looked back to the Roman Republic as a model. He recommended rulers who were wise and creative as well as capable of being cunning and ruthless. "That is how Rome rose to power and conquered the world," Berlin describes Machiavelli's views, "and it is the absence of this kind of wisdom and vitality and courage in adversity, of the qualities of both lions and foxes, that in the end brought it down."[16]

Now, against this, Berlin says, Machiavelli "sets . . . the notion of Christian virtues—humility, acceptance of suffering, unworldliness, the hope of salvation in an afterlife—and he remarks that if, as he plainly himself favours, a state of a Roman type is to be established, these qualities will not promote it: those who live by the precepts of Christian morality are bound to be trampled on by the ruthless pursuit of power by men who alone can re-create and dominate the republic which he wants to see. He does not condemn Christian virtues. He merely points out that the two moralities are incompatible, and he does not recognise any overarching criterion whereby we are enabled to decide the right life. . . . He simply leaves you to choose—he knows which he himself prefers."

For Berlin this was a "shock" because it made him realize that "not all the supreme values pursued by mankind now and in the past were necessarily compatible with one another."

And, so, Berlin says he became a pluralist. And with that perspective he recognizes that every society has its own special character, creating its own special understanding of the world, of itself, and emphasizing certain traits and capacities of the human personality. Thus the Homeric Greeks may have been "cruel, barbarous, mean, oppressive to the weak; but they created the *Iliad* and the *Odyssey,* something we cannot do in our more enlightened day." And what is true across time and across cultures is also true between individuals. "You believe in always telling the truth, no matter what," he says, whereas "I do not, because I believe that it can sometimes be too painful and too destructive." So "We can discuss each other's point of view, we can try to reach common ground, but in the end what you pursue may not be reconcilable with the ends to which I find that I have dedicated my life."[17]

The essence of life, therefore, for Holmes and Berlin and others like them, is the "collision of values." We must learn—in Berlin's words—that we "cannot have everything, in principle as well as in practice."[18] In this way Berlin concludes his essay, and it would seem embarrassingly simplistic were it not said against the background of what he had said before and what we know he had lived through.

Morality and Commitment

And now I want to explore why this perspective of Holmes, Berlin, and others ultimately does not satisfy, is seriously incomplete, and therefore does not account for the tensions of real life.

The critical problem with the recommendation of self-doubt, or of an acceptance of multiple truths and of pluralism, is that it must end somewhere. Yet exactly where the perspective or disposition of self-doubt and pluralism appropriately ends and what we might call reasonable commitment to belief takes up is not easy to identify. As powerful as the Holmes and Berlin perspective is about life, in appreciating the strength and the danger of beliefs and the impulse to intolerance and in articulating the need for greater self-consciousness of our incapacity to hold truth in our hands and, even when we can, to implement it in an imperfect world, that perspective simply cannot provide a full and complete guide to life. At some point we will draw the line and insist on having our way, insist that the book is closed and the mind settled.

Of course, once that is pointed out, everyone acknowledges it as if it were obvious—even Holmes and Berlin. Thus, Berlin, at the conclusion of his essay, after recommending that we must all be "pluralists," after recognizing that "there are many different ends that men may seek" and that these ends bring out different aspects of the human character, the human potentiality, and that these are "in some profound, irreconcilable ways, not combinable in any final synthesis," so that we must always be ready to "compromise" and to accept "trade-offs," Berlin says, finally, in the penultimate paragraph, that certainly there are "if not universal values, at any rate a minimum without which societies could scarcely survive." There can be no compromise, he acknowledges, when it comes to "slavery or ritual murder or Nazi gas chambers or torture . . . or mindless killing."[19] There is, in other words, an end to tolerance, an end to the open-mindedness of the posture of "pluralism," a point at which it is proper, even required, that one insist on having your way, insist that others comply.

When Berlin comes to the subject of commitment to belief, however, his heart isn't in it. He doesn't overlook it, he's far too smart and sensitive for that, but his very considerable and subtle powers of intellect seem to grow dormant as he enters this region of human experience. And, for all these advocates of self-doubt and self-restraint, whether it be Mill or Holmes or Berlin (or others), that failure is perfectly understandable, once one appreciates their personal life experiences against which they think and write. It is hardly surprising that our most compelling warnings about the connections between belief and the darker regions of the human personality come from the pens of individuals who, in one case (Mill), was raised from infancy under the tutelege of an autocratic father on a single intellectual and emotional diet of Benthamite utilitarianism, who in another (Holmes) fought and was seriously wounded in the Civil War and lived through the rabid intolerance of the Red Scare, or who in still another (Berlin) witnessed firsthand the barbarism beneath the ideologies of fascism and communism. In the face of these firsthand encounters with the suffocating and cruel tendencies of true belief, is it any wonder that they would pursue self-doubt until they even flirted with relativism? Because their personal lives brushed up against *one* of the most destructive sides of the human personality, these individuals seem possessed of a need to articulate a vision of life that is more open-minded, more self-doubting, more accepting of the variety of life, more willing to see the possibility of multiple truths in life, than the visions of those who, never having encountered the tyranny of the zealot, are eager to embark on the reformation of mankind and ready to commit themselves whole-heartedly to schemes to improve the human race.

But, whatever the reason for the partial vision of pluralists, the fact remains that life is not only learning to be conscious of the potential destructiveness of belief, it is also learning and embracing—and being able to *act* on, which also means *insisting* on—a basic code of morals and justice. And that, it turns out, is not a simple or straightforward matter either. To do the right thing, even when we clearly see it, often involves costs our weaker wills will not bear, despite the scoldings of our nobler sentiments. To make matters worse, the right thing is, unfortunately, often unclear in life, which means not only that we experience a good deal of anxiety about what to do but, more importantly, our weaker sides are provided with ready cover for choosing to do nothing.

All this has acute relevance when you live in a time, as we do, in which (what Berlin called) the "minimum" is being renegotiated. Many if not most of the matters about which intolerant-mindedness is claimed today relate to another great strand in our intellectual and cultural heritage, namely our great project of equality and civil rights. This tremendous social effort to redefine relationships between groups within the society involves using both legal and social power to change both legal rules and social attitudes.

Now, as the early civil rights movement, spurred on by the Supreme Court's decision in *Brown v. Board of Education* (1954), successfully completed its goal of ridding the society of virtually all legal, or what is known as *de jure*, forms of racial discrimination, attention has inevitably shifted to the next source of segregation and discrimination, that which originates in the hearts and minds of people and not in legislative and official corridors. Today, and this has been true now for many years, the problem of racism in American society is primarily a problem of attitude, of mind, not official policy. No official rule makes white and black students, in this university or any other educational institution, eat at separate tables in dining halls, or socialize exclusively within each group. No official policy makes a black student or faculty member suffer a verbal insult at night while walking across the campus. These are problems of attitude, of mind.

And, as the civil rights movement achieved its successes and awakened the conscience of the nation, other groups within the society have naturally been moved to press their "rights" too. For many people it has become clear, disturbingly clear, that we are partially if not largely socially created, so that the sense of oneself within the society, of who one is, of how seriously one may expect to be treated, of what hopes one may entertain of a role in the society, all are the result of how other people see you. The role of women within the society has thus become a major focus. So has the status of Asian Americans, Hispanic Americans, and gay and lesbian persons. While some of the problems of these groups continue to involve discriminatory laws and official acts, for them too the most significant source of discrimination is that which comes from the mind.

Now, it would be naive to think that using social power—by which I mean all the myriad informal sanctions we impose on people every day: censuring, denouncing, shunning, etc.—to shape people's attitudes is not a part—or not a legitimate part—of this process of change. Social coercion only seems illegitimate when the effort is made *to reform* the way we think now, not for enforcing what we already believe firmly to be wrong. No one today, presumably, would think it illegitimate to condemn someone who refused to associate with another person just because of the color of that person's skin. We would express disgust, collectively if we could, and employ what social powers we possessed to make him reform his conduct, and his attitude. We would not say, "Well, there are different ways of life, and each has its own virtues and vices, and I am in no position to judge whether the racist's life is inferior and it would be wrong of me under the circumstances to in any way coerce him into changing."

But, of course, it was not always this way. If we had lived in, say, the 1930s or '40s, our objection to this behavior, and the attitude it reflects, would probably have been only that it was impolite, or imprudently inflammatory, not morally repugnant. "Reasonable" people then believed that they had a "right" not to associate with black people, the "right" to choose their own society, just like "reasonable" people in the 1950s were convinced that it was appropriate to fire people from their jobs because they thought the precepts of communism or socialism superior to those of capitalism. We now feel very differently. Our attitudes, as it were, toward those attitudes have changed. That happened in part through reason, but it also happened, and continues to happen today, through the exercise of social coercion. People who continue to think that way are made to feel the consequences of private sanctions, of being personally "disliked," or "unwelcome."

That is how it should be. That is how the moral conscience has been created and recreated over time. And now the same process continues. We are in the midst of a great social Reformation, a Reformation of attitude, which, in my view, is generally all to the good. It is an appropriate and desirable step in following the aspirations of our social and political principles. I am not persuaded by those who say or imply that the civil rights project has moved into the realm of the ridiculous—when even blondes are now joining the chorus of victims. There are ridiculous claims, but I see no reason why we should think that our attitudes as a society are perfectly fair-minded and that we can with self-satisfaction shelve our principles of equality of opportunity and respect for the dignity of the individual. I see many valid claims being made today and many on the horizon. It is tiring, to be sure, but surely it is worth it.

There are, of course, many who try to divert attention from these legitimate efforts at refining fairness by employing a variety of tactics. The trivializer focuses on the excesses any reformation is bound to produce—Should "manhole" be replaced with "personhole," they say, and explode with laughter, as if they have thereby shown the entire effort to make a common language more inclusive, more *common*, to be absurd. The obtuse won't deal with the merits of the reformer's claims because they can't get by the intolerant-mindedness with which the claims are advanced, a frame of mind reformers almost inescapably fall into as they continually do battle with the existing status quo (though that does not mean it is inappropriate to object to the state of mind with which claims are made).

But the central observation I am trying to make at the moment is that we are in the middle of a great Reformation, that it is a Reformation of mind and attitude, and appropriately so, and that like any Reformation it is filled with confusions and uncertainties about how we want to reform ourselves and others. As in any revolution, there is confusion and uncertainty about what of the past, of the old regime, to jettison as tainted and what to preserve and carry forward. And there is confusion and uncertainty about how exactly to revise the incredibly intricate interactions of our daily lives. Drawing the lines between treating women as sexual objects and being latter-day Puritans is, unfortunately, not always self-evident.

Here's the main point: Belief and its tendencies are a great concern of our culture and give rise to the felt need to inculcate self-doubt and self-restraint. But there is also a minimum, a floor of principles to which we legitimately will demand adherence. And inside the process of defining these basic principles of morality and justice, which is ongoing and changing, the call is for belief and commitment. There our fear is of apathy and timidity, of not having the courage of our convictions, or even the courage to have convictions, of being the "reasonable" people who in the past accepted as normal what we now regard, thanks to the heroic efforts of the few who brushed aside the arguments of the pluralists and demanded conformity to their visions, as immoral and unjust.

We live with this abiding tension of needing to be more self-doubting and at the same time becoming even more committed to our basic principles.

Academic Freedom and Intellectual Values

In this complex world, there is, I believe, a special role for the university. It is a role that focuses more on the correction of the impulse to intolerance than on the need for commitment to belief. All institutions, all professions, indeed all individuals, have ideal images toward which they orient their behavior. For me the image of the university, what gives content to the principle of academic freedom or intellectual and artistic values, involves a profoundly important process of suspension of belief, which produces an open mind and a sympathetic imagination that bravely explores the paths of human thought and experience, as well as nature, without reserve. It is not standardless; it is guided by notions of reason and truth. But it is continuously self-reflective, even about what we take to be "reason" and "truth." Intellectuals, artists, scientists, are watchers—always looking for what seems to make no sense, for what's surprising, for what's foreign, for what's hidden. And so the healthy academic community has its own special sounds, the sounds of sentences: But is that true? Maybe there's something to that. Let me think about it. I wonder. That's interesting. I've changed my mind.

The university strives to be this way, it must be quickly added, not because it is the only way to improve our understanding of the world. The life of action, of commitment to belief, with all its sharp conflict, has its own way too of giving off the sparks of truth. But the approach of intellectual freedom is one distinctive method, and in a world so largely organized around the other approach the special character of the university is all the more useful to preserve, as wilderness is so much more precious in an urbanized life.

Additionally, the special world of intellectual and artistic freedom in the university also stands as a fixed warning for the rest of society that the commitment to belief has its excesses and must be moderated with self-doubt. In this, I believe, academic freedom shares the same function as the principle of freedom of speech—a special preserve of openness in a society forever on the verge of entering the destructive territory that is Holmes's and Berlin's concern.

So, in these two great pulls of life, the impulse to intolerance and the need for commitment to belief, the university and its principle of academic freedom opts to overcome the former, because it lives primarily in a world of the latter. No claim should be made for it that it is an ideal toward which all human activity should aim, nor that it is the only way—or perhaps even the best way if one had to choose among several—to achieve its goals (i.e., truth, understanding). It is, rather, an extreme extension of a single strand of the human character, justified in being extreme by its location in a human universe that tends toward extremes in other directions. It is fit for its purpose, but its purpose is justified by its location in a larger world.

The defining characteristic of the university, therefore, ought to be the *extraordinary* degree to which it is open to ideas.

The Vulnerability of Academic Freedom

But there are many reasons why this ideal of intellectual freedom is so vulnerable in the real world. The contemporary university is inextricably entwined in the political and moral issues of the day. That is partly because social change often begins with society's youth, and it is at the university that youth tend first to become politically active and to seek social change. It is also partly due to the actions of the university itself. Driven by financial needs to seek the assistance of outside individuals and institutions, the university must deal with donors who insist on supporting only research or programs with a high degree of "relevance." There is the risk that deans and administrators within the university will themselves tend to internalize this value, which gradually undermines the ideal of open and unconstrained intellectual inquiry. Finally, the university is itself an actor, not only a body of individuals pursuing ideas in the abstract. The university decides which faculty to hire and which courses to require and offer.

But there is something even more profound, I believe, than any of these pressures that continually threatens to erode the ideal of academic freedom. It stems from a dilemma deep in the psyche of the enterprise, and I want to close my lecture by trying to grasp it.

The ideal of academic freedom is a way of life. It exercises and emphasizes certain sides of the personality, of the mind, and those parts, through exercise, gain strength and prominence. As such, it is character shaping. Some of us—this must be said—even become quite ridiculous, in our own special ways. The suspension of belief, the openness to ideas, necessarily, or inevitably, I think, is achieved only through a process that involves some mental distancing from the real world consequences of choices, from pain and suffering, in the way that a surgeon develops a numbness to the knife. Most importantly, the capacity for fixed commitment and decisive action tends to atrophy with a developed character of self-doubt and open-mindedness. And the capacities for dealing with a less-than-perfect world, and a less self-doubting world, are also diminished. (The effective politician, for example, must shed the potentiality for intellectual embarrassment, which is absolutely central to the identity of the true intellectual.) The absence of any or all these qualities will, in some settings, be unattractive and even sometimes disqualifying. To put the matter sharply, intellectuals are good at thinking through a problem, but never to lead, and probably not even to join, the platoon.

Berlin is right about this, there are different ways of life, each with its own distinctive calls on our capacities and each with its own unique contributions and achievements. And he is also right that our wish is to deny that reality, to seek to have everything, to be everything. Yet we cannot. And within the world of academic freedom there will, because of this, forever be discomfort with the incapacities generated by the way of life of heightened awareness of ignorance, of self-doubt and open-mindedness. Not only discomfort but efforts—often even desperate efforts—on our parts to deny that truth about our condition and to prove that we are capable of commitment to beliefs.

Like many people of genius, Holmes expressed these tensions so powerfully because he suffered from them so acutely. He almost lusted after self-doubt, because he was repelled by the behavior of true believers (among whom, significantly, he counted himself when he served as a soldier in the Civil War). He "detested," he said, the person who "knows that he knows" and who "catches postulates like the influenza";[20] and yet he also felt some deep admiration for those who saw clearly a truth and pursued it even to the point of sacrificing their own lives. Sometimes, he seemed to face up to the potentially enervating consequences that self-doubt has for commitment to action. On one occasion, in a letter, he forged an ideal of what he hoped he could be, what I have called for this lecture the open-minded soldier: "[T]ake thy place on the one side or the other," he recommended, "if with the added grace of knowing that the Enemy is as good . . . as thou, so much the better, but kill him if thou Canst."[21]

Given what we know about how the mind works in war, whose participants more than at any other time must summon the will (or the courage) to act, the image of combining this action with an intellectual character of self-doubt and sympathetic imagination has always seemed to me vivid and powerful (though not, I should add, its drift toward relativism). Its seeming improbability reveals its central and profound message.

But whether one should take this as a viable ideal toward which all should strive or (following what I believe are the implications of Berlin's argument, which he does not pursue) as a hopeless holding on to incompatible ways of life, I remain ambivalent. I am inclined toward the latter, the less sunny, view. To act is to darken the periphery of our vision. To regain the periphery we sacrifice the single-mindedness that is the spring of the will to act. And, if that is true, then to try to have both states is to have neither as well as we might, producing perhaps a kind of oscillation between mediocre states of both.

That is not to say, however, that the will and capacity to act effectively is entirely destroyed in the intellectual world, only that it is diminished. And, as I mentioned a moment ago, the university must act. It has an intellectual center, in which the principle of academic freedom reigns, but it also has a workplace, residences and a system of faculty and course selection that is created by choice. And whenever it does act, I believe the university most follows and reinforces its special social identity by aspiring to be Holmes's open-minded soldier.

This leads me to close with an illustration of what I have in mind and a paradox for the university and the principle of academic freedom. The dilemma is this: Among the actions we are periodically called on to take is that of deciding whether to maintain the principle of academic freedom itself or to modify or abandon it altogether. Yet, if it is true that the practice of academic freedom diminishes the capacity to act, then the principle is especially vulnerable to attacks from without, as well as from psychological tensions from within (for reasons I have already suggested); or its defense will be taken over by those more accustomed to action but whose defense paradoxically will violate the very spirit of the enterprise. I see this happening all the time with freedom of speech. As the challenge grows to the prevailing rule that extremist or highly offensive speech is protected—it being pointed out that the harm of these speech acts is greater than generally acknowledged, that further exceptions to the First Amendment can safely be created, and that the specter of McCarthyism is now more behind us than we think; arguments which though I disagree with them, are perfectly reasonable and debatable positions—the challenge is frequently met with a closed-mindedness, a pig-headedness, that makes me wince.

What we must understand is that the soul of academic freedom, just like the soul of freedom of speech, resides not in particular rules or outcomes but in a spirit with which we approach life. It is a spirit that is born of a wariness of the dangers of belief, but that recognizes the importance of belief and commitment too. It is a spirit that while stretching in one direction, for perfectly good social reasons, lives comfortably with the disabling consequences of that course. Above all else, it seeks a capacity of understanding of the world, and of the consequences of our actions in it, that tries to come as close as we can to Holmes's open-minded soldier.

NOTES

This essay originally appeared in *Michigan Quarterly Review* 32 (winter 1993): 1–19.

An earlier form of this essay was delivered as the second annual Davis, Markert, Nickerson Lecture on Academic and Intellectual Freedom, sponsored by the University of Michigan Senate, April 20, 1992.

1. *Cohen v. California*, 403 U.S. 15 (1971).

2. *Tinker v. Des Moines Independent Community School District*, 393 U.S. 503 (1969).

3. 403 U.S. 21.

4. 393 U.S. 509.

5. *Bethel School District v. Fraser*, 478 U.S. 675 (1986).

6. *Hazelwood School District v. Kuhlmeier*, 484 U.S. 260 (1988).

7. The University of Michigan speech code was declared unconstitutional in *Doe v. University of Michigan*, 721 F. Supp. 852 (E.D. Mich. 1989). The only other university speech code to be considered in the courts is that of the University of Wisconsin, which was also declared unconstitutional in *UWM Post v. Board of Regents of the University of Wisconsin System*, 774 F. Supp. 1163 (E.D. Wis. 1991).

8. For an elaboration of this point, see my book, *The Tolerant Society: Freedom of Speech and Extremist Speech in America* (New York: Oxford University Press, 1986).

9. *Abrams v. United States*, 250 U.S. 616, 630 (1919) (Holmes, J., dissenting).

10. Edmund Wilson, "Justice Oliver Wendell Holmes." In *Patriotic Gore* (New York: Farrar, Straus & Giroux, 1962), 762.

11. Ibid., 764.

12. Isaiah Berlin, "The Pursuit of the Ideal." In *The Crooked Timber of Humanity* (New York: Knopf, 1991), 1.

13. Ibid., 13–14, 15.

14. Gerald Gunther, "Learned Hand and the Origins of Modern First Amendment Doctrine: Some Fragments of History," *Standard Law Review* 27 (1975): 757.

15. 250 U.S. 630.

16. Berlin, "Pursuit of the Ideal," 5–6, 8.

17. Ibid. 9, 12.

18. Ibid. 17.

19. Ibid. 10, 11, 17, 18.

20. Wilson, "Justice Holmes," 777.

21. Gunther, "Learned Hand," 757. In a letter to Hand discussing his thoughts before "the statute of Garrison on Commonwealth Avenue, Boston," Holmes says that if he were "an official person I should say nothing shall induce me to do honor to a man who broke the fundamental condition of social life by bidding the very structure of society perish rather than he not have his way—Expressed in terms of morals, to be sure, but still, his way." As the "son of Garrison," alternatively, he should find himself thinking differently, taking the view that "every great reform has seemed to threaten the structure of society,—but that society has not perished, because man is a social animal, and with every turn falls into a new pattern like the Kaleidoscope." As a philosopher, however, he would believe them to be "[f]ools both, not to see that you are the two blades (conservative and radical) of the shears that cut out the future." But it is the "Ironical man in the back of the philosopher's head" who is given the last word, saying of the philosopher that he was the "[g]reatest fool of all" for not seeing that "man's destiny is to fight" and urging him to "take thy place on the one side or the other, if with the added grace of knowing that the Enemy is as good a man as thou, so much the better, but kill him if thou Canst."

Dirty Minds, Dirty Bodies, Clean Speech
Catharine R. Stimpson

. . . Civil, or social, liberty: the nature and limits of the power which
can be legitimately exercised by society over the individual. A question seldom stated and hardly ever discussed in general terms, but
which profoundly influences the practical controversies of the age
by its latent presence, and is likely soon to make itself recognized
as the vital question of the future.
> —*John Stuart Mill*, On Liberty, *(1859)*

I leave you the will to fight, the desire to live; the right to anger, to
love, to the erotic, to joy, to transform silence into language and
action. I leave you a litany for survival.
> —*Audre Lorde, "The Blessing,"* Program,
> *Audre Lorde Memorial Service,*
> *Cathedral of St. John the Divine,*
> *New York City (January 18, 1993)*

I am honored that the Senate of the University of Michigan has invited
me to give the third annual Davis, Markert, Nickerson Lecture on Academic and Intellectual Freedom. For the Lectureship has a vital, double purpose. First, it reminds us of the courage of three very good and
admirable men: Chandler Davis, Clement Markert, and Mark Nickerson. In 1954 they chose to test the legitimacy and constitutionality
of the House Un-American Activities Committee and were punished
for it by country and university. The actions of these men, because
they enlarged the field of freedom, were a gift to all of us. Next, the
Lectureship represents an act of restitution for these men and the University's rededication to academic freedom. In 1990 a Senate Assembly Resolution declared that "academic and intellectual freedom are
fundamental values for a university in a free society. They form the
foundation of the rights of free inquiry, free expression and free dissent that are necessary for the life of the university."

I share the spirit of this resolution—as my acceptance of the Senate's invitation signifies. My perspective is not that of the professional historian nor of the legal scholar. Indeed, as I read law review articles about civil liberties, civil rights, and the First Amendment, I feel like an intruder on someone else's ancient, rampant family quarrels. Instead, my perspective is that of a citizen devoted to civil liberties, civil rights, the First Amendment, and feminism.[1] My professional interests are in culture, literature, women's studies, and education. These interests have taught me that original, important work can emerge from brutal confinements and censorship. Beauty is often born from a bleak and filthy matrix. I have also learned how great a price such births extract.

I have selected a form at once familiar and idiosyncratic: the journey. It begins in the citadel of staunch faith in freedom, but then departs in order to wander through doubts and ambivalences, mostly on a road that meanders geographically through our campuses and intellectually through postmodernism. At the end, I return to the citadel, bringing some arguments for its defense. So doing, I illustrate the mission statement of the Michigan League, printed on a card in its guestrooms, "Serving the Present, Preserving the Past."

To begin the jog with an autobiographical anecdote. When I was younger, my devotion to the First Amendment and academic freedom was strong but theoretical, casual, even lazy. In the early 1970s, however, I was up for tenure, my tenure up-for-grabs. Although my struggle for tenure was long and painful, I was not tested as rigorously as Davis, Markert, and Nickerson were. Ultimately, tenure was mine, not because of any crushingly self-evident and transcendental personal worth, but because some strong people fought for me. Their resolve kept me in academic life, and, in wandering and cloud-like moments, I sometimes wonder what I would have become if my supporters had been less stalwart and successful. A law student, perhaps. For the first time, I wish to tell "My Tenure story" publicly. I do so, not out of self-indulgence, but because my story serves as a small prophecy of the condition of academic freedom today. I began my teaching career at Barnard in the early 1960s and was first a lecturer, then instructor, then assistant professor. During those years, the tenure system at Barnard changed. Columbia University, of which Barnard was a part, got far more say. I was a member of the first cohort to go through the new procedures. This mattered. In bureaucratic institutions, the precise nature of the bureaucratic structures always does. People were feeling their way and feeling their oats.

However, three other elements in the mini-series of the Stimpson Tenure Case were weightier. First, during the late 1960s, Columbia University was the setting of a famous student uprising on the part of African-American and radical white students. I was never a central player. Indeed, on the night of the first police bust, I was home preparing a class, ironically on Dostoevsky's *The Possessed*. Nevertheless, I did support the student causes and joined peaceful picket lines around the buildings that students and some faculty had occupied. Members of my department who opposed the strike told me to get off the lines, warning me that it "would be better" for me if I did. I stayed on. A few years later, these people vigorously opposed my tenure. Mindful of the fallacy of *post hoc ergo propter hoc*, I cannot prove that I was being punished for exercising my right to political speech, but I suspect I was.

Next, I did women's studies, then so Utopian. I was teaching courses about women and culture. I published a paper on the relations between black movements and women's movements. Ah, said the administrator at Columbia who oversaw tenure and promotion matters, Professor Stimpson is in women's studies. Candidates for tenure and promotion must be in a discipline. Women's studies is not a discipline. Therefore, Professor Stimpson cannot be a candidate for tenure and promotion. His syllogism, which attempted to exclude me *a priori* from consideration, was no empty intellectual exercise. He did not want me, a rejection that tested academic freedom in a time of intellectual ferment. For surely, academic freedom protects both political speech and fresh intellectual speech, if such speech is rigorous and reasonable. To be fair, it was not entirely muddled and thick-headed for people to ask about women's studies as a field in the early 1970s. Women's studies *was* new, untested, full of wild nymphs who have since calmed down and large claims that have since been recalibrated.

The third element was far uglier. After the remote control of institutional interest had clicked off the channel showing the Stimpson Tenure Case, a participant-observer in some of the meetings told me a story. My sexuality, she said, had become an agenda item. The discussion was not whether I was an appropriate role model for students but what I might do, on the couch or in a bed, what possible gestures, what possible caresses. Some of the professors who were to vote on me had fantasized about my body—overtly, voyeuristically, lasciviously, maliciously. According to my witness, the most voyeuristic, lascivious, and malicious had cast their negative votes most happily. My witness confessed, guiltily, that she had not spoken up. Even now, I cannot think of these scenes, or more accurately, of the account that I was given of them, without anger and shame. What was at stake was more than the freedom of my ideas and speech. My body was at stake. The dirty minds of my opponents were making my body dirty and then voting as if their speech were clean and cleansing. I could not speak back, for I did not know that there was bad speech to answer. My opponents, ironically, were in camera, in a closet called "departmental committee."

Each of the three elements of "My Tenure Case" foreshadowed an issue about intellectual and academic freedom alive on campuses today. Together, these elements make the contemporary situation of these freedoms unique and uniquely volatile. To outline them:

First, the historically notorious assaults on artistic, intellectual, and academic freedom continue within the United States and without. The domineering censors are churches, including the systematic efforts of the radical religious right to take over local politics; the state, from local to national agencies; and, to a far lesser degree, the university. Certain figures have become emblematic of the fight against these assaults. Think, for example, of Robert Mapplethorpe or, on a far grander scale, of Salman Rushdie. Our historians document the sad, stupid, destructive record of such assaults, of Edith Wharton indexed by the FBI in 1945 because her novel *The Age of Innocence* was on a list of books of someone "undergoing a security clearance" (Robins 1992, 447). Partly because of the persistence of such assaults, partly because of the influential role of the modern university in the arts, in 1990 the American Association of University Professors issued a statement, "Academic Freedom and Artistic Expression," which extended academic freedom to cover artistic and imaginative expression as well as scholarship and teaching. The history of freedom of speech alone warns us against relying naively on the state as its guardian. Getting in bed with the state can be worse than getting in bed with an elephant. It is more like rolling around with a dull-bladed but slashing guillotine.

Second, the contemporary university is generating an even greater ferment of ideas in the early 1990s than it did in the early 1970s. Whether new ideas cross disciplinary borders or stay within, these novelties put great demands on people's capacity for fair academic judgments. "Traditionalists" can viscerally react against and suspect the new. For their part, the carriers of the new can viscerally react against and suspect traditionalists. When this Battle of the Books occurs, both camps can ignore academic freedom, an earnest referee whistling away on the sidelines.

Two well-known sets of ideas have become closely intertwined with the discussions of academic freedom. One is postmodern theories of language. Growing from ancient roots, these theories, often deliriously, tell us of the power of language (our systems of meaning) to construct reality. If language constructs our world, the old binary distinction between word and deed, speech and conduct, blurs and threatens to dissolve. A word veers toward the status of deed; speech veers toward the status of conduct. The hoary bit of folklore "Sticks and stones can break my bones, but words can never hurt me" becomes a bitter joke. Not only do words hurt. Words give sticks, stones, and bones their meaning.

The second set of ideas, replete with internal conflicts and arguments, has to do with groups that history has harmed and marginalized, the subordinates in history's hierarchies. In the United States, these groups include women, racial and ethnic minorities, representatives of once-colonized countries, and gays and lesbians. Gay and lesbian studies is, in turn, part of the new study of sexualities. Mostly, membership in one group or more is the consequence of having been born with one body or another, one sex or another, one race or another.[2] In its way, although people dispute whether homosexuality is genetic fate or existential choice, membership in the group of gays and lesbians is also a statement about the body. In placid and respectable poses, none of these bodies is legally obscene, but even so, a grazing gaze can choke on them.

In brief, because this second set of ideas has to do with history, power, gender, race, and sexualities, it is utterly charged with meanings and emotions, which roil the ill-tempered unconscious as well as the well-tempered mind. These ideas and images address intimate as well as public life. Robert Mapplethorpe's most notorious photographs elegantly transgress against conventional prohibitions against sex between men, sex between men of different races, and eroticized sadomasochism among men, no matter what the race.[3] These new ideas and images then present their audiences with challenges different from those that traditionally heterodox political and religious speech do. For various reasons, which people cannot always acknowledge, it can be wretched to let these new ideas and images breathe freely. They may seem, may feel, unclean. We all realize that a flag-waving patriot hates a flag-burner. We have not fully registered how a homophobe with tenure responds to scholarship that marches out of Queer Nation.

These ideas also provide an oppositional analysis of painful and persistent cultural constructions of the body: for example, that some bodies are dirty, some clean; that the black, brown, red, or yellow body is less worthy of respect than the white; that women of all races and all members of "minority" races are nothing but body, no mind, no speech but sighs and, with luck, a song. If I happen to live in a body that has been so culturally constructed, it is peculiarly hard to hear these constructions presented in a non-oppositional fashion, as if they were true or possibly true. I am not an armored institution. I am neither a church nor a state. Nor am I a symbolic object, a flag or a cross to be burnt. I am a person, dwelling in my flesh, who will die when its electrical impulses cease to race through brain and nervous system.

This peculiar hardship helps to breed a prickly suspicion about the modern consensus on free speech. Kathleen Sullivan, whom I very much respect, has written that this consensus rests upon two pillars: agnosticism and materialism. Agnosticism means that "government may not pick and choose among ideas, nor enforce an official orthodoxy by making political heresy a crime." This arrangement will "respect human autonomy, advance the truth, facilitate democracy, or some combination of the three." So far, so good, so very good.

Materialism means that speech is a privileged form of conduct. It may not be "curtailed in order to protect people from psychic injury or emotional distress." Sullivan continues, "True, speech may be banned when it will cause real material harm, but the danger that speech will cause such harm must not be loosely hypothesized" (Sullivan 1992, 36). Sexually harassing speech does material harm. It stops students from finishing a course; it stops workers from earning the paycheck that will pay for food and shelter.

The prickly suspicion escalates into a rash on the question of materialism. For the consensus seems indifferent to the half-life materialism of speech about the body, speech that wraps itself around the body and threatens to become the body's shroud and skin. I tell myself to shrug it off by being thick-skinned, both genuine virtue and survival skill. Being thick-skinned is much better than being thick-skulled. Nevertheless, how can I not sometimes resent the energy it takes to grow and don a carapace? Moreover, the consensus seems indifferent to materialism in a second sense, that is, the strong and palpable connections between having money and exercising one's freedom of speech, especially if one wants to be heard beyond a little booth at Burger King. Catharine MacKinnon is right when she pungently states, ". . . the marketplace of ideas is literal: those with the most money can buy the most speech, and women are poor" (1987, 140).

My third issue is inseparable from my second. Postmodern theories of language might have appealed to the contemporary academy no matter who was on the faculty or in the student body. Among the forefathers of these theories are the Sophists, who were, I believe, white men. However, the proliferation of ideas about history, power, gender, race, and sexualities has occurred, in part, because of the new demographics of the academy. We not only read about women. We women, of all races, are here, asking for our place in the curriculum. Significantly, in 1986, women became the majority of the students who earned a bachelor's or a master's degree. We not only read about the African diaspora or Mexican field labor. Minority students are here, asking for their place in the curriculum. The social relations, as well as the syllabus, of the classroom are changing.

It is a tribute to the American academy and its current commitment to academic freedom that a Catharine Stimpson of the early 1990s would most likely have a different tenure case from the Catharine Stimpson of the early 1970s—if we were forced to suffer the appalling arrival of my carnal *doppelgänger*. Nevertheless, our new ideas and demographic diversities are a cause of two well-known sieges against the citadel of intellectual and academic freedom: the antipornography movement and the ban hate speech movement.[4] Each has a different object. The antipornography movement seeks to outlaw pornography, which it construes, far too narrowly, as hate speech against all women. The ban hate speech movement seeks to outlaw hate speech, primarily but not exclusively against minorities of both genders. Each has its own political allegiances and alliances. The antipornography movement has a right-wing branch. The speech code movement apparently does not.

The two movements, however, have much in common. Both argue that language powerfully constructs the world and its daily agonies. Therefore, changing language will reshape the world and diminish those agonies, especially the pain and suffering of the powerless. Both movements tend to describe the powerless as victims rather than as survivors. So doing, both invert the standard Utilitarian calculus. Instead of asking how to increase the greatest good for the greatest number, they ask how to diminish the greatest harm for a great number. No one should deny that hate speech can enforce and ritualize patterns of subordination. "Our law," writes Catharine MacKinnon of the MacKinnon/Dworkin ordinance which would make pornography a violation of women's civil rights, "is about getting some people off the backs of other people" (MacKinnon 1987, 195). Both movements also fear the current rise of hate speech. Certainly, more and more racial epithets and incidents (such euphemisms) have greeted students who are Jewish or members of racial minorities. Certainly, too, pornography is spreading geographically, to the newly-liberated countries of Eastern Europe, and electronically, on videocassettes and computer networks.[5] Both movements, finally, have brilliant advocates and passionate followers.

Indeed, largely because both movements oppose real harm, they have been able to provoke an ambivalent and divided response in many of us. We dislike opposing the opponents of pain and suffering. Seeing an eroticized image of a woman hustled through a meat grinder, hearing a vicious cry of "Nigger," "Slant-eye," or "Kike"—this engenders anger, anxiety, fear, disgust, dismay. It also stimulates a fierce desire for other and better worlds purged of such images and sounds. In her tremendous poem about rage, "The Phenomenology of Anger," Adrienne Rich writes, "I would have loved to live in a world / of women and men gaily / in collusion with green leaves, stalks" (Rich 1973, 30). Our reluctance to oppose the opponents of pain and suffering is a reverse twist on civil libertarian attitudes during the Skokie March: the distaste at having to support the Nazi supporters of Jewish pain and suffering.

Aiding and abetting this ambivalence is a second—about the role of emotion in public life. The antipornography and ban hate speech movements pump up and run on the fuel of feeling. They push certain emotional buttons in order to push their cause forward and push serious objections out of the way. As Wendy Kaminer, a feminist who defends the First Amendment, writes in a burst of polemic and realism, "Rational argument is no match for highly emotional testimony. But it may be wishful thinking to believe that penalizing the production and distribution of hard-core pornography would have much effect on sexual violence. . . . It would, however, complicate campaigns to distribute information about AIDS, let alone condoms, in the public schools. It would distract us from the harder, less popular work of reforming sexual stereotypes and roles. . . . The promise of the anti-porn movement is the promise of a world in which almost no one can buy pornography and almost anyone can buy a gun" (Kaminer 1992, 118).

Stimulated by "symbolic, nonrational expression," emotions help to create and sustain social change that I want (Massey 1992, 114). The image of the state and university pummeling three good men because of their beliefs outrages me. This is a charge to the battery of my defense of academic freedom. However, emotions, as they wash over and through us, can wash out tolerance. Feelings blind and deafen us. The cries of women taking back the night have been strong and potent, but, on a march or two, I have feared them, because they have reduced the registers of human voices to a yell for cosmic vengeance. One of the great values of free speech is that it lets every emotion hang out, but hang out to dry in the hot light of scrutiny.

Knotting with these two ambivalences is a third, provoked by some of the more vocal, affluent defenders of free speech. I think, for example, of editorialists in the *Wall Street Journal.* On the one hand, they do defend intellectual and academic freedom. However, the defender of my cause is not necessarily my buddy. Often, the defense of free speech has seemed self-righteous, preachy, noble words from comfortable people who have themselves never felt the sting and lash of hate speech. Often, too, the defenders of free speech pick their battles with suspect care. They will revile a campus that has tried to craft a constitutional code of conduct and initiate a multicultural curriculum. They fall silent when Major League Baseball, on February 3, 1993, fines Marge Schott, the owner of the Cincinnati Reds, $25,000 for making racial and ethnic slurs in private conversations and, in addition, demands that she complete a course in multicultural sensitivity training.[6]

Then, too, some of the defenders of free speech have been egregious actors in the P.C. Follies, a show that seems to have been running as long as *The Fantasticks* and in which I have had a bit part. As bit player, I have said consistently that the American campus has not always defended free speech and academic freedom well, up to and during the past decade. Moreover, proponents of the antipornography and ban hate speech movements are open about their hope of pruning back the First Amendment. Nevertheless, charges that the American campus has become a totalitarian boot camp, with left-wing drill sergeants, have been dangerously erroneous and inflammatory, so much so that I often suspect that the liberal defense of free speech has become a supremely ironic cover for an attack on liberal higher education. The accusations of campus malfeasance have taken hold, to such a degree that the label "You're P.C." can now be slapped on like a gag. Richard Perry and Patricia Williams have sardonically written of ". . . those who are apparently unable to distinguish between a liberty interest on the one hand and, on the other, a quite specific interest in being able to spout racist, sexist, and homophobic epithets completely unchallenged—without, in other words, the terrible inconvenience of feeling bad about it. . . . [The] effective message is: 'I have the right to express as much hatred as I want, so you shut up about it'" (Perry and Williams 1992, 228).

So weakened by ambivalences, I recently reread Chapter 4 of *The Gospel According to Matthew*. Jesus, who has fasted for forty nights and days, is fragile from hunger. The Devil then draws nigh. He offers Jesus three temptations: to prove that he is the Son of God by transforming stones into bread; to prove that he is the Son of God by throwing himself from the parapet of the temple and then having angels rescue him; and to become the king of the world, if he will but pay homage to the devil. Fancifully, blasphemously, self-aggrandizingly, I adapted these temptations to my ambivalences about intellectual freedom. My first temptation is to prove that I am the daughter of justice by using law to transform hatred, fear, and ignorance into good feelings, respect, and knowledge. My second is to prove that I am the daughter of justice by asking law to rescue me from making arduous, lengthy efforts to reform our communities. My third is to believe that I can heal ancient sufferings and build peaceable kingdoms—if I will but cease to pay homage to the First Amendment.

Jesus, of course, resists temptation and answers the bad speech of the Devil with the good speech of Scripture. I trotted off to look for more good speech in support of freedom. My technique was to interrogate that postmodern magister figure: a computer print-out of bibliographical data bases. There I discovered an overwhelming apologia for freedom, with bite and edge, an essay by a law professor previously unknown to me: "Hate Speech, Cultural Diversity, and the Foundational Paradigms of Free Expression" by Calvin R. Massey. Massey analyzes three approaches to the gnawing problem of hate speech: the civil libertarian, who finds suppression of hate speech "generally an impermissible restriction upon the content of speech"; the egalitarian, who supports suppression of hate speech; and the accommodationist, who "walks an uneasy tightrope" between the two. Because of their scope and lucidity, combined with an awareness of the monstrosities of history, Massey's arguments knocked this civil libertarian, tempted by accommodationism, off the oscillating tightrope of her ambivalences and back on the track of civil liberties.

Massey then proposes three fundamental principles for the "place of law governing free expression in a heterogeneous society": the culturally authoritarian; the pluralist, who preserves diversity through preserving group diversity; and the individualist, who, like John Stuart Mill in *On Liberty*, preserves diversity through preserving individual diversity. Demonstrating the dangers of cultural authoritarianism and pluralism (as he defines it), Massey argues for the individualist principle. Applying this principle, the rules against hate speech are the same for the university and for the larger society. All that "can be permissibly controlled . . . would appear to be speech that is directed to specific targeted individuals and is plainly so *personally* abusive that it is likely to incite violence." In addition, hate speech directed at a captive audience—for example, a student in a dormitory room—would be unprotected.

Massey so bowled me over that I became suspicious of my cheering enthusiasm. To test my agreement with him, I read a contrasting piece, an "outsider's argument" for greater restrictions on the First Amendment, this by Richard Delgado and Jean Stefanic (1992). In "Images of the Outsider in American Law and Culture: Can Free Expression Remedy Systemic Social Ills?" they focus on racism, but their argument, presumably, would apply to sexism, homophobia, or anti-Semitism. Reading the essay posed a second test as well. Would I, a white woman weaned on the American ethic of individualism, become guilty and defensive? If I did, how would these emotions control my reading? Would guilt drive me to obsequious agreement or belligerent disagreement?

The Delgado/Stefanic argument is no less vital for being familiar. Racism is an overwhelming, constitutive fact of United States history. Whites underestimate it, fail and refuse to see it. One cause of racism—among its roots, branches, and poison leaves—is language, the huge symbolic systems with which we construct social meaning and individual identity. These systems incorporate our narratives, art, artifacts, and everyday gestures. To be sure, Delgado/Stefanic admit that language can be counter-hegemonic and destabilizing, but our dominant narratives are almost impossible to dislodge. "We interpret new stories in light of the old. Ones that deviate too markedly from our pre-existing stock are dismissed as extreme, coercive, political, and wrong." Our speech is too tainted to serve as an instrument of change. As Audre Lorde said, we cannot dismantle the master's house with the master's tools. The powerful, moreover, will not give up. Among the master's tools for shoring up his home and bank is a manipulation of the First Amendment.

Although Delgado/Stefanic are tempted to agree with Derrick Bell that our irredeemable racism will never end, they do offer four remedies: 1) Act against racism; 2) Remedy past mistreatment, through such policies as affirmative action and reparations; 3) "Employ and empower minority speakers of color and expose ourselves to their messages." However, the essay warns, approach neoconservatives with skepticism, including such neoconservatives of color as Richard Rodriguez, Steven [*sic*] Carter, Thomas Sowell, and Shelby Steele; 4) Suspect "remedies for deep-seated evils that rely on speech and exhortation." Indeed, go beyond suspicion. Out-law speech that is "demonstrably harmful" to persons of color.

My sense of the wrongs of this argument was not that of the constitutional lawyer. I am Massey's amateur reader, not his colleague. My nervousness began with Delgado/Stefanic's coercive and dismissive attitude. Some minority speakers are acceptable; some are not. Period. Speech must meet one test and one test only: it does not demonstrably harm a minority speaker. Period. Finally, I could not accept the Delgado/Stefanic picture of the ways in which people act as cultural agents. Attempting to show the limits of the defense of free speech, Delgado/Stefanic create a category they label the "empathic fallacy." This "consists of believing that we can enlarge our sympathies through linguistic means alone. By exposing ourselves to ennobling narratives, we broaden our experience, deepen our empathy, and achieve new levels of sensitivity and fellow-feeling. We can, in short, think, talk, read, and write our way out of bigotry and narrow-mindedness."

Of course, speech alone will not erase bigotry and narrowmindedness. Speech and speech alone is a prescription for failure from one of society's more sentimental or stupid pharmacists. However, the insufficient can also be necessary. Such is the case with speech. Moreover, Delgado/Stefanic drastically sell short the power of minority speech—written, visual, oral, musical. Even under the greatest of political and cultural duress, even under the greatest deprivations of freedom, people have broken out and spoken out. They have used language, be it speech or the silence that speaks. Language has been an act of resistance, self-empowerment, and community. Eleanor Holmes Norton once said, "When my people had nothing else, they had speech" (Norton 1991). In the first female slave narrative in the Americas, "The History of Mary Prince, a West Indian Slave," Mary, beaten beyond endurance, has run away. Her father returns her to her master. Mary remembers her choice between death and speech. "I then took courage and said I could stand the floggings no longer; that I was weary of my life. . . . He told me to hold my tongue and go about my work, or he would find a way to settle me. He did not however, flog me that day" (Andrews 1988, 9). Simplistically, Delgado/Stefanic describe the present day: ". . . even when minorities do speak they have little credibility. Who would listen to, who would credit, a speaker or writer one associates with watermelon-eating, buffoonery, menial work, intellectual inadequacy, laziness, lasciviousness." Of course, many whites do stereotype blacks exactly in this way, including some of my New York City neighbors and Rutgers University students. However, my neighbors and I voted for David Dinkins as mayor of New York City. My students read *Mary Prince* and abhor slavery. They listen attentively to rap music. Last summer, reading my hometown newspaper, the *New York Times*, I saw three names on the fiction best-seller list: Terry McMillan, Alice Walker, and Toni Morrison, all African-American women.

Just as Delgado/Stefanic's politics of minority victimization demands the devaluation of minority discourse, their politics of majority victimizing demands the devaluation of empathy and a moral response to the victim's story. They project readers/listeners as passive consumers of language, incapable of resistance and moral imagination. Like speech, empathy alone is an inadequate remedy for prejudice and injustice. Empathy has, however, a double efficacy. It permits people to experience, if vicariously and bloodlessly, what the pain of the Other might be like. Pictures of napalmed Vietnamese children, running in flames down a road, did help to inspire revulsion against the Vietnamese War. Pictures of sexual violence provoke horror and revulsion against it as well as a possible imitative itch. Simultaneously, empathy with the wronged enables people to imagine a world without wrongs that shimmers as a political goal. Utopias and dreams have been more than dunes in a desert of history.

A few years ago, in my essay "Meno's Boy (1991)," I concluded that banning hate speech, hateful though it is, would be a dual error: it would violate the principle of free speech and fail to end hate speech. In sum, it would mar the good and leave the bad intact. Moreover, I wrote, a ban on hate speech would legally freeze society into two blocs: the newly-silenced harm-givers and the newly-protected harm-receivers, majority whites and minority people of color, or, in the case of pornography, all men and all women. Not only does this bloc-thinking completely dissolve the individual into a class, a man, for example, into "men." Such a ban, instead of stopping hate speech, would divert it into more subterranean outlets and make the hate speaker less accountable. What such a ban would stop is time. For it assumes that things as they are are things as they were; that things as they are are things as they will be. The meanings of race, however, have changed and will change over time. The meanings of gender have changed and will change over time. A ban based on our current understandings of race and gender would be as ineffectual as a concrete jetty is in halting the erosion of a sandy beach.

After reading Massey and Delgado/Stefanic, at such odds with each other, I revisited my argument in order to amplify it. Massey's work is deeper than mine. He also reasons within the well-built framework of the law while I do so within the roughly-hewn framework of a notion of culture. Nevertheless, my support of intellectual freedom is compatible with his work. Mistakenly, I suggest, the advocates of the legal suppression of pornography and hate speech subscribe far too rigidly to one version or another of modern identity politics. Today, the organizing principle of identity politics is membership in a historically disadvantaged group, defined by race, ethnicity, gender, or sexual preference. To be sure, identity politics has vigorously animated social and cultural reforms. Feminism would not have happened unless some women identified themselves as "women" in their public activities. Yet, a grievous flaw of identity politics is its quickness to insist that each of us belongs to one group; that our identity (our sense of self and self-in-the-world) flows solely from membership in this group; that we must remain with the group—come thick or thin, hell or high water—and that we must look at everything through a lens this group has ground.

One sorry result of identity politics gone all rigid is the presence of fundamentalist perceptions as distorted as those that proclaimed the globe was flat or the center of the universe. I once listened to a woman issue a formal complaint about having to read Andrea Dworkin in a women's studies class. "You don't want Dworkin on a feminist theory syllabus?" I asked incredulously. "Why? You have to know about her." I was told that the images of women in Dworkin's books were demeaning to this student as a woman. I disagree with Dworkin, but I had to yelp ferociously in her defense, "Dworkin writes about demeaning images in order to expose them and refute them." "But they're there," my avatar of identity politics said. "They demean me, and I don't want them there."

For better or worse, our identities are neither fixed nor monolithic. One source of Audre Lorde's importance was her complex self-positioning as African-American and lesbian in terms of identity; feminist, black civil rights worker, and supporter of indigenous people in politics; poet, autobiographer, essayist, and mythographer in literature. A postmodern cliché refers to our fluid, multiple, shifting identities. Some clichés, though, become clichés because they say something. Each of us does belong to several classes that might conflict with each other. Each of us does cross and criss-cross borders (psychological, social, cultural, national) as easily as the jet stream does. Our individualism partly springs from the specific equation of our multiplicities. Each of us has a multiplicity of our own.

How would I then respond to a ban on hate speech and pornography? According to the justifying rhetorics of these bans, I am a white woman, and therefore both racist and victim. Am I simultaneously to ban speech from the part of me that is race, as if it were an isolate, and ban speech about the part of me that is gender and sexualities, as if they were isolates? Or do I, far more beneficially, use free speech in order to talk within myself, talk to others, and negotiate a pluralistic identity within a democratic community? As Richard Perry and Patricia Williams have written, it is time to initiate a *perestroika* of personhood, to make a world in which all of us "in our multiple, overlapping, individual and collective identities can come to terms" (1992, 230). Language, freely deployed, is our most creative tool of restructuring. For it maps these identities, no matter how imperfectly, and bridges them, no matter how inadequately.[7]

Such a moving picture of identity is a necessary element in the multiplex theater that contains democratic politics and culture. Dolt though I am, I am aware of the linkages between politics and culture, whether defined anthropologically or aesthetically. Women's studies, cultural studies, the New Historicism—all seek to excavate these linkages. They are as unbreakable as those between crusts of rock and gasses in a volcano. I am also aware that culture has a politics and politics has a culture. Nevertheless, democratic politics and culture are partly different. A democratic politics must obey the rule of law. A democratic culture demands some roguish individualism, a freebooting, free-wheeling, rascally contempt for genres, conventions, and institutional power. A democratic politics must support freedom but still reduce the suffering and inequities that befall its citizens. A democratic culture must have freely-produced narratives that dramatize suffering, a repertory theater of cruelties and punishments. I think, for example, of narratives of gay sado-masochism. Such cultural productions meet a number of psychic and artistic needs: the need to project personal rage, disappointment, loss; the need for catharsis; the need to ventilate a will toward power and powerlessness; the need to transgress, an act inseparable from human creativity and progress; the need to represent history fully; the need to confront the human compulsion toward destruction.

These comments suggest some of the ways in which a democracy uses cultural freedom. Whether citizens of a democracy or not, people as constructors of meaning are beyond firm, complete social control. As users of speech, speakers and listeners, people manage to wiggle free. Because the consequences of this freedom are both awful and sublime, I think of our capacities with despair and celebration. A democracy's formal commitment to freedom of speech is a welcome enlargement, enhancement, and protection of what people seem to insist on doing anyway. We use speech as we do, not only because of the plasticity of the brain as it interacts with the world, but because of the intricacies of discourse. The relationships between "representation" and "reality" are as complex in their way as those among the elements of postmodern subjectivity. We cannot bifurcate "representation" and "reality" and then declare that a representation accurately mirrors reality. For example, we cannot decree that a Mapplethorpe photograph reflects gay male sexuality. "Representations" and "realities" are constantly mingling with and shaping each other, a process that various human agents knead and massage. Nor can we bifurcate "a representation of a fantasy" from our "fantasy life" and then declare that a representation accurately mirrors our collective fantasy life. For example, we cannot decree that a page of *Playboy* represents every man's fantasy of any woman's body.

In particular, the genres of irony, satire, and parody defiantly resist literal interpretations, and do so with zealous and ghoulish delight. Indeed, because irony, satire, and parody are so treacherous and messy and tricky, they have historically served as subversive weapons against such powerful institutions as church, state, corporation, family, and owner. An ironic kiss on the cardinal's ring is never just a kiss. Today, these genres are following their traditional mission of giving wannabe censors of all ideological stripes the fits. How should one interpret the skits of the television show, *In Living Color?* Does it malign blacks and gays or not? What about the Alison Bechdel comic strips portraying lesbians? Do they malign lesbians or not? Or what about the Simpsons? Do they malign family values or not?

In brief, people do their own thing in the interstices between representations and the represented. As Jennifer Wicke writes, criticizing aspects of the 1980s antipornography movement and its embrace by the radical right, "Such a politics involves a deep fear of representation, in the form of imagery or words, and supplants a mediated understanding of human culture. Boiled down to pornography, this entails assuming that representations are precisely what they represent—there is no . . . zone of fantasy, cultural play, or even just framing going on" (Wicke 1992, 27).[8] Arguably, each of us is at our most individualistic and in the most sensitive "touch" with our bodies when we operate, cognitively and affectively, in this zone of fantasy and play. The freer public speech is, the more openly a person can express and confess to these operations. The quality of one's effusions will range from the original to the banal, the healing to the pernicious. If pernicious, they will be out there—to be ignored or answered.

Such individualism is a vital sign of our general creative and interpretative capacities. Crucially, significantly, whether in democratic states or non-democratic regimes, each of us scripts and interprets dramas of suffering differently, each in our way. Each of us scripts and interprets dramas of pleasure differently, each in our way. Obviously,

I am not endorsing a wholly anarchistic theory of interpretation. Our historical situations, our interpretative communities, and the structures of mind do together ground us. Nevertheless, because we have a degree of creative and interpretative freedom, no one can wholly predict or control how I am going to read a text, image, scene, or event. Nor can anyone wholly predict or control how I am going to speak about a text, image, scene, or event. This individualism, plus the depth of the history of human cultures, means that *everything and everyone* has more than one meaning. A woman is not only a whore; she is also the Virgin Mary spreading her hands for the Holy Spirit or for the Baby Jesus. No regulation of speech will work because all such regulations have, at their cold heart, a theory of human behavior that denies these cognitive and cultural realities.

As I jog back to the citadel of the defense of intellectual and academic freedom, I am still anxious. Am I, despite my history, a kissing cousin to the people whom I criticized earlier: comfortable people, mouthing noble words, who have never been gagged, who have never had the bit of the more powerful jammed into their mouth? If I am, I now address myself as well as them. Obviously, a founding father of my commitment to individualism and liberty is John Stuart Mill. I did revisit the fourth chapter of my good father's text *On Liberty*, "Of the Limits to the Authority of Society Over the Individual." As Mill thinks through the relation of the individual to society, he writes firmly about each individual's obligations and responsibilities. Each of us must equitably bear our share of the defense of society and the protection of its members from "injury and molestation." He then claims that there are cases in which we can punish the injurious and molesting by opinion, a form of speech, rather than by law. Education, in particular, works by "conviction and persuasion." In brief, the good speech of educators must drive out bad, including the bad speech of the boorish, cruel, and obstinate.[9]

Mulling this chapter over, I find Mill a guidebook to the citadel, but I wish to paste a warning on the cover. Educators, educate yourselves. Recognize the frustrations and pain that partly drive good people to argue for constrictions on the First Amendment. Obey a protocol of hard listening as well as the principle of freely speaking. Hear the victims' stories and understand why some victims are cynical about the First Amendment. If educators do not, our advocacy of free speech, no matter how passionate, will lack persuasiveness. The advocates of bans on speech will then couple with our weakness to produce a monstrous offspring.

How, much later, from the citadel, would I judge the educators in that room in New York who debated, not only my career, but my body? If their speech had led, directly and demonstrably, to a dirty negative vote on my tenure, I would judge them worthy of lawsuits filed from here to John Stuart Mill's deathbed in Avignon. If they were only fantasizing, albeit in a crude and cruddy and curdled way, I would judge them molesters and answer back. If they were to have spoken publicly, I would judge any educator who had answered them back a fair guardian of the First Amendment. For such guardianship would have reassured me that the erotic need not be a source of powerlessness and that language, clean and dirty, can be bread and bulwark for the body of democracy.

NOTES

This essay originally appeared in *Michigan Quarterly Review* 32 (summer 1993): 317–37.

Parts of this paper build on Stimpson, "Meno's Boy (1991)." Throughout I will use speech as a synonym for cultural activity, which includes academic discourse, the arts and letters, the media, and everyday language.

1. During the fights within feminism over the issue of pornography, I have belonged to groups that support the First Amendment such as the Feminist Anti-Censorship Task Force (FACT) and the Working Group on Women, Censorship, and 'Pornography,' which the National Coalition Against Censorship has recently formed.

2. Because I am aware that the body is socially as well as genetically constructed, my statement is not an endorsement of biological essentialism. Significantly, as Audre Lorde's career shows, some of the most vibrant contemporary cultural productions are coming from people who belong to more than one of these groups and who write from such a position.

3. Goldsby (1990) is an important analysis of Mapplethorpe's representation of black homoeroticism and statement of the need to explore race and racism in lesbian and gay male communities.

4. Recently, the proponents of legal restrictions on the First Amendment in order to curb pornography and hate speech met in order to discuss an alliance (Wilkerson 1993). The bibliography about the legal, cultural, and political fights over pornography is now extensive. Some recent items include Childress (1991), an able review of three books about pornography; Kappeler (1992), a model of radical feminist bias but with some useful information; Leong (1991), a general review of efforts to control pornography that ultimately argues against censorship from any point of the current ideolog-

ical spectrum; and Sullivan (1992), a review of three books about obscenity that, too, suspects state interference and feminist antipornography measures. The bibliography about campus speech codes is also long, but among its recent additions are Dessayer and Burke (1991), an attack on speech codes; Michelman (1992), a "democracy based argument against the Hyde Bill"; Neuborne (1992), which presents a theory of "idealized pluralism" that would permit controls on hate speech under very, very controlled circumstances; and Watterson (1991), a careful reading of the conflict between the First Amendment and the suppression of hate speech.

5. DeLoughry (1993) is an account of the policy decisions campuses must make because of the spread of obscenity, pornography, and violence against women on computer networks.

6. However, Berkow (1993), a sports columnist, did defend Schott's First Amendment rights.

7. In the future, I would like to relate this notion about the relation between free speech and community to Dean Lee Bollinger's ideas about the relations between free speech and the tolerant community. See Lee C. Bollinger (1993, 1–19).

8. Michelman makes a compatible point: "Given our society's predominant notions of the appropriate scope of both public artistic expression and . . . scientific debate, there are countless potential contributions to such expression and debate that cannot, without fatal loss of point and meaning, be completely purged of possibly racially stigmatizing content" (1992, 343–44).

9. One might think of using Mill to justify the outing of gay and lesbian people who carry on sexually in the closet while cannibalizing gays and lesbians in public.

WORKS CITED

"Academic Freedom and Artistic Expression." *Academe,* July/August 1990.

Berkow, Ira. "Schott Punished for Wrong Thing." *New York Times,* February 4, 1993, B8.

Bollinger, Lee C. "The Open-Minded Soldier and the University." *Michigan Quarterly Review* 32, no. 1 (winter 1993): 1–19.

Childress, Steven Alan. "Reel 'Rape Speech': Violent Pornography and the Politics of Harm." *Law and Society Review* 25, no. 1 (1991): 177–214.

Delgado, Richard, and Jean Stefanic. "Images of the Outsider in American Law and Culture." *Cornell Law Review* 77 (September 1992): 1258–1297.

DeLoughry, Thomas D. "Colleges Try to Devise Policies on Obscenity on Campus Networks." *Chronicle of Higher Education,* January 27, 1993, A27.

Dessayer, Kathryn Marie, and Arthur J. Burke. "Leaving Them Speechless: A Critique of Speech Restrictions on Campus." *Harvard Journal of Law and Public Policy* 14 (spring 1991): 565–82.

Goldsby, Jackie. "How to be Colored Me." *Out/Look* 9 (summer 1990): 8–17.

Kaminer, Wendy. "Feminists against the First Amendment." *Atlantic Monthly*, November 1992, 111–18.

Kappeler, Susanne. "Pornography Unmodified." In *The Knowledge Explosion: Generations of Feminist Scholarship*, edited by Cheris Kramarae and Dale Spender, 379–85. New York and London: Teachers College Press, Athene Series, 1992.

Leong, Wai-Teng. "The Pornography 'Problem': Disciplining Women and Young Girls." *Media, Culture, and Society* 13 (1991): 91–117.

MacKinnon, Catharine A. *Feminism Unmodified: Discourses on Life and Law*. Cambridge and London: Harvard University Press, 1987.

Massey, Calvin R. "Hate Speech, Cultural Diversity, and the Foundational Paradigms of Free Expression." *UCLA Law Review* 40 (October 1992): 103–97.

Michelman, Frank. "Universities, Racist Speech, and Democracy in America: An Essay for the ACLU." *Harvard Civil Rights—Civil Liberties Law Review* 27 (summer 1992): 339–69.

Mill, John Stuart. "On Liberty." In *The English Philosophers from Bacon to Mill*, edited by Edwin A. Burtt, 949–1041. New York: Modern Library, 1939.

Neuborne, Burt. "Ghosts in the Attic: Idealized Pluralism, Community, and Hate Speech." *Harvard Civil Rights—Civil Liberties Law Review* 27 (summer 1992): 371–406.

Norton, Eleanor Holmes. Luncheon address, annual meeting of the American Association of University Professors, Washington, D.C., June 1991.

Perry, Richard, and Patricia Williams. "Freedom of Hate Speech." In *Debating P.C.*, edited by Paul Berman, 225–30. New York: Dell Publishing, Laurel Trade Paperback, 1992.

Prince, Mary. "The History of Mary Prince, a West Indian Slave." In *Six Women's Slave Narratives*, with an introduction by William L. Andrews, 1–44, plus title page and preface. New York and Oxford: Oxford University Press, 1988.

Rich, Adrienne. *Diving into the Wreck: Poems 1971–1972*. New York: Norton, 1973.

Robins, Natalie. *Alien Ink: The FBI's War on Freedom of Expression*. New York: William Morrow, 1992.

Stimpson, Catharine R. "Meno's Boy: Hearing His Story and His Sister's." *Academe* 77, no. 6 (November–December 1991): 25–31.

Sullivan, Kathleen M. "The First Amendment Wars." *New Republic*, September 28, 1992, 35–40.

Watterson, Kim W. "The Power of Words: The Power of Advocacy. Challenging the Power of Hate Speech." *University of Pittsburgh Law Review* 52 (summer 1991): 955–87.

Wicke, Jennifer. "Postmodern Identities and the Politics of the (Legal) Subject." *boundary* 2 19, no. 2 (summer 1992): 10–33.

Wilkerson, Isabel. "Foes of Pornography and Bigotry Join Forces." *New York Times*, March 12, 1993, B16.

A Stroll along the New Frontiers of Academic Freedom
Walter P. Metzger

During the past fifteen years or so, the widespread enactment of academic rules banning the expression of racial, religious, and ethnic insults (commonly referred to as rules constraining hate speech) and the widespread proscription of gender references and erotic imagery deemed to create a "hostile learning environment" for women (often defined as a form of sexual harassment) have been roiling the American professoriat, reflecting and exacerbating its inner tensions to a degree unmatched by any other tidal campus movement since the student rebellions of the 1960s and early 1970s.

This essay will concern itself with the bearing of these events on the American theory and practice of academic freedom in recent times. It will not be directly concerned with related but separable academic race and gender issues, such as the influence of antidiscrimination laws on the makeup of academic workforces or the impact of affirmative action policies on the rigor of academic admissions standards. Still, the issue it will address—the academic freedom implications of codified speech restrictions and the academic due process implications of the extra monitory and punitive mechanisms they impose—can hardly be called marginal or picayune.

Since, like most historians, I am convinced that the best way to penetrate the present is to build access roads to it from the past, I am going to reflect on how academic freedom has been traditionally defined and defended on its old frontiers before I try to assess how well it is faring on the new.

Fortunately, one need not hunt high and low for that traditional definition and defense. We who are academic are the legatees of an academic freedom rationale that did not become crystallized in this country until 1915, when a committee of the fledgling American Association of University Professors (AAUP), set up by the first AAUP president, John Dewey, and stocked with such academic luminaries as the Columbia economist E. R. A. Seligman, the Harvard jurisprudent Roscoe Pound, and, a star that outshone all others in this setting, the Johns Hopkins philosopher Arthur O. Lovejoy, issued the twenty-page Declaration of Principles: Academic Freedom and Academic Tenure.[1]

The appearance of the Declaration of Principles was a landmark event in the history of the American academic profession.

- It presented to contemporary readers—and bequeathed to later generations—the powerful belief that academic freedom is not a decorative addition but an essential characteristic of a university, the one grace it cannot lose without losing everything.
- It paid homage to words ending with the suffix *-freiheit* but it drew the first distinctly American map of the expressional terrain under academic freedom's protective cover and thus helped break this professoriat's long dependence on attractive but illfitting German atlases.
- It laid down ethical principles and practical proposals that filled a large part of the portfolio of ideas on which the 1940 statement drew. The latter—a historic accord on the tenets of academic freedom and the procedural requirements of academic tenure that was entered into by AAUP professors and Association of American Colleges (AAC) college presidents and was subsequently endorsed by more than one hundred learned societies and administrative associations—was a consensual feat unique in the battle-scarred arena of faculty-administration relations in this country.

From 1915 to this day, the AAUP Committee on Academic Freedom and Tenure (dubbed Committee A to mark both the temporal priority of its establishment and the perceived importance of its subject) has been in full swing almost without interruption. There was one unfortunate operational hiatus between 1950 and 1956, a gap that I daresay is well remembered, and not with fondness, by the three distinguished victims of McCarthyism to whom this series of lectures is dedicated. Having dealt elsewhere with this regrettable default during the cold war years, I will say no more about it here, except to suggest that it had less to do with an organizational failure of nerve, and more to do with the incapacitation of a dominating organizational leader, than the chroniclers of this episode have generally supposed. Down through the years, Committee A has both refined the principles it enunciated in its creative infancy and served as a systematic investigator of allegations by faculty members (they did not have to be association members) that their academic freedom or tenure had been infringed. Undoubtedly, the willingness and ability of Committee A to get down to cases has made it a more significant institution than it would have been had it simply issued pronouncements. Because it has done both, it has been able to clarify and evaluate specific controversies in the light of its stated principles and to amend its stated principles through the edifying factuality of specific controversies.

In the ratiocinative part of its work, Committee A has sought to satisfy a hunger felt by many academics for standards of professional conduct that are more durable than the shifting currents of faculty opinion, more universal than the discrepant norms of the varied institutions that make up what we are pleased to call a system of higher education, and, above all, that are more objective, more scholarly, more judicious than the spinnings of those who incant the free speech religion when—and only when—it momentarily suits their needs. In its case work, Committee A has made a point of treating complainants as fallible supplicants, not as clients; of reserving judgment until it has heard from every party; of publishing case reports based on site investigations that aim to let the chips fall where they may. Admittedly, Committee A has not always been able to live up to the nonpartisan purity it professes. As a dues-dependent professional society destined to vie for faculty votes in collective bargaining elections, the AAUP has an organizational stake in not treating professors in trouble with icy Olympian detachment. On the other hand, Committee A's signature ideals, though prevented by group interests and guild complexes from being practiced to perfection, never did yield to the amoral solidarity of "my coprofessional right or wrong." (These words of praise oblige me to declare an interest: I was a member of Committee A for almost half of its life on earth and for a bit more than half of mine.)

In the limited space I have reserved for historical tourism, I am going to comment on two important contributions of our professional ancestors to the theory of academic freedom. The first pushed out the boundaries of academic freedom further than German theorists had been prepared to go; the second set ethical limits to the exercise of academic freedom stricter than these *Gelehrten* were inclined to accept.

When I think about academic freedom (and it seems to me that I have not gone a week since I started shaving without thinking about it), I visualize a territory divided into three large regions: a region in which faculty members who engage in scientific or scholarly research are allowed to pursue their investigations wherever they may lead without fear of institutional censorship; a region in which academic teachers are allowed to teach their students what they specially know and conscientiously believe, even if those teachings run counter to the ideas and beliefs of those who employ them and pay their bills; and last, but by no means least, a region in which faculty members are allowed as citizens to express their opinions on mooted issues in public forums without risk of retaliation by campus authorities who hold contrary opinions, even if the subject is outside the purview of the faculty member's acknowledged expertise.

Three-part spatial metaphors are no strangers to our culture. No student of antiquity would find them odd or rare: I can still hear myself incanting as a high school Latinist the famous first line of Caesar's war memoirs: *"Gallia omnia in tres partes divisa est."* Anyone up on current events will have no trouble visualizing the three Bosnian ethnic enclaves that existed before the Dayton Accord or the two no-fly zones bordering a third middle zone in post–Gulf War Iraq. And should one run out of Caesarean operations and cartographic analogues, one can always fall back on the resonance between the trizonia of academic freedom and the trinitarian foundations of the Christian faith! Still, despite the triadic tilt of our culture, academic freedom would have been a two-part, not a three-part, invention if the members of the first Committee A had decided to mimic rather than just admire German thought. In imperial Germany, a university professor accorded the privilege of *Lehrfreiheit* (professor freedom) had the right to teach and conduct intellectual inquiries in his specialty without seeking the prior consent of state ministers of education or church officials. But he was granted no special immunity from prosecution or disemployment in his civil, as distinct from his professional, role; indeed, insofar as he was required as a high-level civil servant to swear allegiance to the Crown and to be circumspect in his private affairs, he was subject to special constraints. At first, a number of Committee A members, particularly Seligman, arguing in the German manner, were reluctant to extend the protections of academic freedom to professors who, by venturing beyond their disciplines, might well find themselves beyond their depth. Some members were afraid that the general public would not understand why a professor should have more protection than a janitor when both had the same academic employer, addressed the same public issue, and spoke their minds with the same want of gnostic qualification. It took Lovejoy's analytic gifts to persuade his colleagues to abandon these misgivings and vote for an inclusive threefold shield. In the end, the report they wrote declared that academic freedom protected a certain class of professionals, no matter where or on what topic they chose to express themselves, and not simply certain types of expression that were within the repertory of that class.

Several considerations helped bring the committee around to this conclusion. One had to do with the urgencies of professional recruitment: in a society that placed a high value on citizen participation in public life, a profession committed to zonal ordinances that might effectively curb those activities would be at a competitive disadvantage in attracting talented and strong-minded persons. The second consideration had to do with the fact that all the professors who appealed to the AAUP for assistance in its natal year had gotten into trouble for expressions of opinion that had little to do with their specific fields. Lovejoy had discovered, when he went off at his own expense to investigate faculty complaints throughout the country, that faculty members openly critical of their administrations were, of all who ran risks by speaking out, the ones most likely to become an endangered species. His report to Committee A on the dismissal of eighteen faculty members from the University of Utah in 1915 showed how readily a thin-skinned president could confuse faculty criticism of his policies with faculty disloyalty to his person, and disloyalty to his person with insubordination, a cardinal sin for which dismissal was the surest cure.

What Lovejoy observed in that distant day would be ever so. Once it was decided that academic freedom included ordinary freedom of speech—the AAUP would call it "extramural freedom"—Committee A's work of the guardian variety would be disproportionately devoted to the defense of this tertium quid. A study of 1,500 cases sampled from the files of the committee between 1915 and the late 1970s revealed that most of them raise questions of procedure not of substance: they were tenure cases, pure if not always simple.[2] Among the cases that did raise academic freedom issues, alleged violations of freedom of research were rare and scattered: here a psychologist was dismissed for venturing to survey the sex habits of his students; there a research team in an agricultural college drew fire from the dairy industry for declaring oleomargarine nutritious; elsewhere a professor in a Catholic women's college was expelled by the reverend mother president for writing a novel that some alumnae deemed risqué. Only in part can the paucity of cases be explained by the tendency of scholarly and scientific grievants to seek assistance from their disciplinary society rather than from the transdisciplinary AAUP. Some weight should be given to the fact that the bulk of academic research is carried on by only a small fraction of the professoriat and that a relatively small population at risk is likely to produce a comparably small incidence of complaint, and to the fact that scientists communicating with scientists are not often overheard or, if overheard, are not often understood, by potentially hostile outsiders. Privacy and safety have no better friend than an impenetrable technical vocabulary. Finally, one must bear in mind that those who publish scientific works that disturb the world (and they are not innumerable) tend to be associated with universities that praise them for their intellects and benefit from their celebrity. Complaints to the AAUP were not likely to emerge from academic prodigies who earned rapid promotions and were awarded government grants and prestigious chairs.

More academic freedom violations were brought to the attention of Committee A by professors who claimed that their teaching freedom had been infringed. In the period covered by the survey, cases of this kind were mostly incubated in places of lesser rank: in denominational colleges that imposed doctrinal restrictions not only on the teaching of theology, Bible study, and church history but also on the teaching of biology, Reformation history, and sexual ethics; in tax-supported state universities that were pressured by local citizens to close an offensive student play or remove a controversial student work of art; and in institutions of diverse types that laid off teachers and discontinued programs, ostensibly in the interest of economy but suspiciously for the purpose of purging faculty troublemakers or expanding administrative control.

The cases that fall into this category, though not petty in consequence or small in number, are not consequential or numerous enough to support the common view that academic freedom confronts its most serious threat in the academic classroom. The Committee A record shows that administrations of leading American colleges and universities were seldom censured by the association for attacking a syllabus or lecture offered by a regular faculty member (they were perhaps less circumspect when it came to the presentations of outside speakers); the administrators of undistinguished colleges and universities, although more likely to curtail academic freedom in the classroom by exerting prior restraint (that is, by not appointing controversialists or heretics to sensitive teaching positions), seldom ran afoul of the AAUP by punishing the dispenser of abrasive or errant doctrine in the classroom after the fact.

In large part, the sparseness of cases in this category can be attributed to an unwritten code of classroom manners that gave the academic teaching site the shielded quality of a confessional. For years, in all but the most high school–like places, it had come to be taken for granted that professors had almost proprietary control over the venues of instruction that were assigned to them; that properly socialized faculty members never entered a colleague's teaching space uninvited; that reputable administrators would think twice before they visited occupied classrooms on their tours of unannounced inspections; and, above all, that well-brought-up students would not deliberately and persistently spill the beans about what went on behind closed classroom doors. The police docket of Committee A suggests that the student restiveness and riotousness unleashed by the early civil rights movement and the Vietnam War weakened the ability of academic teachers to live sheltered lives. But the turmoils of the 1960s and 1970s do not seem to have greatly increased the frequency with which teachers were punished for remarks they made or readings they assigned in class. A heavier blunt attack on teaching freedom would not occur until what was left of the classroom as a propaedeutic sanctuary broke down in the 1980s and 1990s, when (for reasons I will later touch on) many faculty members overcame their scruples against didactic eavesdropping, many administrations set up special offices that legitimized classroom prying, and students willing to inform against their teachers arrived in critical mass.

It is in the third zone of academic freedom, the one providing a safe haven for civil liberties, that Committee A has done the bulk of its business since 1915. It was here that the most banal motive for silencing professors—the refusal of campus authorities to suffer criticism of their policies or persons—would be repeatedly exhibited; it was here that repressive actions of enormous gravity—the purging of pacifists and German Americans from American campuses during World War I and the dismissal of so-called Fifth Amendment Communists from American universities after World War II—would erupt with dramatic force.

During its first forty years, Committee A labored in its vineyard of good works with precious little help from the law. At the tail end of the cold war and ever since, the law has increasingly become a partner in this libertarian enterprise—many regard it as the decidedly senior partner—with consequences for academic freedom of enormous weight.

Before I take leave of the distant past, I want to allude to the second principle our professional ancestors deeded to posterity—the brave, if not startlingly original, idea that in no zone should academic freedom be taken as an absolute. "There are no rights," Lovejoy and company stated in the 1915 declaration, "without corresponding duties."

> The liberty of a scholar to set forth his conclusions, be they what they may, is conditioned by their being conclusions gained in a scholar's method and held in a scholar's spirit; that is to say, they must be fruits of competent and patient and sincere inquiry; and they must be set forth with dignity, courtesy, and temperateness.

The language in which the limitations were cast would undergo nuanced changes as it traveled from the professorial monologue of 1915 to the faculty-administration duet of 1940. Thus, where the earlier document warned teachers not to take "unfair advantage of the student's immaturity by indoctrinating him with the teacher's own opinions," the later document, less afraid of the purposeful Svengali than of the rambling polemicist, warned the teacher "not to introduce into his teaching controversial matter which has no relation to the subject." And where the earlier writers tried to raise the standard of academic public discourse by admonishing professors to avoid "intemperate" and "sensational" rhetoric, their followers put their plea for verbal propriety more affirmatively: a faculty member, the AAUP and AAC representatives wrote in 1940, "should at all times be accurate, should exercise appropriate restraint, should show respect for the opinions of others, and should make every effort to indicate that he is not an institutional spokesman."

As these linguistic tinkerings suggest, it was not easy for libertarians to formulate speech restrictions that would neither overshoot nor undershoot their mark and that would satisfy every interest at the drafting table. But the close resemblances between the two documents suggest that the same professional sensibilities were at work on each. Both the authors of 1915 and those of 1940 believed that faculty members, as professionals, were bound to comply with standards of decorum that did not apply with the same force to nonprofessionals. Both believed that members of the academic profession were not only embarked on careers but were committed to a *calling*, a term that brought to mind the divine mission of the clerical profession from which the academic profession sprang. Doubtless, there was something narcissistic about these attempts to specify the terms of professional good behavior. The persona idealized in these documents looked a lot like the white Anglo-Saxon, Protestant, middle-class men who produced it. But the values these academics gave praise to—civility, collegiality, rationality, tolerance, scholarly poise, mutual respect— were not, I would argue, ethnocentric; they were—dare one say so in this era of perspectivalism?—universal.

Yet was this not a dangerous course for freedom fighters to take? Is it possible to proscribe the uncouth expression of ideas without precluding the expression of unpopular ideas? To the latter question, a famous negative answer had been formulated in the mid-nineteenth century by the great philosopher of civil liberty John Stuart Mill, and it still stands as a critique that must be reckoned with by those who think they can quarrel with form without censoring or punishing content.

In his magisterial *On Liberty*, Mill decried as risky and hypocritical the bien-pensant belief that *what* we say can be dissociated from *how* we say it. Beyond the seemingly disinterested demand for mannerliness, Mill detected a masked ex parte motive:

> [T]he denunciation of . . . invective, sarcasm, personality, and the like . . . would deserve more sympathy if it were ever proposed to interdict them equally on both sides; but it is only desired to restrain the employment of them against prevailing

opinion; against the unprevailing [opinion] . . . they are likely
to obtain for him who uses them the praise of honest zeal and
righteous indignation.[3]

The authors of the 1915 statement were Mill's heirs and disciples:
if they were not deterred by his warning that restrictions on "manner," like restrictions on "matter," may compromise freedom of
speech, this was surely not because they had never heard the warning
or because they had heard it but disagreed with it. They believed, however, that its practical corollary—to protect expressive freedoms, persons in positions of authority should be as permissive on issues of style
as they should be on issues of content—was not a tenable one in a university. For Mill, the battle for human liberty was waged between two
antagonists, the individual and society; he did not deal with the more
complicated situation of the individual who seeks a license to speak
his or her mind while adhering to the norms of a profession. For the
AAUP authors, high standards for verbal deportment in the classroom
and the public arena had to be established, not because the risk of substance abuse was so negligible that it could be ignored but because, in
a profession that sought and rewarded moral character as well as intellectual ability, that risk was to some degree inescapable.

Nevertheless, the early theorists of academic freedom did try to
lessen the risk that speech will be judged professionally inappropriate
only by those who find it ideologically objectionable. One of their ways
of ensuring that expressions of opinion would not fall victim to parti-
san clamorings for decorum was to make it clear that their "shoulds"
and "should nots" were not intended to be hard-and-fast rules of verbal conduct that the faculty had to follow as a condition of employment but were meant, rather, to serve as admonitions—pieces of
advice to unseasoned colleagues who might otherwise suppose that
academic freedom was a way of saying "anything goes" and assurances
to skeptical outsiders that this profession had the ability and desire to
police and upraise itself.

In the spirit of their distinguished forerunners, but going a step
beyond them, later incarnations of Committee A would conclude that
any attempt to *codify* punishable speech offenses posed a threat to academic freedom. In this sensitive area, detailed and exhaustive penal
codes were thought to possess inherent liabilities: they were likely to
retain proscriptions that outlive their original raison d'être; they were

likely to be called on to make room for some faction's or generation's new pet peeve; they were likely to be applied so literally and mechanically to specific cases that the motives of defendants, and the quality of their entire record of service, would receive short shrift.

Finally, and most important, these AAUP professors sought to protect academic freedom from specious appeals to good taste by giving the faculty a decisive role to play in the dismissal process. In 1915, Lovejoy and company, like other star professors in the Progressive era, were still sufficiently under the spell of the ideas of faculty self-governance they had picked up in their student days abroad to propose that the faculty and only the faculty be empowered to judge what was and was not a capital speech offense. "Lay governing boards," they declared, "are competent to judge . . . charges of habitual neglect of assigned duties on the part of individual teachers, and also grave moral delinquency. But in matters of opinion, and of the utterance of opinion, such boards cannot intervene without destroying the essential nature . . . of the university." Here the founders did not pass on to their successors an enduring legacy: the conservative chill that passed over academe after World War I put an end to talk of syndicalist solutions to academic problems. But a milder version of that idea did survive and prosper—the belief that meaningful faculty *participation*, not in the ultimate stage but in the early and middle stages of the dismissal process, was a vital professional deterrent to lay intolerances and mistakes.

I have lingered lovingly and long—perhaps too long—on the canonical inventions of the past. The time has come to consider the threat to academic freedom posed by contemporary speech codes, using the classical tradition as a measuring stick and moral guide.

That the threat to academic freedom posed by speech codes is grave and possibly lethal is not so obvious that it goes without showing. For one thing, most hate speech codes (including the one enacted at the University of Michigan and kept on its books until a federal district court judge struck it down) have been explicitly aimed at the provocative slurs of students and not at the epithetical rhetoric of professors. Ever since 1915, when the concept of *Lehrfreiheit* (professor freedom) was decoupled from the concept of *Lernfreiheit* (student freedom), the standard professional answer to the question of "who is entitled to academic freedom?" has been "every academic and no one but an academic," an answer that would seem to bolster the notion that hate speech codes are of no real professional concern. For another thing, the conceptual foundations of antisexist speech codes, far from originating in the academy and bearing its distinctive stamp, were imported into institutions of higher learning from the external world of work and thus gain credit as a benign general regulation from which professors have no right to be exempt. But the codes themselves warn wary readers that they should not be taken quite so lightly.

Consider the hate speech code enacted at the University of Michigan, a fairly typical example of the genre. It sanctioned the disciplining of students for "any behavior, verbal or physical, that stigmatizes or victimizes an individual on the basis of race, ethnicity, sex, sexual orientation, creed, national origin, ancestry, age, sexual status, handicap, or Vietnam-era veteran status." Although the professors and administrators who wrote this code may have the limited objective of putting a lid on the abusive speech heard at fraternity drinking parties, and although the document referred solely to student crimes and student punishments, this enactment did not hold the Michigan faculty harmless. Determined to give bigotry no hiding place in the university, the authors laid down no rule that would protect the privacy of campus conversations and made no mention of a professional function or activity that was categorically beyond its reach. The forbiddances specified in this document applied with equal force to the published word and the spoken word; they applied to everything a student said, not just to other students, but to anybody, including teachers; they applied, at least inferentially, to everything the student's interlocutors said in reply, for a code could hardly raise the standard of tolerant discourse if it were simply a one-way street.

Given the sweep of this regulation, it could hardly have left any professor on the Michigan faculty secure in any one of academic freedom's major zones. The list of protected groups spanned so many cultures, histories, and life experiences that no scholar in the liberal arts and probably few researchers in the natural sciences could be certain that their published works would not violate a legislated taboo. The written and missing words of the document might well have excited fears that classrooms would not be off-limits to patrols by the politesse police. (It was no accident that the plaintiff in the legal action that resulted in the demise of the Michigan speech code was a graduate assistant who feared that his freedom as a teacher, not his freedom as a student, would be abridged.) And group insults uttered in porous public settings are probably more likely to be recalled, and are surely less likely to be excused, when they emerge from faculty than from student throats.

In any case, the professional ill effects of speech codes are not exhausted by a reckoning that considers nothing but the interests of practitioners. Even if the Michigan regulation had been crafted to apply exclusively and unambiguously to students, it would have warranted professional concern. It conveyed to impressionable minds all sorts of miseducative messages: that the right way to deal with words we find discomfiting is not to dispute them but to suppress them; that any characterization of a group that hurts the feelings of its members is out of bounds, which is as much to say that, on such topics, only speakers who utter pleasantries are in the clear, that, though truthfulness serves as a defense against a charge of defamation in the law, in the academy it apparently does not; that, consequently, in the academy, belittling comments about minorities and women, even if veracious, may properly be declared unspeakable, and falsehoods about such groups, provided they are flattering, are OK; and, finally, that academic teachers are so professionally incompetent, so unable to gentrify student discourse through preachment and example, that the only thing they can do about the intolerances and stereotypes of their students is to confess to failure and hurl an index prohibitorum at them.

The rules enjoining sexual harassment apply unequivocally to faculty members (among others) and thus more than hate speech codes are obviously awash in academic freedom issues. Consider, in this regard, the policy statement on the books of the University of New Hampshire (UNH). Like all drafters of academic policy on this subject, the code writers at UNH had no tolerance at all for faculty members who offered pedagogical rewards such as high grades in return for student sexual favors, an act whose vileness is commonly but inadequately portrayed by the cool Latin phrase quid pro quo. Surely, everyone, even the truest of true believers in academic freedom, would regard that behavior as a serious breach of professional ethics. Again, like all framers of sexual harassment codes, the UNH drafters prohibited assaults by a teacher on a student's person in the form of "unwelcome touching, petting, pinching, and leering." These acts are gross violations of a client's privacy and dignity that the criminal laws of most countries including ours punish and that the ethical pronouncements of all human services professions sternly reprehend. The code writers included a third test of sexual harassment, a standard that had been invented by Catharine MacKinnon, a feminist law professor, in the 1970s, was endorsed by the Equal Employment Opportunity Commission (EEOC) in 1980, and was adopted by a great many institutions of higher learning thereafter. This third provision placed out of bounds any expression by a faculty member that, "intended or not," had the effect of interfering with a student's performance or of creating a "hostile or offensive . . . academic *environment*." In an effort to illustrate without exhausting the kinds of speech that ran afoul of this provision, they referred among other things to the repeated use of "sexually suggestive objects and pictures," "graphic comments about a person's body," and "derogatory, gender-based humor." With this third prong of sexual harassment, and with these illustrative interdictions, the academic freedom fat was thrown into the academic censor's fire.

The hostile environment test was designed to deter not acts of sexual aggression aimed at particular individuals but prurient utterances and graphic displays that gave off an insalubrious miasma. Probably, the UNH code writers were trying to hit at the calendar art and locker-room talk that accompany the cruder forms of male bonding, but what they wrote managed to call into question the academic acceptability of any word, idea, artifact, or image presented by a teacher that (1) is thought to have an undue sexual connotation by an unspecified fraction (possibly a very small minority) of a (not necessarily captive) student audience; (2) makes an unspecified part of that fraction feel demeaned or embarrassed, emotions that are said to be in some way incapacitating; (3) at the same time makes them irritated and emboldened enough to lodge a complaint with an administrative office set up to receive complaints and counsel complainants in hearings before joint faculty-student panels; and (4) is presented by the teacher so often or in the company of so much like material that it can be interpreted as part of a pattern of purposeful behavior and not as an anomaly. A not very measured response, one would have to say, to the problem of Archie Bunkerism at that university.

Obviously, not every hostile environment code produces the academic freedom disaster it seems to court. Goodwill and good sense, blessed counterweights to regulatory frenzy, often see to it that references to female pulchritude as a source of art and as a force in history are not banished from academic scholarship or discourse and that representations of the human figure, so central to the study of human culture, are not forced into hiding by arbiters of good taste. But a system of rules whose principal aim is to protect the audience from the speaker (rather than the other way around, which all civil libertarians steeped in the law, and most toilers in the vineyard of academic freedom, would insist on) starts out on the wrong foot. And it does nothing to correct itself when it answers Juvenal's ancient query—"Who will guard the guards?"—by appointing midlevel administrators who do not have much academic experience to review charges of faculty salaciousness brought by college students who do not have much life experience.

No profession can be expected to speak energetically and coherently on every issue that affects it. But on an issue that affects it profoundly, every profession can be expected to plead in the chambers of the powerful and in the court of public opinion for a verdict favorable to its interests, and every mature profession can be expected to do so by drawing on the wisdom of its sages and on practical lessons taken from its lengthy life. However well intentioned, academic race and gender speech codes—rising like dandelions in the springtime *hic et ubique;* impinging on all the delicate relationships that academics form with students, administrators, and one another; presuming to pronounce on issues of faculty obligation, comity, and decorum that ethicists have wrestled with for ages—clearly affect the academic profession profoundly. Yet, oddly and I believe significantly, in the vehement disputes that erupted over the rights and wrongs of race and gender speech codes the voice of the academic profession was not strongly heard.

On these matters, the AAUP spoke in public tardily and haltingly. Until the Michigan and Wisconsin hate speech codes were declared unconstitutionally vague and overbroad,[4] Committee A swung irresolutely back and forth on the basic question of whether racial insults could be proscribed by penal codes without violating academic freedom. In 1992, after courtroom defeats had taken the wind out of the sails of the hate speech codifiers, Committee A and the Council of the AAUP finally issued a statement on this subject for publication.[5] It warned that "the line between substance and style was . . . too uncertain to sustain the pressure that will inevitably be brought to bear upon disciplinary rules that attempt to regulate speech"; it cast doubt on the ability of an institution to protect academic freedom when it is forced by rules of its own making to "distinguish permissive expres-

sion of hateful thought from what is proscribed as thoughtless hate";
it insisted that the only safe way for a college or university to combat
insensitive speech, as distinct from violent, threatening, and disrup-
tive acts, was through the processes of education—"the means it uses
best." A wonderful statement. But the inconclusive debate that for
years delayed the delivery of these pronouncements contradicts the air
of easy certitude with which they were belatedly expressed.

On the hostile environment test, the AAUP had more to say offi-
cially and said it sooner. In 1976, it had promised, for the first time formally, to put the discriminatory treatment of academics close to the
top of its agenda. Thereafter, in amicus briefs, the AAUP national
office supported the claim of faculty attorneys that sexual harassment
was a form of gender discrimination and was thus illegal under the
civil rights acts, and its redoubtable Committee W on the Status of
Women followed the EEOC in inserting the hostile environment test
into the definition of sexual harassment.[6] But what the AAUP notably
did not do at any time was to acknowledge publicly that the hostile
environment test was inimical to academic freedom.

This was not because doubts about the practical wisdom of turn-
ing American colleges and universities into environmental protection
agencies were never raised in these councils. They were, sometimes
quite vociferously, not least of all in meetings of Committee A. But
spirited internal debates, even by keepers of the academic freedom
flame, did not bring about a change in policy: the association never
publicly disavowed the hostile environment test.

Committee A did investigate and report on one full-blown hostile
environment case—the case of a tenured professor, J. Donald Silva,
who was suspended from teaching for two years by the administration
of the University of New Hampshire (of all places!) for having used
sexually suggestive metaphors in a class on English composition and
for having made some possibly erotic (mostly cryptic) comments to
students outside the classroom. In the report, which was on the whole
exculpatory of Professor Silva, Committee A authors dwelled on the
procedural errors of the administration, especially on its shift of the
burden of proof from the accusers (where the AAUP had always held
it belonged in disciplinary hearings) to the accused (where the AAUP
had repeatedly said it did not).[7] But they ducked the question of
whether hostile environment statutes are inherently at odds with academic freedom principles and contented themselves with the lesser

finding that academic freedom was imperiled by the *manner* in which the statute was applied. Because that statute is the one I cited a moment ago as a prime example of censorial overreach, the failure of the authors to address its substantive defects (or even to detail its provisions) has to be seen as meaningful omission, not as aimless neglect. Indeed, even when they spoke of its procedural defects, they remained in an avoidance mode. Blaming a technical flaw in the sexual harassment code for the fact that the hearing committee found Professor Silva guilty of harassment simply on the strength of the students' complaints, they suggested that a redrafting of the procedures section would be enough to prevent the next tribunal from rushing precipitously to judgment. The point they did not make would have gone to the heart of the matter: if the head and fount of a professor's offending lies in the perceived offensiveness of the environment he creates, the mere fact that somebody took offense would in itself be proof of a misdeed, and a hearing panel would not be remiss if it thought that a number of such adverse testimonies—in this case six—warranted a conclusive judgment of guilt.

I hope I have not given the impression that I alone among the members of Committee A was quick to see how the movement to regulate campus speech was trampling on its highest ideals. Lest I do seem to be patting myself on the back for having seen the light while my committee colleagues dwelled in darkness, let me hasten to say that much time passed before I came to realize how much the speech codes threatened the academic freedom of faculties and yet more time before I tried to convert this realization into concrete policy. Let me also disavow any suggestion that, in failing to rise to this occasion, the AAUP markedly differed from its peers. The history and constituency of the AAUP give unique significance to the weakness of its response, but its weak response was not unique. The higher education division of the National Education Association (NEA) and the academic division of the American Federation of Teachers (AFT)—two organizations that represent American faculty members as collective bargaining agents— were quicker than the AAUP to issue policy statements critical of speech codes, but their leaders were no less divided on these issues. There was, to be sure, the National Association of Scholars, a loose aggregation of faculty members that was born in the fires of the speech code controversy and that denounced these regulations as violations of academic freedom—with no ifs or buts. More decisive than the

AAUP, more strictly professorial in its membership than the NEA and the AFT, this group was nevertheless ill equipped to speak for the profession on this matter: it was too young to invoke the authority of past achievements, too small to enjoy the power of impressive numbers, and too heavily stocked with bitter-end conservatives to enjoy the reputation for disinterestedness that would-be professional prolocutors, if they hope to make a lasting mark, must possess. Finally, to correct any misimpressions, I should make it clear that the abandonment of professional reference points, which I hold to be a cardinal characteristic of life on academic freedom's "new frontier," was not a default of professional leaders alone. Anyone who tuned in to the clamorous debate over academic speech codes in any part of academe would have needed unusual acoustical sensitivity to hear references to Committee A's case law or its landmark texts.

In a well-known A. Conan Doyle story, Sherlock Holmes, taking note that a dog failed to bark at intruders when he would have been expected to, presumed that if he could explain this nonevent, all the remaining mysteries in the case would be cleared up, too. My curiosity has also been aroused by the aphasia of some usually noisy dogs (or, as I might have put it, since I am talking about academics, by "the silence of the lambs"). In the limited space at my disposal, I am going to try to explain, taking a leaf from the methods of the mastermind of Baker Street, why the academic profession did not protect academic freedom by speaking out more forcefully against academic hate speech codes and the environmental sexual harassment test. Three explanations, none of them mutually exclusive, seem to cover the possibilities:

1. That the dog, though trained to bark, lost its confidence that barking really mattered, so it barked no more
2. That the dog did bark but could not be heard over the louder vocalizings of a more impressive canine that had recently moved into the neighborhood
3. That the dog did not bark at the sight of marauders because it was too caught up in a far-ranging dogfight to attend to its sentinel duties

In the following paragraphs, I consider the merits of each explanation for reticence, adapted, of course, to the peculiarities of a different animal species.

1. In a collection of essays on the future of academic freedom (a work that worries mightily over whether academic freedom *has* a future), Louis Menand postulates that the rise of "epistemological relativism," which denies the possibility of discovering "objective truth," has produced a "paradigm shift" that has undermined the philosophical foundations of and hence the professorial commitment to academic freedom in the "postmodern" world.[8]

In my view, this way of accounting for the failure of the profession to assert itself on the "new frontier" gets one thing right—the academic speech code war was, at bottom, an outgrowth of cultural and philosophical conflicts generally kindled outside the academy—but it gets almost everything else wrong. The theory and practice of academic freedom surely rest on a complex of sustaining faiths, but faith in the attainability of fixed and final truths, the epistemological starch in the doctrinal tests of confessional universities and totalitarian party platforms, plainly is not one of them. Nor is it true that American professors no longer aspire to discover truer and truer things; even those who are skeptical about the existence of a mind-independent reality and express doubt about the possibility of escaping the perspectival warp of texts are known to pride themselves on getting things straight. No one doubts that postmodern ideas have consequences (their ability to rattle and sunder departments of English literature makes that indisputable), but entertaining these ideas has not, as far as I can tell, led any department of English or any other department of instruction in America to raise the salaries of its members who peddle falsehoods and call them truths. Finally, it flies in the face of common experience to suppose that academics would relinquish an advantageous privilege because they could not give it a philosophical rationale. If a professor ever threw away the protective shield of academic freedom because he or she no longer credited its epistemic premises or if a president did not get rid of an annoying gadfly because he considered gadflying "socially constructed," the instance does not readily come to mind.

2. Did the law, unaccustomedly vociferous, drown out the profession on free speech issues in this period? The answer, I think, is yes, but only up to a point. Had the same issues arisen four decades earlier, before the right of public employees to express their views on matters of public interest without fear of retaliation by their employers was wrapped in the protective folds of the First Amendment, the decibel differences between law and profession would not have been great. As

late as the late 1950s, faculty members dismissed from state colleges and universities for having engaged in unpopular political activities were stymied in their quest for legal remedy by the prevailing judicial doctrine that public employment was a privilege, not a right, and could thus be offered, qualified, or retracted by an agent of the state on any reasonable ground without raising a valid constitutional objection.[9] But as it happened, a turnabout in constitutional law that many academics had wished for but few had dared to predict was in the offing. The Vinson Supreme Court, amenable to severe restraints on civic freedoms in the name of national security, was succeeded by the Warren Court, bent on building constitutional barriers against the return of McCarthyite excess. The privilege-in-employment doctrine, used in 1952 to uphold the constitutionality of a New York antisubversion statute called the Feinberg Law, was abandoned in 1967 by a new majority that climaxed a reversal of course by striking down that very statute.[10] The First Amendment, once a blocked artery for those trying to extend the freedoms it guaranteed to the sphere of state employees, became an open and inviting highway that was increasingly substituted for the road taken by Committee A, especially by academics in the public sector. Meanwhile, faculty members in private institutions of higher learning, who were constitutionally defenseless against the punitive intolerance of their employers, became more successful in winning breach-of-contract suits, as the old judicial habit of consigning major personnel decisions to the at-will discretion of employers gave way in the era of antidiscrimination laws and the growth of legally protected faculty unionism to stricter judicial scrutiny of employer-employee relationships in the private sector.

By the time the speech code controversy erupted, a large part of the complaint constituency of Committee A had learned to seek satisfaction first in court, on the assumption that a judicial arsenal stocked with subpoena powers, contempt citations, discovery rights, and court-mandated reinstatements or money damages would do more for them than a professional armory filled with philosophical declarations, on-site investigations that had no power to compel testimony, and naming-and-shaming ceremonies that relied only on moral suasion to induce reform. To be sure, filing a suit in court and mailing a complaint to the AAUP were not necessarily mutually exclusive actions. Most professors who made use of legal weapons were probably glad that professional weapons were at hand as well, especially since the latter, while not theirs to control, was theirs for the asking and at no money cost. Still, there can be no doubt that the terms of the public debate over academic speech codes were set by decisions of the courts and not the case reports of Committee A.

Nor can there be any doubt that the classic cause of academic freedom was in important ways strengthened by this development. To cite one example: the Lovejovian commitment to institutional neutrality was resoundingly echoed in the Court's repeated holdings that the First Amendment does not permit agents of the state to discriminate against speakers because it disapproves of the contents of their speech. True, the relationship between professional principle and constitutional law did not always run smoothly. In *Chaplinsky v. New Hampshire* (1942),[11] the Court had exempted from the content-neutral principle a class of speech it called "fighting words"—words that "by their very utterance inflict injury or tend to incite an immediate breach of the peace"; in *Beauharnais v. Illinois* (1952),[12] it had upheld the conviction of a speaker who violated a state statute prohibiting "group libel," defined as words uttered in a public place that "portray depravity, criminality, unchastity, or lack of virtue of any class of citizen, or [that subject] any race, creed, or religion to contempt, derision or obloquy." These distant decisions were made much of by defenders of academic speech codes, who claimed that they bestowed on their handiwork the moral authority of the Constitution. On this score, they were overconfident. In a series of subsequent court decisions involving hate speech ordinances, federal judges whittled down the *Chaplinsky* doctrine to the point where "fighting words" lost constitutional protection only when they brought their addressee to fisticuffs and not when they simply breached decorum. Judicial second thoughts reduced the *Beauharnais* doctrine to the status of a relic by applying it once and never again. For these saving revisions, academic freedom owed the law a substantial debt.

Yet I confess to a certain unease about a profession that has to wait for the law to correct itself before it acts on a matter of crucial importance to it. For the fact is that law and profession do not in many ways see eye to eye on the issue of academic freedom. The law says that, where there is no state action, an institution of higher learning is constitutionally incapable of committing an academic freedom offense; the profession says nothing of the kind but accepts the burden of confronting private as well as public miscreancy. The organized profession says that academic freedom is only for academics; the law says that First Amendment freedoms are for academics and everyone else. The result is that academics resorting to the legal system to protect their expressional rights come up against balance-of-competing-interest arguments and judicial standards of review that are tailored to persons in occupations that have different needs and take different stands.

Academic freedom was the winner when the Supreme Court, in cases not involving universities, narrowed the definition of "fighting words." But academic freedom was the loser when the Supreme Court, in a case involving the work culture of a savings bank, legitimized the use of hostile environment as a test of sex discrimination and when the lower federal courts followed suit in discrimination suits challenging the legality of male behavior in shipping yards and business offices.

As though universities were indistinguishable from business firms in the quantity and quality of intellectual freedom they required, campus proponents claimed the courts, by these rulings, settled the hostile environment issue in their favor once and for all. This ruling probably had a profound effect on public and professional opinion. But does one have to be an odd contrariant to ask, in a paraphrase of Saint Matthew, what is a profession profited, if it shall gain a world but lose its own voice?

3. I turn at the end to a nagging question: Was the battle over speech codes regarded by vocal controversialists as a battle over the scope and limits of academic freedom (in which case the profession would be presumed to have a vital stake in it) or was it viewed as a set of local skirmishes in a far-reaching and multifaceted cultural war (in which case academic freedom—and the profession's enduring stake in it—would be of no more than tangential importance to articulate partisans on either side)?

A review of the rhetoric of this debate would strongly favor the latter conclusion. The trademark tendency of the most ardent endorsers of the codes has been to commend them for the contribution they make to a variety of left-leaning noble causes. For those persuaded that an uncivil tongue is a major ally of discriminatory practices in employment and education, the surpassing merit of anti–hate speech codes was that they shored up the beleaguered policy of affirmative action and stiffened the flagging enforcement of federal civil rights laws against the mounting assault on them throughout the land. For those convinced that the subjugation of blacks and women is a consequence of their feelings of powerlessness, the greatest glory of these regulations was that they encouraged the victimized to stand up to their victimizers, cast off disabling self-images, and achieve the kind of psychic liberation that had long been promised but had not yet been achieved. And for those given to sweeping civilizational analyses, the most praiseworthy feature of these regulations was that they were part of the struggle to rid society—particularly Western society—of the cultural ills of patriarchy and imperialism, diseases that are presumed to incubate in the speech habits of white American males.

Opponents of academic speech codes do not make their case for externalities in these terms, of course; still, for them, too, the urge to explain academic events in nonacademic terms has been irresistible. Typically, their way of treating academic speech codes has been to view them as alarming examples of the depths to which leftist politics in America tend to sink. On the assumption that rules protective of specific groups attest to the coerciveness of those groups, they have lashed out at black nationalists, militant feminists, and Third World chauvinists for seeking yet another permit to cow and silence their opponents, and they have argued that, by stiff-arming the academy into accepting speech codes, the advocates of these rules demonstrate the readiness of the liberal mentality to insinuate Big Brother tactics into ostensibly philanthropic do-good plans. At their most expansive, conservative critics of speech codes have contended that the epidemic spread of these devices throughout the system of American higher education betrays the ineradicable affection of intellectuals for the latest in radical chic, a tropism that had been notoriously exhibited by American professors in the 1960s when they pandered to the foibles of the countercultural generation, and was displayed again a generation hence when they appointed the same enrages, now armed with Ph.D.'s, to junior teaching positions and then undertook to mentor their ascent to positions of tenured power. At an earlier time, such dark suspiciousness of academic networking would have been put forth under the heading of "La Trahison des Clercs" or the "Communist conspiracy." In the post-Comintern era, buzz phrases of this kind are not available. But the code critics of the right, never at a loss, have come up with a stigmatizing near-equivalent: they accuse the supporters of speech rules of acceding to "political correctness," a put-down with anti-Stalinist connotations that can be put to limitless use.

How does the breadth and intensity of these hostilities help explain the feeble professional response to speech codes? Let me count the ways. First of all, the spotlight of attention fell on supporters and opponents of speech control to whom the defense of academic freedom was of some concern but not of prime concern; because they were for the most part faculty members who ranked high among their colleagues on the scale of social consciousness, their subordination of the virtue of free speech to the cardinal virtues of other causes cost the profession dearly. Second, the entry of the minorities—and, more massively, women—into the ranks of the academic profession in recent times has assured the procode leadership of mass support. (The anticode leadership was not so favored by demography, but it did benefit hugely from the recent intellectual rightward shifts.) Leaders of the organized profession, hitching their wagon to the star of neutral principles, could count on no demographic or social trend that would swell the ranks of their supporters. The profession's freedom fighters did not know but had painfully learned that battle lines on the new frontier should be drawn, against what foe and in whose behalf they would have to fight and by what definition of a casualty they would count their losses. This inexperienced uncertainty was deeply disorienting to them. By the lights of 1915, a violation of academic freedom was a crime designed and executed within the confines of an academic institution. Dissident professors were the victims, trustees and administrators were the culprits, the power of dismissal was the weapon, the loss of employment was the fatal wound. The great lesson of the free speech story is that violations of academic freedom can also be committed by professors: academics had to repeat Pogo's imperishable words, "We have met the enemy and they are us."

But there were also, I should hope, further lessons to be learned from all of this: that love of academic freedom for its own sake is a sublime emotion, even if it raises the risk of getting caught in the cross fire of left-right politics; and that, for those who find it impoverishing to live by bread alone, living with faith in the worth of professionalism is well worth a try.

NOTES

1. "1915 Declaration of Principles: Academic Freedom and Academic Tenure," *Bulletin of the American Association of University Professors* 40, no. 1 (spring 1954), 90–112.

2. Loya F. Metzger, "Professors in Trouble: A Quantitative Analysis of Academic Freedom and Tenure Cases" (Ph.D. diss., Columbia University, 1978).

3. John Stuart Mill, *On Liberty* (1859; reprint, Indianapolis, Hackett Publishing Company, 1978), 51.

4. *Doe v. University of Michigan,* 721 F. Supp. 852 (E.D. Mich. 1989); *UMW Post v. Board of Regents of the University of Wisconsin System,* 774 F. Supp. 1163 (E.D. Wis. 1991).

5. "A Preliminary Report on Freedom of Expression and Campus Harassment Codes, Approved by Committee A," *Academe* 78, no. 4 (July–August 1992): 30–31.

6. *Meritor Savings Bank v. Vinson,* 106 S. Ct. 2399 (1986).

7. "Academic Freedom and Tenure: University of New Hampshire," *Academe* 80, no. 6 (November–December 1994): 70–81.

8. Louis Menand, ed., *The Future of Academic Freedom* (Chicago: University of Chicago Press, 1996).

9. Cf. *Adler v. Board of Education,* 342 U.S. 485 (1952), 34, 1.14.

10. *Keyishian v. Board of Regents,* 385 U.S. 589 (1967), 34.

11. *Chaplinsky v. New Hampshire,* 315 U.S. 568 (1942), 36, 1.17.

12. *Beauharnais v. Illinois,* 343 U.S. 250 (1952), 36, 1.21.

Academic Freedom and the Merits of Uncertainty
Linda Ray Pratt

Alexis de Tocqueville thought Americans the least philosophical citizens in the Western world but nevertheless a people of great certainties. Although they appealed only to the individual efforts of their own understanding, they did so with sublime confidence. The American practice "of fixing the standard of their judgment in themselves alone" led them to "readily conclude that everything in the world may be explained, and that nothing in it transcends the limits of understanding" (1956, 144). Whether in religion or politics, they found their assurances within themselves. The business of their science was to discover truth and put it into practice. Their plain and direct way of speaking assumed that language could tell it like it is. Their predilection for engineering rested on the certainty that two and two were always four, and that all things were commensurable. In 1831, perhaps only a prescient Frenchman like Tocqueville would have dared to deconstruct American certainties.

In such a society both knowledge and opinion were held in an equilibrium of contradictions: knowledge one did not have was viewed with suspicion, but knowledge one did have was truth. Opinion one did not believe was just another person's view, but opinion that was one's own was rule. Universities would, of course, be revered or reviled, depending on whether they confirmed one's knowledge and conviction or denied them. Academic freedom, the special condition that was to permit colleges and universities the free expression of ideas without threat of punitive action, carries within its traditions these same contradictions. For some, academic freedom is justified because faculty have truths to tell, and the truth and its prophets must be protected. For others, academic freedom is the condition necessary for the revision of truth by skeptics and dissenters from the accepted wisdom. Academic freedom then exists precisely because the truth is not certain, or stable, and the intellectual work of the academy is always to challenge our understandings. In one interpretation academic freedom is about passing on knowledge; in the other, it is about revising it.

For much of the history of academic freedom in the United States, both interpretations have flourished. Indeed, the interaction between certainties and uncertainties drives the academic enterprise. Left to ourselves, we have bumped and rubbed along in a spirited but largely open contest of ideas, losing our balance and perspective mainly when outside political forces intruded on the economic security necessary for ready participation in the dialogue. In times of repression when such forces as the McCarthy inquisitions destroyed the academic equilibrium by endangering the security of our jobs, we could turn mean or silent, betraying our profession either through punishing colleagues we found threatening or refusing to speak up against what was happening. More often, however, we have been united in our understanding of professional standards, and, through organizations such as the American Association of University Professors (AAUP), we have sought to advance a definition of academic freedom that protected those who believed they had the truth to tell and those who wanted to question it.

Unfortunately, not all of our critics have understood that academic freedom is premised as much on the absence of truth as on the presence of it. Lynne Cheney's parting shot at the professoriat on leaving her post at the National Endowment for the Humanities was a pamphlet called *Telling the Truth* (1992). It was about how we did not. Cheney recognizes that new "theoretical approaches" are afoot and concedes that they "can enhance the study of literature and other subjects" (23). Yet for her a belief that "truth" is a social or cultural construct corrupts the integrity of intellectual inquiry and reduces teaching to political manipulation. "The idea that there is no truth to pursue has a corollary: There are no standards to meet" (25), she writes. Without the reality of objectivity, without certainties, faculty in her view have no basis for academic freedom. Those who share her belief profoundly believe that faculty today are imposters in the temple of learning, having, by our own admission, no gospel with which to redeem the time. Without truth, according to our critics, we are left with opinions, the advocacy of which translates as politics. Cheney's logic is, we might say, profoundly American as she reflects the assurances Tocqueville described when she draws on her own understanding and from that point publicly and powerfully judges the world.

For many of us, however, Cheney and others who share her view voice a deep misunderstanding of intellectual work. The nature of academic discourse and the freedom that protects it never depended in principle or practice on certainties. If truth were our currency, we would have little need for academic freedom; a good censor in the defense of ideology or theology would serve instead. But truth is not stable or absolute, and academic freedom protects the space in which to revise and reconsider it. Where "truth" cannot have, indeed, must not have, the status of ideology or dogma, the highest standards of intellectual freedom must prevail—that is, the freedom to pursue alternative truth, to ask the shattering question, to challenge the status quo, to critique hallowed beliefs, to expose error, and to redefine what knowledge is in light of new learning. In short, to be uncertain. The uniqueness of the academy in society is to house just these unsettling and always revisionary forays into the untrammeled spaces of thought.

From one perspective the history of academic disciplines in this century has been the story of certainties becoming unglued. "Things fall apart; the centre cannot hold," the poet Yeats writes in 1920, reflecting on a world whose principles of order seemed to be dissolving. In discipline after discipline we can trace the unfolding of scientific and theoretical developments that introduced uncertainty where certainty had once prevailed. In language and literature the certainty that words represented real presences dissolved in nineteenth-century linguistics. What philologists such as Max Muller and W. D. Whitney started by defining the meaning of language as a social construction, modern neogrammarians including Ferdinand de Saussure were to carry even further. By 1916 Saussure was saying that language was a network of relations whose meaning was defined by its users, not by any organic link between words as signifiers and the things they signified. This theory of "linguistic autonomy" was, as Linda Dowling (1986, 80) puts it, "another sort of metaphysical rupture" that robbed words of their certainty and literature of its claim on expressing universal truth.

If poets were no longer bardic figures whose imaginations drank the milk of paradise, then what were they, and what was the status of the literary creation? From the 1830s on, the best minds were uncertain. Even Eliot, who became certain that the Incarnation was real, knew that words perish and decay amid imprecisions that cannot be stilled. Those less certain than Eliot of a logocentric universe would not say that temporal words in their artistic pattern and form resonated with a supernal harmony or embodied universal truths. In the first half of the twentieth century, literature was preoccupied with what a portrait of the artist would be; in the second half of the century, literature was preoccupied with what literature itself would be.

Even in math, which to the popular mind is the most precise of all measures, scholars learned the lesson of uncertainties. I remember as a schoolgirl my own delight in the certainties of Euclidean geometry. It is just as well that no one told me then that mathematics was an elegant fiction, an intellectual invention, and that there might be more than plain and solid geometries, which, of course, we did not use in the plural. By the 1830s, however, mathematicians such as Carl Friedrich Gauss and Nikolai Lobachevski had already seen that Euclidean geometry was "not the geometry of the universe" (Guillen 1983, 109). As Michael Guillen explains it, the possibility that "a mathematically sensible geometry could be derived from a postulate that was apparently not a self-evident truth" implied that "mathematics is a mere invention of the human imagination and not a body of universal truths based on common sense" (109).

But Gauss and Lobachevski were only the beginning of a revolution that continued into the twentieth century. Consider the case of Gottlob Frege, who, like George Eliot's Mr. Casaubon in search of the key to all mythologies, thought to gather all arithmetic into his massive two-volume *Fundamental Laws of Arithmetic.* But in 1902, after many years on the project and as he neared its completion, Bertrand Russell, philosopher and mathematician, observed a flaw in the fundamental logic of Frege's work. In a postscript to the second volume, Frege wrote, "A scientist can hardly meet with anything more undesirable than to have the foundation give way just as the work is finished" (quoted in Guillen 1983, 15). In the 1930s Kurt Godel argued "that complete certainty was never to be encountered in mathematics by any route founded on traditional logic" (Guillen 1983, 18). But as late as 1981 Morris Kline, in his book *Mathematics: The Loss of Certainty,* would note that in practice if not in principle mathematicians today still "write and publish as if uncertainties were nonexistent" (quoted in Guillen 1983, 20).

Some of you perhaps heard in my title an echo from physics. In 1926 Werner Heisenberg formulated the uncertainty principle that, as Stephen Hawking says, signaled the end of "a model of the universe that would be completely deterministic" even as it initiated the new field of quantum mechanics (1988, 55). Although Heisenberg's principle specifically addressed the relationships of position, velocity, and mass of particles, as metaphor it, too, suggests a world in which measurement itself is variable and a number of different outcomes are always possible. In this world of uncertainties, the unavoidable unpredictability of things means nothing is absolutely fixed. Hawking is one of the few who still project a goal of "complete understanding," but he acknowledges that if that complete understanding comes, "then we would know the mind of God" (175).

For most of us, knowledge is the collective work of human minds. It is as close to truth as we can get or as we may want to be. Our contemporary definition of knowledge relies on how we understand the other elements of a system in which not all things are stable. Heisenberg's principle moved physics from classical to quantum, and Saussure's principle moved language from diachronic to synchronic—that is, from a system in which meaning exists in a pattern of historically determined developments to one in which meaning is constructed from a set of relationships existing at a particular moment. These scientific and linguistic developments toward uncertainty of measurement and meaning, and perhaps others we could trace in other fields, were unfolding at just the historical moment when academic freedom as a concept moved first to self-conscious definition and then to codification of protective practices. The intellectual revolution in disciplines that Thomas Kuhn sees as a change in our paradigm of knowledge and order and the defining of practices that we call academic freedom make an important intersection in the figure of John Dewey.

Dewey was already a major figure in pragmatist philosophy and professor at Columbia University in 1915 when he became a founding member of the AAUP and then its first president. In James Kloppenberg's book *Uncertain Victory* (1986), Dewey is a central figure in the "generation of radical philosophers" whose work in the early part of this century formed a new school of thought. Though trained in "both the idealist and empiricist traditions," these philosophers "carefully avoided fruitless attempts to reconcile the irreconcilable; they tried instead to jostle philosophy into a productive confrontation with doubt" (27). Dewey was on the faculty at the University of Michigan in the 1880s and 1890s before going on to the University of Chicago and then in 1904 to Columbia. Kloppenberg notes that in a March 27, 1892 speech before the Students' Christian Association at Michigan, Dewey made one of his earliest formulations of truth as "created on earth by man's thought, reason, and activity" (43). For Dewey democracy was the vehicle through which humanity could best create its time-bound and culturally constrained truths. Society's forms of social organization were the setting in which religious or moral values were made functional (44). Knowledge was provisional, and politics a form of cultural problem solving (45). Kloppenberg saw these early radical philosophers as both liberating and burdening the scholars who would follow them. He writes, "When they cut the moorings to uncertainty, they simultaneously liberated the imagination and imposed an awkward responsibility on the thinkers who would presume to provide guidance in such an uncertain universe of ideas" (46).

Part of the "awkward responsibility" of those who sought to provide guidance in an uncertain universe of ideas fell on those professors who were to define the principles and practices of academic freedom. The 1915 "General Declaration of Principles" of the newly organized AAUP bears the stamp of Dewey's ideas. According to the document, the university "should be an intellectual experiment station, where new ideas may germinate and where their fruit, though still distasteful to the community as a whole, may be allowed to ripen." (Van Alstyne 1993, 400). Such intellectual fruits must be the produce of a scholar's methods, of "competent and patient and sincere inquiry, and they should be set forth with dignity, courtesy, and temperateness of language" (401). University teachers, the document tells us, should, when giving instruction on controversial matters, "set forth justly, without suppression or innuendo, the divergent opinions of other investigators" (401). They should cause their students to become familiar with the best published expressions and, "above all, remember that [our] business is not to provide . . . students with ready-made conclusions, but to train them to think for themselves, and to provide them access to those materials which they need if they are to think intelligently" (401). The document reminds faculty that many of our students are "still relatively immature" and that we must "guard against taking unfair advantage of the student's immaturity by indoctrinating him with the teacher's own opinions upon the matters in question" and before the student has sufficient knowledge and judgment to form his own opinion (402). Yet, the document is forthright that it is the duty of instructors to spark in students "a genuine intellectual awakening and to arouse in them a keen desire to reach personally verified conclusions upon all questions of general concernment to mankind, or of a special significance for their own time" (403). Such intellectual awakenings must be brought about by "patience, considerateness, and pedagogical wisdom" (403). Professors should not be terminated for setting "their students to thinking in ways objectionable to the trustees," and classroom "utterances ought always to be considered privileged communications" (403).

The "General Declaration of Principles" is equally clear about the role universities must play in society and the danger to our credibility if we corrupt the practices that earn us the right to make the campus "an inviolable refuge" from the tyranny of the public, the politicians, and the commercial world. Universities face a growing demand for technical knowledge and the training of experts. Even in 1915 democracy was also confronting "grave issues in the adjustment of men's social and economic relations [that] are certain to call for settlement in the years . . . to come" (Van Alstyne 1993, 399). The document cautions that universities will not be able to meet these responsibilities if we do not adhere to scholarly standards of research and opinion. The warning from this founding statement is clear: "To the degree that professional scholars, in the formation and promulgation of their opinions, are, or by the character of their tenure appear to be, subject to any motive other than their own scientific conscience and a desire for the respect of their fellow-experts, to that degree the university teaching profession is corrupted; its proper influence upon public opinion is diminished and vitiated, and society at large fails to get from its scholars" the service necessary to the general good (397). The scholar's discourse should place knowledge before action, assess the "complexity of social problems," take a long view, and have a reasonable regard for experience (401). Without these characteristics, the university will not be able to fulfill "its most characteristic functions in a democratic society," which are "to help make public opinion more self-critical and more circumspect, to check the more hasty and unconsidered impulses of popular feeling, to train the democracy to the habit of looking before and after" (401).

Three things strike me as I study this "General Declaration of Principles" by the 1915 Committee on Academic Freedom and Tenure:

(1) the absence of abstract language about truth and the presence of descriptions of an exploratory academic practice, (2) the expectation that scholarly discourse should be temperate and that teachers must exercise patience and discretion in order to allow students to develop their own opinions, and (3) the insights that sound so contemporary about the interaction between the universities and a troubled democratic society. Eighty-five years after this founding document of the AAUP was written, there is nothing I would want to throw out except the use of the generic *he.* Indeed, there is much here I would like to see more widely and sincerely practiced in our profession.

The label of political correctness has been used so loosely and in so many kinds of accusations from left and right that the only thing I am certain it represents is a challenge to the way one pursues one's politics. In 1956 when Jessica Mitford published her little satire called "Lifeitself-Manship, or How to Become a Precisely-Because Man," she perhaps produced the first glossary of politically correct "current usage." Numerous examples refer to "the correctness" of a policy or an "incorrect perspective" (1977, 323–33). Her target was, of course, the Communist Party's habit of correcting the views of its members and disciplining or even expelling those who would not accept correction. For an object lesson in political correctness from the 1950s, we need only look at the Stalinists on the left or the McCarthyites on the right.

The intellectual life of the academy has always been under scrutiny and subject to controversy, but accusations of political correctness go beyond the familiar public hostility to new ideas or our political views. These attacks impugn the ethics of the profession as well as condemn its presumed political perspective. We are accused of substituting indoctrination for teaching, of manipulating our students for political ends and thus violating their academic freedom in the act of corrupting our own.

All the accusations have not been without foundation. Several convinced me that there was substance to some of the criticism. One episode involved a job candidate who was Jewish. When a few members of the department that was interviewing him began to wonder if he had "correct" views on the Palestinians, his chance of being hired was endangered. Another sign of PC tactics appeared in our school paper, which ran an ad from Accuracy in Academia. It read, "Frosh Beware! Liberal Nebraska Professors Want to Control your Minds!" It pictured a bearded professor who had decorated his classroom with a bust of Lenin, a map of Europe divided between the Imperialist West and Holy Mother Russia and her satellite paradises, and posters against nuclear power and in celebration of May Day. The professor is saying, "Hey, A little political bias in the classroom is unavoidable." Accuracy in Academia promises to alert concerned students of the "latest atrocities of the Thought Police" and concludes, "Through our Dead White Males program (you know, Washington; Lincoln, Jefferson, etc.) we'll pay you cash for your story leads and articles." Both of these examples are to my mind legitimately labeled "political correctness" in that neither of them is concerned about the intellectual issues or quality of the academic work and both seek a punitive or intimidating action against someone because of his or her views.

Political manipulation in the classroom is not a function of where one is on the political spectrum. Some argue that including non-canonical works in the curriculum will lead to the "deculturation" of America and conclude that those who teach outside the canon must have the political intention of subverting American values. But questions about what constitutes the culture or cultures of America are equally valid, and they cannot be raised for discussion if one must accept without question the supposed "culture that unites, even defines" the real America (George Will, quoted in Frank 1993, 133). From my vantage point in the past few years as first vice president and then president of the AAUP, I have seen enough action on both ends of the political spectrum to believe that political correctness comes in every ideological variety, and its practitioners can as readily be administrators and students—or government figures—as faculty.

Nothing in recent years has so undermined the public's respect for the academy as the PC controversy. Yet, despite overt political examples such as the ones I have mentioned, the locus of the controversy resides in the contemporary theoretical and methodological developments we have been discussing. Sometimes they are called poststructuralism, postmodernism, or neopragmatism. Sometimes they are clumped together by the unread as "deconstruction." Without question these theories are intellectually controversial and have broad implications for how one constructs the political and cultural world. But many reject these theories or find them threatening to the presuppositions of the disciplines. It does not mean that such ideas do not belong in the university and its classrooms or that teachers and scholars who work in these areas are "politically correct" merely on the basis of their interests.

The intellectual content of the current controversies should neither alarm nor surprise us. These controversies have, in fact, been a long time in development and rise out of the scholarly work of our disciplines—and so do the academic practices that should guide us in our world of uncertainties. I refer in particular to those practices that protect faculty from being fired at will, the peer review process that judges both our merits and the appropriateness of our professional conduct, and the investigative procedures that adjudicate grievances. In an essay Richard Rorty (1996), a neopragmatist philosopher in the line of Dewey, argues that philosophical presuppositions about the nature of truth may have little to do with social practice. He finds that philosophical propositions "turn out to be rhetorical ornaments of practice, rather than foundations of practice," because philosophical views are "just not tied very closely either to observation and experiment, or to practice," and we have "much more confidence in practice" if that practice has been observably effective (22). He uses as one of his examples the attitudes toward oath taking as they evolved from promise making carrying divine sanction to today's legal practice of telling the truth in court, regardless of one's belief about God. Rorty strongly defends academic freedom as a set of practices that are our best chance to have healthy and free universities. I am sure, reading that 1915 "General Declaration of Principles" of the AAUP, that John Dewey thought the same thing, and I am also sure that the history of the past eighty-five years of academic life in this country as opposed to those in almost any other nation you want to cite will provide the evidence that on the whole Dewey and Rorty are right.

Those practices that define academic freedom allow us to resolve in actions the philosophical differences that we could never resolve as intellectual questions. The intellectual historian Thomas L. Haskell (1996), who is in deep philosophical disagreement with Rorty about the nature of truth, for example, locates the practice of academic freedom within disciplines that act as "communities of the competent." The development of disciplines and then departments as "a distinct community of competent investigators" provided "the keystone of professional autonomy" (46). Peer judgment could either determine the "collective warrant" for one another's ideas or "deflate all truth claims unable to win communal support" (46). "The price of participation in the community of the competent," Haskell says, "is perpetual exposure to criticism" (47). Haskell may take more comfort in the truth claims of scholarship that survives this open and competitive process of peer review than Rorty would ever wish to embrace, but both of them accept the practice by which academics evaluate our work and reward our colleagues as the best way we have to handle such issues.

Because academic freedom is defined by practice, it is not perfect, and we must ask how it works and what we can do if it does not. In my role as president of the AAUP I was occasionally confronted with hostile assertions that academic freedom and tenure protected professors who made the most absurd kinds of assertions. The example most often cited was the historians who do not think the Holocaust really happened. I always asked my questioner to name the reputable university that employed such a historian or which journals and conferences had featured such papers. The case of historians who do not believe the Holocaust really occurred is the evidence that academic practices do work. The communities of the component have not extended the collective warrant that would give such ideas any legitimacy. The First Amendment protects the right of anyone to say such things, and the profit motive may lead some publishers to authorize such books, but the academy circumscribes the right to talk with the responsibility to do so with sound and scholarly opinion that can win communal support. A similar defense of academic practice might be made about the place of creationism in the science curriculum. The Religious Right can buy all the television air time it can afford to discuss creationism, and it may be able to bring politicians to their knees in an election season, but in our universities we are teaching evolution. The practices that give academic freedom a functional role are how we manage to withstand the organized ideologues of intellectual error.

But, of course, we do not always manage either to judge wisely or to withstand interference. Our refuge then is in adjudication, either locally in faculty governance or nationally through our professional associations. The historian Joan Scott (1996) points out the tension "between academic freedom as an historically circumscribed relationship and an enduring universal ideal" (165). Cases happen in particular and usually complex specific circumstances, and Scott reminds us that it is the process of adjudicating what happened and why "that articulates historical meanings" and defines ethical practice (166). In her conclusion she defines academic freedom as "a tense mediation of relationships" (178). "With it, we are not always spared the punishment that orthodoxy metes out to its critics; without it, the critical function of scholarship and the possibility it represents for change would be lost" (178).

If our principles and practices have always reflected a concept of academic freedom that protected both the truth claims and the truth questions, if academic freedom was always defined in communal decisions of participants in the field, how is it that we have sometimes faltered so far from our ideal, and how is it that a public that appears to grant us this space in thought so often thinks that we violate our own principles? The answer, I believe, lies in a loss of the traditional equilibrium or balance that stabilized disciplinary changes even when confronted with theoretical upheaval. In practice, as the historian of mathematics observed of his colleagues, until recently most academics in this century still wrote and published as if uncertainties were nonexistent. Now, they do not. The uncertainties that had in theory redefined the meaning of knowledge have now significantly redefined the nature of disciplinary work in many fields. And the universities in which we work are also changing rapidly. The traditional university, which was an instrument of emancipation through education, now also serves the economic and corporate power structure, which has little interest in the free exchange of ideas and little patience with the niceties of academic practice. The pace of change is unsettling, and many of the directions we see the university taking are unwelcome. In such a climate it is easy to lose one's balance, or one's temper, and the social imperative to improve our world may seem a justification for doing so.

People such as myself still believe that the university must be the resource and refuge for the free exchange of ideas, that if that function is absorbed in a new commercialized or vocationalized university where assessment of instructional efficiency for economic development is the measure of our success we will have no barricade against the technocratic world of an international commerce. But a critic of the university such as William Spanos argues in his book *The End of Education* (1993) that liberal reform initiatives themselves are complicit in supporting the power goals of a hegemonic state. He rejects "the renewed appeal to disinterested inquiry by liberal humanists in the university." In his view these reforms are "ultimately intended to recuperate the lost authority of humanism by way of a more subtle practice than heretofore" of a hegemony that "constitutes a microtechnology of the disciplinary society intended to make those on which it is practiced the bearers of their own oppression" (xiv–xv). Spanos believes that the ideal of a disinterested humanist inquiry mediated through the disciplines is "grounded in metaphysics" (xv). Spanos is naive in his understanding of both the presuppositions about the contingent nature of knowledge inherent in academic practice and the need to believe in the value of disinterestedness before one can usefully aim at objectivity in our practice. He calls for collaborative practice but scorns it exactly where it has functioned best. For Spanos the university is one of the "inspection houses" that normalize deviants by means of surveillance. This is a loaded rhetoric, but labeling peer judgment surveillance does not make it that. It is only when that peer judgment abandons a reasonably objective standard of what might be intellectually credible within the scope of our knowledge that we are in severe trouble. Of course, when we make the political implications of one's work a central criterion, or when we demand more work from colleagues than they can reasonably produce to win their place in the institution, then we give Spanos his point.

The uncertainty theories that mark the modern development of so many of our disciplines necessarily opened us wide to the variables of relativism. At the same time, however, the relativist context delimits the boundaries of our relativism. The meaning assigned words is relative, but to a specific culture and historical moment. Mathematical measures are relative, as is the movement of particles, but within the parameters of space, mass, and velocity. Ethics are relative, but adjudication gives them cultural definition. The Other, whether defined by race, class, culture, or gender, is separate and mysterious, but surely we do not believe that all Others are locked away from us in an alien state of unpenetrable unintelligibility. To think so is to abandon the hope that political action and cultural understanding have any force to change our world. As one critic notes, to abandon the idea of interpretative validity of some general criteria between my culture and the Other's is to conclude that I cannot, and therefore need not, think about how they relate (Mohanty 1992, 129). If knowledge fails to open understanding, it will end in closing doors, in either frustration or indifference. The question before us is not whether things are relative, uncertain, different, separate, Other. The question is what practices can best develop areas of understanding that can strengthen our sense of belonging to a human community.

I do not believe that healthy academic practices include flame wars, political correctness, ideological insistence, or hate speech. To the extent that our professional practice has participated in the rhetorical extremes that characterize our national politics and what passes for debate on such television shows as *Crossfire* or even *The MacNeil-Lehrer Newshour*, we have added to the murk and mire of the cultural discourse. Mark Dery suggests that flame wars, those "vitriolic on-line exchanges" that flourish on e-mail talknets, offer a "glimpse of mainstream culture a few years from now" (1993, 559, 564). Because he also describes them as "witless" rants or "demented soliloquies" in which hostilities accelerate because combatants can insult with impunity, we should perhaps ask ourselves whether the presence of flame wars in academic discourse is an omen we should read with care. The relativism inherent in our knowledge, the theoretical principles of uncertainty in our fields of study should tutor us in an academic discourse that is more tentative and exploratory than insistent and sure. In the face of our uncertainties, should we not stand before our students and our colleagues with humility instead of arrogance? Is our practice open, flexible, and tolerant to new ideas and new voices? Do we, as those founders of academic freedom in 1915 urged, speak to each other with "dignity, courtesy, and temperateness of language"? Do we remember that we are a community and that the people up and down the halls are our colleagues in a mutual enterprise that is more committed to high principles than it has ever been to monetary gain? Do we, in short, make a merit through practice of our inherent intellectual uncertainties?

The historian Eric Hobsbawn has labeled the twentieth century the age of extremes, and the rhetorical extremes of our public dialogue would seem to support him. Extremes of rhetoric are, of course, strategies to replace the truth function. Where we have not been able to believe philosophically, we have substituted an insistent advocacy that was rhetorical, political, and moral. Critics who understand the conflict between the uncertainties of our theory and the insistence on our ideas often view us with contempt. Those who do not understand the conflict often view us with distrust.

An age of uncertainties is an age of anxieties in which fears multiply because the laws we need to limit them are themselves open to transformation. Determinant worlds require only that we adjust to the inevitable; uncertain ones require that we think and act and that we do so without assurances that thought and action will prove effective or even look wise in retrospect. It is hard to act morally without assurances that we can do good. As T. S. Eliot reminds us, everyone is ready to invest money, but most are looking for dividends. Our universities are on a collision course with the American psyche because the public wants certainties, dividends, skills, information that will stabilize the future for our culture and ourselves. Our institutions of education are more eager to offer all that we know and can teach to an anxious world than ever before, but our theoretical, philosophical, and scientific understanding is increasingly that the nature of knowledge is problematic and contingent. Increasingly, we shall need our academic freedom to protect the space in which to be uncertain, the space in which to hang possibilities that do not reconcile, the space in which to explore the connections that might be built between differences, the space in which to adjudicate an ethical outcome when opinions are in conflict. In our age of extremes we have unfortunately made words such as *accommodation* and *compromise* into demeaning labels for betrayal. The tragic irony of our time is that at this historical moment in which consensus is a virtual impossibility, our society idealizes it, almost demands it, at the same time it makes television entertainment out of our discord.

If our universities are not places where the communal exchange and evaluation of ideas can flow freely, where teaching and learning are conducted with consideration of the rights of students and colleagues, then I am not sure there will be any place in our society where such conduct is the practice. We will not get it in Congress, and we will not get it on television. And even if the extremes of our national discourse do not encourage a society of hatred and suspicion, they will obscure the pursuit and dissemination of knowledge that might help us.

The poet W. B. Yeats once wrote, "All empty souls tend to extreme opinion. It is only in those who have built up a rich world of memories and habits of thought that extreme opinions affront the sense of probability. Propositions, for instance, which set all the truth upon one side can only enter rich minds to dislocate and strain, if they can enter at all, and sooner or later the mind expels them by instinct" (1971, 317). Education is still the way most of us build up rich worlds of memories and habits of thought. Academic practice is still the training ground that best enables us to evaluate propositions that make improbable truth claims and to expel the foolish and the false. Our declaration of principles was designed with a material world in mind, and our practices have history to back them up. Academic freedom in its practices provides the model and the means by which knowledge changes and grows in a highly politicized world that does not want uncertainty and difference. It was Nietzsche who said, "We would not let ourselves be burned to death for our opinions: we are not sure enough of them for that. But perhaps for the right to have our opinions and to change them." Our practices give us room to be right and to be wrong, to harbor tradition and to foster revolution, to defend truth and to debunk it. If we listen to our history and honor our principles, they are certain to be our surest guidepost through our uncertain future.

WORKS CITED

Cheney, Lynne. *Telling the Truth*, 23, 25. Washington, D.C.: National Endowment for the Humanities, 1992.

Dery, Mark. "Flame Wars." *South Atlantic Quarterly* 92 (fall 1993): 559–68.

Dowling, Linda. *Language and Decadence in the Victorian Fin de Siecle*, 80. Princeton: Princeton University Press, 1986.

Frank, Judith. "In the Waiting Room: Canons, Communities, 'Political Correctness.' " In *Wild Orchids and Trotsky*, edited by Mark Edmundson, 125–49. New York: Penguin, 1993.

Guillen, Michael. *Bridges to Infinity*, 15, 18, 20, 109. Los Angeles: Jeremy Tarcher, 1983.

Haskell, Thomas L. "Justifying the Rights of Academic Freedom in the Era of 'Power/Knowledge.' " In *The Future of Academic Freedom*, edited by Louis Menand, 43–90. Chicago: University of Chicago Press, 1996.

Hawking, Stephen W. *A Brief History of Time*, 55, 175. New York: Bantam, 1988.

Kloppenberg, James T. *Uncertain Victory*, 27, 43–46. New York: Oxford University Press, 1986.

Mitford, Jessica. *A Fine Old Conflict*, 323–33. New York: Knopf, 1977.

Mohanty, Satya P. "Us and Them: On the Philosophical Bases of Political Criticism." In *Critical Conditions Regarding the Historical Moment*, edited by Michael Hays, 115–45. Minneapolis: University of Minnesota, 1992.

Rorty, Richard. "Does Academic Freedom Have Philosophical Presuppositions?" In *The Future of Academic Freedom*, edited by Louis Menand, 21–42. Chicago: University of Chicago Press, 1996.

Scott, Joan. "Academic Freedom as an Ethical Practice." In *The Future of Academic Freedom*, edited by Louis Menand, 163–80. Chicago: University of Chicago Press, 1996.

Spanos, William V. *The End of Education*, xiv–xv. Minneapolis: University of Minnesota Press, 1993.

Tocqueville, Alexis de. *Democracy in America*. New York: Mentor, 1956.

Van Alstyne, William W., ed. *Freedom and Tenure in the Academy*, 397, 399–403. Durham, N.C.: Duke University Press, 1993.

Yeats, W. B. *The Autobiography*, 317. 1938. Reprint, New York: Collier, 1971.

A Federal Trial Judge Looks at Academic Freedom
Avern Cohn

Introduction

Thank you for that kind introduction, Dr. Hollingsworth.

I first came to Ann Arbor as a student in January 1942. I left in March 1943, on being drafted into the U.S. Army. I returned in September 1946 to begin a three-year stint in the Law School. Neither when I entered as a freshman in the College of Literature, Science, and the Arts (LS&A) nor when I returned as a freshman in the Law School did I imagine I would one evening be speaking to the faculty as the annual Davis, Markert, Nickerson lecturer. I am humbled by the privilege.

Although I alone am responsible for what I say tonight, I must express thanks to a number of persons whom I have spoken to in recent months, including: Peggie Hollingsworth, Elsa Kircher Cole, Jon Cosovich, Thomas Moore, Tom Roach, Carl Dibble, and particularly Professor Ted St. Antoine. Professor St. Antoine came to the Law School after my time. I regret not having the opportunity to be his student.

As you know, I am not an academic. I am not a scholar. In Cass Sustein's words in his book *Legal Reasoning and Political Conflict* (1996), I am not given to high-level theoretical thinking. Rather, almost always I think low level and deal with incompletely theorized agreements.

This is unusual territory for me. Customarily I speak mostly to lawyers—some even say I mostly bark at lawyers. I also talk to judges and law students. When I go outside the profession it is to answer questions and defend judges against the accusation that we too often do dumb things—which is partially true—and have too much power—which is also partially true.

The lecture is an important event in the life of the university and the community. Its spirit is expressed in the enabling resolution:

The protection of academic and intellectual freedom requires a constant reminder of their value and vulnerability.

The Davis, Markert, Nickerson Lecture is a continual reminder of things past. Had the university authorities apologized for their sins and made amends, as some of you urged, we might not have this reminder. Apologies, even with reparations, do not undo past wrongs, as the Japanese who were interred during World War II tell us.

A third-century rabbinic sage, Reshi Lakish of the Academy of Tiberias, said:

Each generation has its own interpreters; each generation has its own teachers.

Tonight I am an interpreter and a teacher from a perspective you have not heard from before.

What I propose to do is first tell you something about me personally, not because I am particularly exciting or unique but because I believe I am the paradigm—or close to the paradigm—of a federal district court judge, one of the six hundred who regularly make decisions, many times affecting the academy, in the ninety-four judicial districts that make up the federal court system in the United States. We are real people. Then I will tell you something of the federal court system in which I operate. And I remind you there are also fifty state court systems in the United States, each with its own particular procedures and each with its own particular jurisprudence. In this connection you should know that the vast majority of the cases in which the university is a party, for whatever reason, start and finish in the state courts of Michigan and particularly the Washtenaw County Circuit Court here in Ann Arbor, as we have recently seen.

After that introduction, which I believe is an important predicate to any discussion of academic freedom in today's environment of judicialization of institutional personnel matters, as David Adamany, president of Wayne State University, has put it, I will talk about the events of the 1950s here at Ann Arbor, review briefly the prior lectures, and go on to talk about academic freedom before and since World War II, describe the university in federal court, and offer some concluding thoughts.

I will be speaking largely anecdotally and selectively, and I want to make three points at the beginning. First, so far as academic freedom is concerned, my inquiries tell me the university is in a generally healthy condition. This is so even in light of the concerns President Duderstadt spoke of in his farewell letter last June and even in the face of the fact that the defining quality for one of the nominations for regent at last summer's Republican state convention appears to have been the competing candidates' position on a university policy regarding distribution of condoms on campus. Second, I do not see the challenges facing the academic community today to be nearly as serious as those of the 1950s. Third, the years before World War II did not display a more hospitable environment to academic freedom than today. Until the courts began to view academic freedom through the prism of the Constitution, particularly the First and Fourteenth Amendments, the only protection of academic freedom in public universities and colleges was contractual and jawboning. And today academic freedom at private colleges and universities is still largely protected only by contract and jawboning.

My Persona

I have been a federal judge for seventeen years. I came to the bench from private practice through the confluence of several events taking place more or less at the same time. Jimmy Carter, a Democrat, was president. I had been active in the Democratic Party and in Jewish and general community affairs including bar activities. The Senate was under Democratic control. Don Riegle, in whose campaign I had been active, was the senior U.S. senator from Michigan. There were five positions open for appointment. I had strong support from the leadership of the Jewish community in Detroit and particularly those who had strongly backed Senator Riegle in his 1976 election effort. I was acceptable to organized labor even though I was a partner in a corporate law firm, and Mayor Coleman Young endorsed my candidacy. My particular skills as a lawyer or my potential for being an erudite and wise judge were certainly not as important as the factors I have just mentioned.

Now, what do I bring to the bench? What makes up my persona as a judge? These are important matters in my decision making. Ninety to ninety-five percent of all cases in federal court are likely to be decided the same way regardless of the judge. Ten percent or fewer are likely to be decided more by the persona of the judge than by their facts or rules of law because in these few cases there is no particular course laid out to follow. In a book published by the University of Michigan Press, *The Federal Judiciary and Institutional Change,* Barrow, Zuk, and Gryski (1996) discuss how alternating party control of the Congress and presidency, together with an accelerating turnover of judgeships, and what they describe as a constant acculturation of new judges through record-breaking growth, affect decision making in a system initially thought to be politically independent and stable. There are liberal judges and there are conservative judges, and these casts of mind do not come about after a judge takes the bench.

There are two quotations I am partial to in talking about the differences in the personas of judges. The first is from an English judge of the 1920s:

> The law as laid down in a code, or in a statute or in a thousand eloquently reasoned opinions, is no more capable of providing all the answers than a piano is capable of providing music. The piano needs the pianist, and any two pianists, even with the same score, may produce very different music. (McCluskey 1987, 7)

The second is from Chancellor James Kent, an early-eighteenth-century New York state judge:

> I was master of the cause & ready to decide it. I saw where justice lay and the moral sense decided the cause half the time, & I then sed [*sic*] down to search the authorities until I had exhausted my books, & I might once & a while be embarrassed by a technical rule, but I *most always found principles suited to my views of the case.* (Kent 1897, 210)

Now what determines the way I play the piano and the music I produce? What determined my moral sense when, for example, I looked at the facts and what I thought to be applicable in *Doe v. University of Michigan* or *United States v. Baker,* two cases with which I am sure you are familiar? Of course, my years as a judge give me a body of experience, as does my understanding of the facts and my reading of the rules. But more is involved. Had I followed the late judge Jerome Frank's advice and been psychoanalyzed when I came to the bench I might better know. I have not been psychoanalyzed, so I must speculate.

I know my life history plays a role. I come from an upper-middle-class socioeconomic background. I, like my father who practiced law for more than sixty years and graduated from the Law School in 1917, went through the Detroit Public Schools and took my law degree at Michigan. My political background is liberal Democrat. Some say I was a yellow-dog Democrat—that is, had a yellow dog been the Democratic candidate I would have voted for him or her. My religious background—Conservative Judaism—certainly has helped shape my thinking process. The three years I spent in the Army, all in the United States, give me some humility, although it may have faded with the years. My age at investiture, fifty-six, and the fact that I have life tenure and my pay cannot be reduced, and that I still worry about being right are of significance. I had street experience as a lawyer before I came to the bench. In my early years as a lawyer, I accepted criminal assignments when there was no pay. My experiences at the bar—my public service assignments—are all factors that contribute to the way I play the judicial piano.

This is the background I brought to the bench. As for what I am as a judge, it is really for others to tell you. I will tell you that when recently asked by the *Detroit Jewish News* the way I view myself as a judge, I said:

> Some judges have an imperfect heart: they are harsh, vindictive, narrow. I like to think of myself as having, not a perfect heart—but the absence of an imperfect heart.

There is a difference in persona among judges; that is a fact of life. James Boyd White (1985), in *Heracles Bow*, puts in this way:

> Of course one may properly argue against the results of particular cases and, more deeply, against a judge's institutional or political premises, and one may properly criticize technique as well. But any judge brings a set of basic values and orientations to his or her work, and it is hard to fault someone for having a different set from one's own.

The Federal Court System

There are at least fifty-one court systems in these United States. Each state has its own system, as does the federal government. Many disputes can be handled by either system. Most of the major constitutional disputes, particularly those with significance to the academy, are in the federal system. They begin in the district court and may come into court at the behest of a citizen or a taxpayer, a student, an academic, or sometimes an institution. A decision by a district judge is sometimes publicly reported but is not binding precedent. At best, it is only an authoritative statement of the law. If a party disagrees with such a decision, an appeal can be taken to one of the twelve regional courts of appeals where three judges review the case and make the decision. A decision at this level is precedential and binding on the district judges with the states comprising the region, and the law can be different among the circuits. In *United States v. Baker*, for example, the government argued that the law regarding threats is different in the Sixth Circuit—that is, in Michigan, Ohio, Kentucky, and Tennessee—than in the Second Circuit—that is, in New York, Connecticut, and Vermont. That is an issue in the appeal now pending from my decision dismissing the indictment.

The Supreme Court is the ultimate decision maker on constitutional matters, but it takes only the cases it wants to decide and frequently leaves differences among the courts of appeals unresolved.

District judges such as me are generalists. We have civil cases and criminal cases. We get our cases by blind draw. What is assigned to us we decide. As an example of the generality of my work, during a three-month period in the spring of this year cases before me ranged over the following:

- A threat to kill the president
- My approval of $1.5 million in legal fees for defense attorneys in a mammoth drug case that included five defendants potentially facing the death penalty
- An invasion of privacy claim involving Jenny Jones showing home movies of a bachelor party
- An accusation against the Internal Revenue Service of wrongful disclosure of tax information

- An alleged illegal police raid in which a television reporter was invited along

I and my colleagues are well housed and well staffed. We have strong support services. We are part of an elaborate governance structure that has at its top a group called the Judicial Conference of the United States headed by Chief Justice Rehnquist, which is composed of chief judges of the twelve courts of appeal and a district judge from each circuit. The conference operates through a multitude of committees that are also well staffed. As a think tank and for continuing teaching we have the Federal Judicial Center. Lastly, in every law school we have at least one academic and sometimes a multitude studying and writing about what we do. We do not lack for critics or critical analysis.

The Events of the 1950s at Ann Arbor

In preparation for tonight, I sought to familiarize myself with the Davis, Markert, Nickerson events. You each have, I am sure, your particular view. Ellen W. Schrecker, in her seminal work *No Ivory Tower: McCarthyism and the Universities*, described very well the environment of the early 1950s when she said:

> The academy did not fight McCarthyism. It contributed to it. The dismissals, the blacklists, and above all the most universal acceptance of the legitimacy of what the congressional committees and other official investigators were doing conferred respectability upon the most repressive elements of the anti-Communist crusade. In its collaboration with McCarthyism, the academic community behaved just like every other major institution in American life. (Schrecker 1986, 340)

The way the administration in Ann Arbor responded was consistent with its history on these matters. In 1935 President Alexander Ruthven, in response to the activities of the National Student League, a socialist organization, said, "attendance is a privilege and not a right" and to make clear the point, wrote a student, who had gained some visibility in his support of the league's views, as follows:

University of Michigan
Ann Arbor
President's Room
July 9, 1935

Mr. Daniel Cohen,
155 S. Broad Street
Trenton, New Jersey

My dear Mr. Cohen:

It has been decided by the authorities of the University of Michigan that you should be asked not to re-enter the University. It has proved to be impossible to persuade you to refrain from interfering with the work of the University and with the work of other students.

Yours sincerely,
(Signed) Alexander Ruthven

Student Cohen was no slouch. He sued the university in the federal district court in Detroit, asserting a rather primitively phrased right of due process and denial of equal protection because of the failure to follow then-in-place procedures for expulsion. Cohen asked for a court order requiring his readmission. The university took the position that Cohen had no legal right to attend. I do not know what happened to Cohen. The court docket shows the case was dismissed by agreement shortly after the university filed its answer. Of particular interest is the fact that Cohen was one of four students, in President Ruthven's words, "of the same persuasion."

While I was in law school in the early winter of 1947, Gerhard Eisler, then reputed to be head of the Communist Party in the United States, was denied the right to speak on university property and the mayor of Ann Arbor canceled a permit for a meeting in Felch Park at which Eisler was scheduled to talk. Eisler then spoke from the steps of a house and eventually had to flee into the house when students began pelting him with snowballs. I can still recall a front-page picture in the the *Michigan Daily* of the house, faces in a window, and a large group of angry students outside.

The reaction to the Davis, Markert, and Nickerson response to the demands of East Lansing Congressman Kit Clardy to name names should have come as no surprise. Professor Davis surely should have known at the time, or at least his lawyer should have told him, that the courts were not likely to rule against the will of Congress. And the result in *Barenblatt*, the case that did him in, was predictable. Professors Markert and Nickerson should have known the weakness of the support they would get for their reliance on the Fifth Amendment. Although the outcome of the administrative process was certain, formalities were followed. The university then, and now, is dependent to a considerable extent on public money and legislative goodwill. At work were political processes; moral judgment was absent.

Prior Lectures

As I now direct my comments more particularly to academic freedom and the courts, let me recall for you the lectures that have preceded tonight's. I am the sixth in the series. All of the lectures have been printed, with the exception of Professor Metzger's. However, Professor Metzger's lecture was extensively reported in *The University Record.*

Professor Robert O'Neil gave a historical overview of academic freedom and discussed current concerns. He urged "resisting notions of what is politically correct or incorrect" and "combatting self-imposed orthodoxy as vigorously as we protested orthodoxy imposed on us from the outside."

Lee Bollinger talked of the impulse to intolerance and what can be done about it and the need to have a floor of principles. He pointed out the special role of the university. Particularly, he said:

> in these two great pulls of life, the impulse to intolerance and
> the need for commitment to belief, the university and its prin-
> ciple of academic freedom opt to overcome the former, because
> they live primarily in a world of the latter.

Catharine Stimpson gave a reasoned argument in support of freedom of speech and why the academy should support the absence of restrictions. She expressed concern with the antipornography movement and the ban hate speech movement.

Professor Metzger talked about the watchdog role of the American Association of University Professors (AAUP). He traced the history of the involvement of the AAUP in protecting academic freedom and noted that much of the combat zone is outside the academy. He observed that it is the AAUP's position that it is not fair for faculty members to indoctrinate students or to introduce controversial matters not related to class subject matter. He concluded by noting that academic freedom is in better shape today than in 1950 and that it would be naive to dismiss the tension between law and the academy. He said, "They aren't always pals."

Last year Linda Ray Pratt looked to the future when she spoke of the merits of uncertainty and cautioned:

> Increasingly, we shall need our academic freedom to protect the space in which to be uncertain, the space in which to hang possibilities that do not reconcile, the space in which to explore the connections that might be built between differences, the space in which to adjudicate an ethical outcome when opinions are in conflict.

Pre–World War II

Now let me get to some particulars. In the early years the difficulty in defending academic freedom—that is, in the words of the *American Heritage College Dictionary*, "Liberty to track and pursue knowledge and to discuss it openly without restriction or interference"—was the absence of support in the law for such a liberty.

The *Yale Law Journal*, in 1937, prompted by the failure to appoint a professor at its divinity school and by the dismissal of the president of the University of Wisconsin, said:

> It is extremely difficult to frame a legal action through which the courts can give relief against such unwarrantable limitations on academic freedom. Academic freedom is not a "property" right, or a constitutional privilege, or even a legal term defined by a history of judicial usages. Moreover, where a case is brought the plaintiff faces the added barrier of judicial reluctance to intervene in the internal affairs of an educational institution, an attitude which is said to limit the court to an examination of the authority, not the propriety, of adminis-

trative action. ("Academic Freedom and the Law," 1936–37, 670–71)

Many of you will recall a New York state court judge barring Bertrand Russell from a professorship at City College at the behest of a group of taxpayers because of the judge's disfavor with what he called Russell's moral character. The public, likely because of Russell's then controversial views on marriage, supported the decision. *Black's Law Dictionary* today uses the *Russell* case definition of academic freedom: "Right to teach as one sees fit—but not necessarily the right to teach evil" (Hamilton 1940–41, 778–79).

In a second article on academic freedom in the *Yale Law Journal*, commenting on the *Russell* case, there was the suggestion, the first I found, of the possibility of arguing a denial of a civil liberty implicating a violation of due process under the Fourteenth Amendment in the way Russell was treated.

Post–World War II

The difficulty before the 1960s was in the lack of appreciation of what the Constitution said about the actions of public officials at public universities and colleges. As the years went on judges began to have a deeper appreciation of what the Constitution, and particularly the First and Fourteenth Amendments, means. I do not intend to trace that history. The first time the words *academic freedom* appeared in a Supreme Court decision was 1952, and since then these words have appeared in some twenty-nine cases, the latest in 1990.

Walter Metzger, in discussing the 1940 Statement of Principles on Academic Freedom and Tenure of the AAUP explained it this way:

Those who wrote the 1940 Statement put their words to paper long before academic freedom had entered the protective folds of the first amendment and some time before academic tenure had acquired strong advocates on the bench or many statehouse friends. Their animating assumption was that the defense of these professional goods would have to lie outside the law, in the perfection of the policies and practices of institutions of higher learning. Their aim was to elevate academic conduct to a high uniform standard; their means—an inventory of "do's" and "don't's"— reflected their belief that, since the law allows academic institutions to be run like so many extraterritorial enclaves imposing rules of their own devising on the native population, the only way to achieve that elevation was through moral, not legal, prodding. That the words they concocted for that purpose might be used to affect the outcome of courtroom battles seems to have been furthest from their minds. (Metzger 1990, 3, 7)

The legal landscape today is far different. For example, the agenda of the American Civil Liberties Union today on issues of academic freedom covers such matters as the following:

1. Access to materials stored in libraries and archives that the donor has restricted
2. Speeches of students relating to nonacademic behavior and taking it into account in degree awarding
3. Racial and gender unrest on campuses and resulting restrictions
4. Disparity in qualification for scholarships among athletic students and other students
5. Excessive governmental intrusion into publicly financed academic activities
6. Religious control over faculty in parochial colleges and universities
7. The military presence on campus—recruiting and training
8. Relationship between tenure and discipline (nonacademic misbehavior)
9. Physical facilities and preference for racially and ethnically oriented programs

The University of Michigan in Federal Court

I would now like to talk about the university in federal court. I will not go into detail. The university is an arm of the state of Michigan and cannot be sued for damages in federal court because of the

Eleventh Amendment, which bars the federal court from exercising jurisdiction over a state. Consequently, the defendants are nominally individual officers and administrators. Also, many cases arise because the university is a rather large corporate enterprise that employs many people. Inevitably, employer-employee disputes arise outside the area of academic freedom and include claims of

- Sex discrimination
- Race discrimination
- Equal pay for equal work
- Collective bargaining disputes
- Breach of contract claims

Also, disputes sometimes arise between the university as a service provider and students as a consumer of such services, such as over tuition.

My research has located about ten cases in my court—one in the 1960s, two in the 1970s, and the rest in the 1980s—that have some particular interest as implicating principles of academic freedom. This is aside from *Doe,* which I will discuss separately.

The first case I found was a 1963 effort by Jackie Vaughn, then a student and now a state senator, to bar Governor Ross Barnett of Mississippi from speaking in Hill Auditorium because of the disrupting influence the speech would have on campus life. Vaughn was denied an injunction on the grounds he did not establish a clear and present danger from the speech and it was not the court's duty to decide who could speak on campus. The university said in opposing the injunction in words that should be remembered and bear repeating in detail:

> The function of the University is the education of the persons who attend. The most important feature of education is teaching and training the student to think so as to choose the true and reject the spurious. Education also extends to the imparting of knowledge but knowledge without the ability by thinking to weigh and choose is not of substantial consequence. It is because of the settled conviction accepted by all free peoples that by thinking, weighing, and choosing the right and the true will ultimately prevail that the great principles of free-

dom of speech, press, and religion are considered to be inalienable rights of the citizen. Every person has the right at all times and places to express his personal views and ideas on any subject. It is for the person to whose attention they come to determine whether sound or unsound. And it is only by having all such views and ideas before a person that he can acquire ability and facility to think, weigh, and choose. To that end Governor Barnett is permitted to address whosoever cares to come. (*Vaughn v. University of Michigan*, docket no. 24586 [E. D. Mich. 1963], 6)

Twice in the 1970s students challenged the denial of their right to continue in school, and twice they lost because the judges found the processes followed passed constitutional muster. In the early 1980s, an assistant professor of engineering challenged a denial of tenure on First Amendment, equal protection, and breach of contract grounds. The professor lost. The trial judge found the decision to deny tenure reasonable in light of deficient classroom performance.

Again in the 1980s, a medical student challenged his dismissal because of academic deficiencies. The student lost in the trial court. The judge said the school authorities had good reason to deny the student the right to take the examination that led to his dismissal. The court of appeals found the refusal arbitrary and capricious and ordered the student back. The Supreme Court of the United States upheld the dismissal on the grounds that university officials have a broad range of discretion in these matters and it is dubious at best to think there is a property interest in university enrollment. One justice wondered why the case was ever litigated.

Another case involved an expulsion for cheating in circumstances in which the student was denied the opportunity to have lawyer representation or a transcript of an administrative hearing. The student lost. The judge found the procedures adequate.

Still another case involved a challenge by a graduate student to the revocation of his master's degree on grounds his thesis was based on fraudulent research. The trial judge agreed, finding fault in the process followed. The court of appeals disagreed, stating that regents had the constitutional authority, to revoke a degree where fraud was involved because "upon the grant of a degree, the university certified to the world that the recipient has fulfilled the university's requirements and this certification continues until the degree is revoked."

The last two cases each involved a law student challenge to a denial of a degree on due process grounds. Neither was successful. The procedures followed, including requiring a polygraph test in one case because the student was thought to have been involved in a fire, were found to be adequate.

These cases, typical of cases from around the country, demonstrate the wide authority given to university administrators in the operation of the university and judge approval of procedures typically followed. It is a rare case in which a student is successful in challenging an academic decision against him or her and almost as rare a case in which an academic will be successful in resisting an adverse decision of a university administration.

Now, as you all know, the university lost in *Doe v. University of Michigan.* This case never should have been heard, and, to the credit of the university, that fact was recognized when it was over. The university, instead of appealing, went back to the drawing board.

I am not going to describe *Doe* to you. I am sure you all know the basics of the case. Also, I have written a somewhat personal account of the case for a 1991 issue of the *Wayne State Law Review,* There are a couple of comments I would like to make. My first inclination was to call the parties into chambers to see if their differences could be resolved. I had done that several years earlier in a case in which the American Civil Liberties Union (ACLU) challenged speech regulations at Detroit–Wayne County Metropolitan Airport. There I suggested the airport authority sit down with the ACLU and see if they could resolve their differences. The effort was successful.

However, two of my colleagues, both University of Michigan Law School graduates, persuaded me otherwise. They were of the view I should deal with the case head on. We all thought that the university, with its wealth of legal talent at the Law School, could not be that far off base. I discovered otherwise.

Second, in my written decision I used the words *academic freedom* only twice and then only obliquely. My concerns were directed to the First Amendment implication of the code in action.

Third, as I look back, what happened was not all that unusual. A political problem existed. The politicians developed a political solution, knowing if it did not work a federal judge would take care of the matter. The regents apparently believed that what they thought was good social policy would be good law. They did not stop to think that what was bad social policy was likely to be bad law. It was simply bad social policy to put civility above freedom of expression as a core value, as C. Van Woodward put it in his 1975 report on free speech at Yale.

Speech codes are still a problem. In 1995 the Court of Appeals for the Sixth Circuit held unconstitutional a speech policy at Central Michigan University. The current issue of the *Northern University of Kentucky Law Review* contains a student note "Campus Speech Codes: Whatever Happened to the 'Sticks and Stones' Doctrine?" The same issue also contains, to my dismay, a distorted description of the events of *Doe* by Lino Graglia, a law professor at the University of Texas, without so much as a mention that I held the speech code unconstitutional.

Conclusion

I am not sure how to conclude. As I told you earlier, I am one of six hundred federal district judges. In the Eastern District of Michigan a case involving the university could end up on the docket of any one of our current complement of eighteen regular and senior judges. I might not see a case involving the university for years to come. The university may not get to federal court on an academic freedom issue for years to come. However, given the complex nature of rules and regulations governing student conduct, faculty-student relationships, tenure, freedom of speech, and the like, it is more than likely that some student or academic, offended by an action taken, or some ill-thought-out administrative action ignoring what the Constitution requires, will come to my court for relief, and academic freedom issues will be part of the dispute.

As constitutional interpretation expands and contracts, so does the concept of academic freedom. Ronald Dworkin (1996) in an essay in *The Future of Academic Freedom*, notes that the phrase *academic freedom* collects different images and associations now than it did thirty or maybe even ten years ago. He says:

> We thought then about leftist teachers and McCarthyite leg-
> islators and loyalty oaths and courageous and cowardly uni-

versity presidents. Liberals and radicals were all for academic freedom. Many conservatives thought it overrated or even part of the conspiracy to paint America red. Now it is the party of reform that talks down academic freedom and conservatives who call it a bulwark of Western civilization. Now the phrase makes us think of insensitive professors and of speech codes that might protect students from their insensitivity. We wonder whether academic freedom forbids such protection, and, if so, whether academic freedom is as important as liberals once thought. (181)

Given the constantly changing landscape of constitutional rights and the scope of academic freedom, it is not safe to predict the likelihood of future cases in court or the course such cases will follow. For example, in a California case last August, setting aside discipline against a professor for having created a hostile learning environment by his sexually oriented teaching methods, the court of appeals said that the courts have yet to determine the scope of First Amendment protection to be given a public college professor's classroom speech. Just last month a district judge ordered to trial a protest by a Temple University professor that he was denied tenure because he protested conditions in a laboratory in which toxic materials were stored. The judge said the protest was protected speech on a matter of public concern and could not be the basis of adverse action. There is no mention in the decision of academic freedom. In this area the same uncertainty also obtains as to private colleges made subject to constitutional limitations in some of the states by statute as in California and by court decision as in New Jersey.

This I do know: judges will continue to differ. Justice Oliver Wendell Holmes said that the life of the law has not been logic but experience. An English judge extended that view when he said that the life of the law has not been experience but common sense. I believe that judgments ultimately are made on a commonsense basis and that most judges strive in that fashion.

I have stayed away from any discussion of the issues of multiculturalism, diversity, and affirmative action in a university setting, and for good reason. These cases have yet to come to court in any number. Thus far two decisions have gotten attention, a University of Texas Law School case and a New Jersey high school case. We are more than likely to get such a case in my court one day. I would like not to have engaged in prejudgment should it come to me. So instead of discussing the pros and cons of these issues, let me finally conclude by describing to you the decision in *Wittmer v. Peters* (681EOP.D. 4119 [7th Cir. 1996], 916) authored by Richard Posner, a noted legal scholar and chief judge of the Seventh Circuit.

The case involved a challenge by a white male to the promotion of a black male to the position of lieutenant in a boot camp for young offenders operated by the Department of Corrections of the state of Illinois. The challenger outranked the man who got the promotion in an examination for the position. The boot camp population was more than 70 percent African American. Only 69 percent of the staff was African American. Expert opinion said the camp could not achieve its goal of rehabilitation with that disparate ratio and that there was an operational need for more African Americans in supervisory positions.

Judge Posner's decision rejected the challenge and upheld the promotion. He said:

> While we may assume that a practice that is subject to the skeptical, questioning, beady-eyed scrutiny that the law requires when public officials use race to allocate burdens or benefits is not illegal per se, it can survive that intense scrutiny only if the defendants show that they are motivated by a truly powerful and worthy concern and that the racial measure that they have adopted is a plainly apt response to that concern. They must show that they had to do something and had no alternative to what they did. The concern and the response, moreover, must be substantiated and not merely asserted. (Wittmer v. Peters 1996, 918)

This is the challenge ahead. Thank you.

WORKS CITED

"Academic Freedom and the Law." *Yale Law Journal* 47 (1936–37): 670–71.
Barrow, Deborah J., Gary Zuk, and Gerald S. Gryski. *The Federal Judiciary and Institutional Change.* Ann Arbor: University of Michigan Press, 1996.

Dworkin, Ronald. "We Need a New Interpretation of Academic Freedom." In *The Future of Academic Freedom*, edited by Louis Menand, 181. Chicago: University of Chicago Press, 1996.

Hamilton, Walton H. "Trial by Ordeal, New Style." *Yale Law Journal* 50, no. 2 (1940–41): 778–79.

Kent, James Chancellor. "Unpublished Letter." *Green Bag* 9 (1897): 206, 210.

McCluskey, Lord. *Law, Justice, and Democracy*. Sweet and Maxwell: BBC Books, 1987.

Metzger, Walter P. "The 1940 Statement of Principles on Academic Freedom and Tenure." *Law and Contemporary Problems* 53 (1990): 3, 7.

Schrecker, Ellen W. *No Ivory Tower: McCarthyism and the Universities*. New York and Oxford: Oxford University Press, 1986.

Sustein, Cass. *Legal Reasoning and Political Conflict*. New York and Oxford: Oxford University Press, 1996.

Vaughn v. University of Michigan, Docket No. 24856 [E.D. Mich. 1963]:6.

White, James Boyd. *Heracles Bow: Essays on the Rhetoric and Poetics of the Law*. Madison: University of Wisconsin Press, 1985.

Opportunity and Academic Integrity
Roger W. Wilkins

Speaking here at Michigan is wonderful for me. It is, in a real sense, a coming home. I entered this university as a skinny, scared seventeen-year-old nearly forty-eight years ago, wondering: "What's to become of me?" Now, after all this time, I know.

I began forging the answer to that question in the seven years I spent here. I love this place. It is where I began in earnest the task of attempting to develop a deep and settled comfort in being a black citizen in a country that insisted on claiming to be white.

My deep affection for this university stems in part from the hard lessons I learned as I began that journey. I experienced Michigan as a white institution, and I had to adjust my spirit in ways that helped prepare me for the soul-jarring contradictions blacks encounter just living in their own country.

I will return in a moment to Michigan and the hard lessons it taught at midcentury and to the lessons I believe it must now work very hard to teach to help prepare this country for the *next* midcentury. First, however, I want to touch on citizenship.

A couple of years ago, I became certain that my sense of Americanness had settled deep inside me during an exchange with a student that occurred during a question period at the end of a debate I had had with a black conservative at George Mason University, where I teach. I interrupted a personal attack the student was leveling at my debate opponent.

"But Professor," the student complained, "he offended me as an African in America."

After commenting on what was required of us as hosts, I then blurted out words I'd never consciously thought before:

I don't think we're "Africans in America." At least I'm not.

What kind of African is born in Kansas City; lives and dies for the University of Michigan football team; loves Toni Morrison, William Faulkner, and the Baltimore Orioles; reveres George Washington and Harriet Tubman; and who, when puzzled by the conundrum of Thomas Jefferson, collects his thoughts while listening to B. B. King?

I am profoundly connected to the ideas, the history, the soil, and the culture of this vast complex and confounding country, and, as an active and concerned citizen, I am deeply disturbed about its future. I have strong ideas about what institutions like this one must do about the problems I see looming in that future. To do that, I need first to talk about the institution I encountered here almost fifty years ago.

In those days, just after Jack Roosevelt Robinson integrated Major League baseball, but before the Supreme Court decision in *Brown v. Topeka Board of Education*, the University of Michigan *followed* American culture. No black person had ever represented this university on the basketball court or on the baseball diamond. Though racial designations were not required on housing forms, we were assigned rooms by race on the basis of the photographs we were required to submit. The student who became my roommate in the second semester of my freshman year was a light-skinned African American with straight hair. The housing authorities did the right thing for the wrong reasons by placing him with a Hindu from New Delhi and a Muslim from Karachi. He was forced to mediate the partition of the subcontinent all over again. In the meantime, he learned enormous amounts about the postcolonial subcontinent and the people who lived there.

I remember encountering no black adults either on the faculty or on the administrative staffs of the university during my seven years here. I was assigned no book, play, essay, or poem by a black author, nor did I have a reading assignment over those seven years that suggested that blacks had done anything of value in the history of the world except for the decision in *Brown v. Topeka Board of Education*, which I studied in law school.

Many of the whites on campus went off to live in their segregated fraternities and sororities. Whatever mixing there was usually ended on the steps of Angell Hall. By necessity, we blacks constructed a segregated social world for ourselves here.

The lessons that both we and our white fellow students learned from this experience were, of course, quite awful ones. The bloated sense of self and the sense of entitlement to unearned privilege was driven deeply into the spirits of our white classmates by the campus culture. For us blacks the answers to the fundamental questions that young people ask themselves were these: Who am I? *A semiperson.* Where do I fit? *At the margins.* What is my role in America? *To be an eternal supplicant.*

Perhaps worst of all, we were encouraged by what we found here to hold on to the belief we had come with: that we had nothing to learn from one another across the racial divide. Whatever we had in our heads on that subject at seventeen or eighteen was sufficient for our adulthood and for our joint citizenship in this country. Unfortunately, despite significant advances, too much of what happens in higher education today teaches, though perhaps less powerfully and pointedly, those same lessons.

There was at least one other set of lessons that the university taught me by following the culture of the time. We students of the 1950s were called the silent generation. We were silent largely because the times frightened most of us. When we did attempt to speak up, we were slapped down. It was a dark time. The ugliest scar was inflicted during my first year here. In February 1950, Senator Joseph McCarthy of Wisconsin delivered the speech at Wheeling, West Virginia, alleging that he knew of a large number of Communists in the State Department and thus gave his name to an ugly period that had already begun.

In my junior year, I was a new member of the student government—the only black—and the chair of its Human Relations Committee. The Student Legislature adopted a resolution, proposed by our committee, that called on the regents and the university administration to resist subpoenas to be issued by the House Un-American Activities Committee directed at Michigan faculty members. Because the House Committee proposed to probe faculty political beliefs and associations, we believed that the hearing constituted a serious violation of academic freedom. Our resolution was brushed aside by university administrators, who said that since this hearing was to occur in Detroit, it was no concern of students, whose interests should not go beyond the campus.

Subsequently, the student government took one more foray into an area of politics that adults found difficult to treat honestly. We believed that fraternities and sororities that had national charters containing racially exclusive clauses were particularly obnoxious at an educational institution. Thus, the Student Legislature enacted a resolution that would have required Greek letter groups to eliminate such charter provisions over a reasonable transition period or face expulsion from the campus.

This action, too, was brushed aside by the administration. This time we were told that property rights precluded any action on our concern. This statement was buttressed by a citation of *corpus juris secundum*. A couple of years later when I got to law school I learned that *corpus juris secundum* was a legal encyclopedia that no one taking an argument seriously would have used as an authoritative statement of Michigan law.

As you might imagine, the idea of dissent in support of principle began to appeal to me as I pondered these actions by people who were supposed to be educating me as a person and as a citizen. I began to internalize active citizenship as a powerful personal value. I surely developed the idea that it was required to probe beneath the conventional wisdom dispensed by society in general or by interested bureaucracies in particular if one were to be in charge of her or his own moral bearings. Lone dissenters of conscience were imprinted on my spirit as the heroes of the time. For that part of my education, I am deeply indebted to Chandler Davis, Clement Markert, and Mark Nickerson, whose acts of conscience earned them seared careers but who simultaneously held up guiding torches for me in that decade of darkness.

Those men lit my way toward others carrying torches along the road. I have in mind here J. Waites Waring, the white federal judge in Charleston, South Carolina, who endured shunning by his local community as he followed what he understood to be the constitutional requirement to admit blacks to full citizenship. They led me to Andrei Sakharov, whose courageous dissent against the Soviet dictatorship made him immortal. And they led me to believe that Martin Luther King Jr.'s finest hour was his dissent from our war policies in Vietnam—despite President Johnson's fury and dire warnings from virtually all of his civil rights colleagues.

My Michigan lessons were thus quite profound. They were that one could love something quite deeply while being aware of and impatient with ugly and glaring imperfections. They were that imperfections had to be addressed, not accepted passively. They were that individual belief in one's own principles and actions taken on those beliefs could make a profound difference. They were that active citizenship is an obligation of people who value their freedom. And they were that institutions teach powerful lessons that matter down through the long decades of the lives they shape.

So, then, what are universities for? Are we simply here to help our students tuck into their souls the best of what has been thought and said as they fit themselves into the world as we have received it? Do we create new knowledge only to help these young people develop a better passive understanding of the world than earlier generations had? Is our function, in other words, to accept the world as it is and simply to equip our students with skills—to enjoy Shakespeare and to be computer literate, for example? Or is it to build some of that new knowledge on what we have come to know as human beings and to help equip our students with our understandings so that they may struggle more effectively with the problems that we believe are sure to come?

Should we not teach them about the dangers of national pathologies? No one could have lived through the last two-thirds of the twentieth century without concluding that untended national pathologies can surely lead to the most disastrous national calamities. The pathologies that festered in tsarist Russia led to the brutalities of Leninism-Stalinism. Pathologies festering beneath Weimar democracy led to murderous Hitlerism in Germany. And untended pathologies have ripped apart the country formerly known as Yugoslavia and the little central African nation of Rwanda.

The dark American time of the 1950s taught that despite our myths about how exceptional we are (and our persistent denials over the centuries of the pathology of racism), the United States is not immune to social pathologies that can destroy lives and rip at the very fabric of our democracy. This vulnerability was understood as early as 1787. At the Constitutional Convention, in urging an end to the international slave trade, George Mason of Virginia told the notables assembled in Philadelphia:

> As nations can not be rewarded or punished in the next world they must in this. By an inevitable chain of causes and effects, providence punishes national sins by national calamities.

Another lesson of the 1950s was that institutional and individual integrity and courage are rare commodities when a nation is in the grip of a fever. And, yet, it is just such clarity and courage that are required to serve free institutions and free people during times of great peril. We professors are a privileged class in society. We have good lives and relative security. There is little excuse for us to fail to be brave or to fail to give back to a country that has treated us so generously.

You may think that my talk about pathologies is a bit overwrought as our nation glides through the decade after the collapse of European Communism while enjoying a prolonged period of economic growth. The trouble is that our ancient problems have not gone away and they threaten to get worse very soon.

Let me illustrate with a story from an issue of the *New Yorker* published just after the presidential election of 1992. A reporter watched the election returns in a working-class bar on the West Side of Manhattan. The noisiest patron was a white man in a bomber jacket who was audibly distressed by the possibility that Bill Clinton might win. He began muttering about the role he thought Jesse Jackson might play in a Clinton administration. As the evening wore on and a Clinton victory became probable, the man became more agitated. Finally, when Clinton's victory was confirmed, the man threw his money on the bar and stormed out shouting: "I'm not going to be a minority in my own country."

I want you to remember that man's rage and fear as we peer into our future. Today the population of the globe is about 5.8 billion people, 75 percent of whom are poor. There are about 265 million Americans: 73 percent of us are non-Hispanic white; 12 percent are black; 10.6 percent are Hispanic; 3 percent are Asian Americans, and fewer than 1 percent are Indians, Eskimos, or Aleuts.

In the middle of the next century—when my daughter, who is now in the eighth grade, is about the age I am now—there will be 8.5 to 10 billion people in the world, and 80 percent of them will be poor. The population of the United States will then be about 394 million, only 52.8 percent of whom will be "white." The 47.2 percent of the population that is "minority" will be distributed this way: 24.5 percent of the American population will be Hispanic; 13.5 percent will be black; 8.2 percent will be Asian American, and 1 percent will be Native American, Eskimo, or Aleut.

The world will be more closely connected and tightly wired. There will be more poor people in the world's population than there are people on the planet today. As we now think of the world's poverty as the cause of enormous problems in immigration policy and the availability of drugs, we should probably remind ourselves that we are only glimpsing the foothills of the emerging world. America will be a much more crowded place with more competition for space and other pressures grinding away at our civility and our senses of personal and international security.

It will, of course, be much harder to think of America as a "white country" or as a new and improved version of Europe. It will be a true world country, a country whose citizens have families with origins on every conceivable spot on the globe.

I would now ask you to think about the man in the bomber jacket who was having an identity crisis in the bar. There are already distressing signs about what our demographic trend might mean for America. I think the Oklahoma City bombing and the national teach-in on militias and white identity groups it generated were deeply disturbing. There are true pathologies at work there. On the far other side of the cultural chasm in America there is gangsta rap. It is a cultural phenomenon that I find profoundly distressing, and I think the companies that profit from it are obscene. Someday scholars of music, poetry, and sociology may tell us that this is a starkly beautiful and artistic representation of the spiritual life salvaged from the rubble of the American ghetto. But I find the murders of the gangsta rappers Tupak Shakur and Biggie Smalls to be representative of the economic and spiritual desolation that our country has dumped on our most vulnerable citizens. We, as a people, take our profits and our income where we can find it and then flee from the poverty and human wastage our social and economic dislocations cause.

Lost lives—whether on the streets of the inner city, in the rapidly growing number of prisons, or in failed elementary schools—are held in contempt in this country. The contempt is shown by the brutal way society rations opportunity and by young black murderers, who are simply externalizing their own contempt for themselves. The murders and the murderers generate increasing amounts of fear of blacks in general and of the black poor in particular.

We thus already have the bookends of a dreadful American calamity. White identity groups are at one far side and black desperadoes who have absolutely nothing to lose are at the other. The only thing necessary for a full-fledged pathology to begin raging is for the pressures of demographic trends to begin to fill up the middle.

My forebodings are not rooted in some ideological denial of the enormous progress in race that this nation has made in my lifetime or the enormous progress this university has made since my time here. America is a far better place today than it was when I was born in a segregated hospital in Missouri sixty-five years ago or when I began my formal education in a segregated one-room schoolhouse four years later. We are surely a fairer and more decent country than we were then, and the education provided by this institution is far richer and more conscious of the realities of the society around it than the Michigan I attended. But that progress was achieved—to borrow a phrase— "with all deliberate speed."

I do not think we have the luxury of time anymore. The demographic shift we are experiencing suggests that over the next fifty years, the very identity of the nation will be up for grabs and that many people will be shaken to their roots. Being a human being is an uncertain, often painful, and frightening business. People seek solace and security in the group identities that may cloak them with standing and some physical and psychic protection. From our earliest history, when it was already demonstrably not true, Europeans insisted that this was to be a white country.

In those days, the world was thinly populated with perhaps only around half to three-quarters of a billion people. From the fifteenth century on, the pace of intercontinental collisions of peoples quickened and human difference became a massive human problem. America's national pathologies began to take shape at Jamestown in 1607. Human difference was even more startling then than now, and difference was taken to mean danger. The earliest English colonists grappled for ways to deal with people who were different from them and finally concluded that domination of the dangerous Other would work best.

Domination required the creation of a culture that justified a good deal of violence and deviousness, and so *otherness* became forever dangerous and inferior, whether in Native Americans, blacks, dark Latins, or Asians. Such people were also pushed to the margins of a busy, thrusting, and increasingly more powerful "white" country. Thus, whiteness provided privilege as well as protection. So the white American identity, originally potent because of primal fears, was pounded deeper into the soul of the nation by the cultural accretions that justified the subordination and marginalization of millions of human beings.

Much of the twentieth-century racial progress occurred on top of and around this seminal racial sludge that lies somewhere near the center of American culture. As the old caste structures have broken down and have lost their force in law and in the superficial structures of civility, the damage done to all of us by our culture has become more apparent as opportunities for people who are not white remain severely restricted. I will deal here only with the damage to whites and blacks, but I am sure that similar assessments could be made of Hispanic, Asian, and Native Americans as well.

Some whites have become more fearful and have retreated into white identity movements of various kinds. Others have become sullenly resentful of any minority advance, which some of them view as personal assaults. Still others have organized highly effective movements to contest the gains blacks and others have made. Some, who believe themselves to be racially decent, continue to behave and to exercise power in the old ways while denying—even to themselves— that they have "a racist bone" in their bodies. While we were once able to believe that prejudice was an individual thing, we have come to see during our thirty-year attempt to live with civil rights laws that the virus of racism adapts to new circumstances, replicates itself in new generations, and affects profoundly how we think, live, and make public policy. Laws liberated millions of white Americans, but they did not root racism out of the culture.

Clearly blacks are damaged as well. In addition to the tangible injuries in the economic, educational, health, and housing spheres, there is also the cultural battering of the soul. That takes many forms. For some of the poorest and least connected citizens, it takes the form of almost total demoralization and a collapse of the family structure accompanied by the horrendous collateral damage I have already mentioned. For others it means lowered self-esteem and a sort of constantly imploding rage. And for still others it means a serious confusion about personal identity.

So, I tell my white students that they need to be much more than a collection of fantasies about the magic of whiteness or about the inferiorities of blacks and others to be fully human. I tell my black students that they need to be much more than the sum of their injuries and their grievances to achieve their full humanity. But for now the injuries to all are there, and they are real and they could surely provide the seeds for a new, intense manifestation of our national pathologies.

As politicians have sensed the powerful reactions to challenges to the white identity of the nation or to the individual identities of white human beings, many have chosen the course of least resistance and have pandered to those feelings. The results—whether on immigration and civil rights issues in California or the ugly and brutal welfare "reform" law—have suggested a national direction that raises possibilities of massive national calamities as the pace of demographic change picks up speed. We are thus faced with the daunting question of whether we can find national leadership with the courage and principled fiber to see us through such dangerous times.

I can think of no more suitable institutions to take the lead than the nation's universities and colleges. Current academic responses to this danger are hopelessly out of date. Questions about affirmative action are being fought out and defeated in the courts and in the political arena on interpretations of the past. As you would expect, in my mind there is no doubt that minorities and women have enormous justice claims on this society, not just for past wrongs but for current discrimination for which, in many cases, no adequate remedies other than affirmative action exist. Powerful and right as I believe these claims to be, they rest on past injustices rather than on the even more powerful claims the future makes on us.

There is also the lumbering, multifaceted debate about multiculturalism. This battle is littered with the bodies of "dead white males" and of their "victims." The struggle can be reduced to terms that make it seem pretty silly, but the dangers that grow out of virulent ethnocentrism are not at all funny. Many people just cannot see other people or other cultures. Instead, they see representations of their own fears and their own needs. They do not try to understand human behavior and motivation because it is more comforting to deal with myths and stereotypes than with the complexities, ambiguities, and gnarled histories that produce the boiling occurrences that we experience as contemporary life.

It therefore seems to me imperative that we change the debate in the society at large about how our business is to be conducted and why. We must also change the debate inside the academy about what we must teach and why. The essential question here is whether we are to follow the culture as universities did in the 1950s, when they permitted careers such as those of Professors Davis, Markert, and Nickerson to be damaged, or whether we should try to *lead* the society because our mission is to educate people, most of them citizens, for a future that, thanks to the demographers, we can now see pretty clearly.

The essence of that mission, in my view, is to *maximize opportunity* and to make vigorous use of educational diversity to produce the extraordinarily able citizenry that will be required to guide America through the profound changes coming in the next few decades.

To chart such a course and to engage in such a dialogue will take courage because not everyone sees the same future or takes the same view of the educator's responsibility. Some disagreement with my view is clearly rooted in deep intellectual conviction that this is not the role of universities. Some might grow out of the traditional American optimism that we are free and creative people, and with the help of our free market, will work things out as we always have. Other opposition will surely be rooted in fear and the need for the crutch of white identity. Finally, some people are not about to give up their privileges, whether earned or not. Wherever the opposition comes from, it will be powerful and often bitter. Great courage and tenacity will be required to sustain the side of the argument I am suggesting.

One of the ways we might define our task is to recall the words of the pioneering black historian Carter G. Woodson, who set out to correct what he called "the miseducation of the Negro." The pathologies lurking just under the tissue of our national civility result from the way we *all* have been "miseducated." They also result from the fact that millions of our fellow citizens are *undereducated* and are therefore easy prey for demagogues.

Not long ago, Michigan's provost, Dr. Bernard Machen, made a statement about affirmative action that I would have applauded wholeheartedly a few years ago but think is too narrow today. He said that the top value at Michigan "is a renewed commitment to diversity and informed affirmative action." Michigan's *University Record* went on to report that Machen said that "[While] there is a 'compelling case to be made about the need to prepare our students' for life in the 21st century, the key reason for the U-M 'is an intellectual one,' which he said is defined well by John Stuart Mill in *On Liberty*—that it is of special benefit to the quality of thought and discourse for many opinions to be expressed."

As the *New Yorker* story about the man in the bomber jacket or my observations of blacks whose horizons are crimped by pain and bitterness demonstrate, there are vast and dangerous numbers of Americans who are not prepared either emotionally or intellectually for the changes we face in the twenty-first century. And many of these people will become parents who will pass their injuries on to their children, thus perpetuating our cultural pathologies. So, I would reverse and enlarge Dr. Machen's vision.

In short, we need to retell the story of human beings in ways that emphasize our membership in the same species and to retell the story of our country in ways that make it clear that however much white domination there has been, the creation of American culture and identity has always been a multiracial enterprise; that we have enormous amounts to learn from each other; and that our greatest achievements as a nation lie ahead of us as we struggle to become the first country on the planet where the entirety of the human species is present and fully respected in the polity.

In calling for such a national discourse and such a curriculum, I am not calling for "victim" studies or courses designed narrowly to raise the self-esteem of one group or another. I am searching for ways to include material in our curriculum that seeks to make students more comfortable with their full humanity (with all the existential peril that involves) and with all other kinds of human beings. In addition to revised intellectual content, this approach would include emotional education to help Americans get through the turbulence of the shifting nature of American identity.

It may help if I give an example of what I mean by emotional education. I learned powerful emotional lessons during the mid- and late 1940s in a Grand Rapids high school in which I was, for much of my time there, the only black student in a population of about 1,100. In this time before the civil rights movement, I learned valuable lessons about white people and about myself.

Even though the customs of the times did not constrain whites from expressing belief in their own superiority or their dislike of blacks, I still learned that whites were not supermen and that many of them were quite likeable. I found that some of them were smarter than I and that lots of them were not; that some of them were better athletes than I but many were not; and that although there were plenty of racist bozos, there were a lot of really decent people as well.

In sum, I learned—deep down in my soul—that whites were human and so, indeed, was I. Those lessons undoubtedly accounted for the fact that I later had the confidence here at Michigan to run successfully first for the student government and then for the presidency of my class. Moreover, a number of my old high school friends say that knowing our family was the most powerful lesson they learned during their high school days and that the experience enriched them in wonderful ways.

That would suggest that we must begin to take what we *say* about the benefits of diversity in education seriously. Effective education for American citizenship cannot occur without a richly diverse student body. Every student should be regarded as a potential educational opportunity for every other student, and students should be made to understand that concept from the very beginning of their educational experience. Students should be given every opportunity and should be encouraged at every turn to meet, mix, and learn with people with different backgrounds from their own. This effort should include living arrangements, educational exercises in the classroom, and extracurricular activities. To the greatest extent possible, we should make sure that students do not retreat easily into the comfortable, but narrowing, habit of spending all of their time with exactly the same kind of people they spent time with in high school—that is, with people from homes, parents, and family incomes exactly like their own.

But to accomplish that on the campus, we must intervene in the national debate on behalf of providing the broadest possible opportunity and explain clearly that our country's future depends on it. We educators were citizens before we were intellectuals, and somewhere deep in our souls as American citizens we all know that we owe a great deal to this country. I think we also know that the imperfections we have accommodated for so long are weakening our nation and sapping the vitality of our democracy. Finally, I think we know that however damaging to the country the silence of my student generation was, our silence or passivity as adult educators in the face of the current threats to our democracy will be infinitely worse.

As the story of Germany in the twentieth century tells us, democracy is both precious and perishable. The Founding Fathers expected us to work hard at being citizens and at taking care of our democracy.

It has been said that a woman encountered Benjamin Franklin on the street in Philadelphia just after the secret Constitutional Convention had ended.

"What have you made in there, Dr. Franklin?" she is supposed to have asked.

Franklin's reply: "A republic, madam, if you can keep it."

"If you can keep it." Our job as citizens and scholars and teachers is to turn out citizens with the emotional and intellectual capacities to "keep" and improve on our democracy. The fact is, I learned to think that was my lifetime job when I was a student here back in the 1950s. For that lesson above all others, I am deeply grateful to the University of Michigan.

Free Speech, Free Press, Free Society
Eugene L. Roberts Jr.

For most of my working life I was a journalist. Only for a bit more than three years, all told, have I worked on a college campus as, allegedly, a professor.

As a journalist I accepted doing battle for First Amendment values as a part of my job. There were battles for access to public records, battles against libel suits aimed at inhibiting public discussion, battles against judges who attempted to gag reporters from writing about what was transpiring in courtrooms, and battles for admission to the meetings of city councils and school boards. I envied my friends in academe, where there seemed to be freedom with less effort and exertion.

True, there were the grave excesses of the McCarthy era and a flurry of rules banning Communist speakers from college campuses during the early stages of the cold war. And campuses became battlegrounds during the Vietnam War. But gradually in most of the 1970s and 1980s, freedom of expression prevailed over the fear of words.

Then, about ten years ago, disquieting developments began recurring on campus after campus—the adoption of speech codes; lawsuits and assaults on the tenure of professors for opinions and, sometimes, fact uttered in the classroom; the seizure of all, or a major part, of issues of campus newspapers; the public burning of publications that angered some students. In some instances, but thankfully not all, college administrations looked the other way.

These incidents escalated in the first half of the 1990s, then subsided a bit, but still they surface to this day, much like a stubborn virus that will not go away. In the past fifteen months, publications have been seized, or burned, or both, on campuses as far-flung as the University of North Carolina at Chapel Hill, Cornell University in Ithaca, New York, and the University of California at Berkeley.

Precipitating incidents have ranged from an editorial against affirmative action to a cartoon against abortion. Sometimes the offending publications were temperate, sometimes intemperate; sometimes facts were correct, sometimes they were not.

All of this, of course, is fully within the scope of freedoms envisioned by the architects of American liberty. More than 265 years ago in the June 10, 1731, issue of the *Pennsylvania Gazette*, Benjamin Franklin had this to say:

> I request all who are angry with me on Account of printing things they don't like calmly to consider these following Particulars
>
> 1. That the Opinions of Men are almost always as various as their Faces. . . .
> 2. That the Business of Printing has chiefly to do with Men's Opinions; most things that are printed tending to promote some, or opposite. . . .
> 3. That it is unreasonable in any one Man or Set of Men to expect to be pleas'd with every thing that is printed . . . [or, I might add, said].
> 4. Printers are educated in the Belief that when Men differ in Opinion, both Sides ought equally to have the Advantage of being heard by the Publick; and that when Truth and Error have fair Play, the former is always an overmatch for the latter. . . .

The words of Franklin, like the guarantees of the First Amendment, have been overlooked too frequently on all too many campuses in the past decade. Freedom of speech, the most fundamental of all democratic values, has been transmogrified again and again into freedom *from* speech—not, I believe, what the drafters of the Bill of Rights had in mind.

In the past decade, speech prevention has often come from groups that have triumphed over or are still struggling against discrimination and unequal treatment. Some—not by any means all—seem to believe speech prevention will secure and consolidate progress. This view flies in the face of history.

The civil rights movement, the women's movement, the labor movement, and the gay rights movement all made major gains precisely because they fully exercised freedom of expression in their struggles. In print. From the podium. In the streets. Freedom of expression was absolutely fundamental to achieving all other rights. How, then, can we take free speech lightly in our colleges and universities? They should be the very citadels of free inquiry and debate—for the left and for the right, for minorities and for majorities, for humanists and, yes, even for bigots.

Consider segregation in the American South. It might still be with us today if not for freedom of the press and the fullest range of expression, especially by black journalists and black students. Let us go back in time to the South in the 1930s, when segregation was as pervasive and as grinding as it ever got. The "whites-only" and "colored" directional signs of segregation were over every drinking fountain, toilet, and train and bus waiting room. No signs were needed at restaurants. If they were located conveniently in a business district or shopping area, they were invariably for whites. Blacks entered white churches and schools to clean them or deliver packages. Blacks came and went as servants at white homes through back doors.

The economic plight of blacks was so desperate that some sociologists described it as *pathological*—a disease of epidemic proportions. Because segregation embodied a caste system, blacks were denied professional or white-collar jobs that would put them with whites on anything approaching an equal footing. To an overwhelming degree, blacks were where the money was not: in cotton rows, in day laboring, and in domestic jobs. They were delivery men, porters, janitors, and charwomen.

As bad as the economic condition was for blacks in the segregated South, their treatment in the courts was worse. Whites were the judges, the jurors, the bailiffs, the court clerks, the arresting officers, the prosecuting attorneys, and the jailers. Only the instruments of execution—the electric chair, the gas chamber, the hangman's noose—were desegregated and used for blacks and whites alike. But in this case, desegregation did not mean fairness. Blacks were far, far more likely than whites to be put to death. Even voting was not a right for blacks. It was at the whim of whites. Some counties allowed it. Some did not. And some counties permitted some blacks to vote and denied the ballot to others. Not even property ownership was safe for blacks. Whites could cheat blacks and steal from them, knowing that when it was white testimony against black in the courts, white almost always prevailed.

There was one right that could be generally depended on by blacks in the South, astonishingly, considering the times. It was freedom of the press. Black weekly newspapers were published by the hundreds in the South and distributed, for the most part, without any sort of hindrance. Northern black newspapers, some as outspoken as any papers ever published in America, could be found in newsstands and mail boxes in every southern state. Between 1827, when the first black newspaper appeared in New York, and 1951, when a detailed survey was made, 2,700 black newspapers were founded—many, many of them in the South. Serving poor and less than affluent communities, most black papers lived hard and died young. The average black paper died after nine years. But collectively they made their mark.

Many of these papers were utterly fearless. They were fierce in their denunciation of discrimination. They berated white hypocrisy. And they built a climate among black readers that paved the way for the civil rights movement.

The gains made by blacks in the 1960s and 1970s arguably would not have been possible had the black press not been free in the 1930s, 1940s, and 1950s—free to distribute, free to advocate over and over that all persons should be equal before the law, in the economy, in education. Free to prepare the black South for an assault on segregation.

Even as astute an observer of the racial scene as Gunnar Myrdal, the author of *All American Dilemma,* was mystified by the reality of a militantly integrationist black press operating relatively freely in the militantly segregationist white South. In a region in which blacks could not be sure of voting, or even of basic property rights, their newspapers were exercising the broadest of latitudes under the First Amendment.

How could this be? Myrdal never came up with a definitive answer. He thought it possible that whites simply did not read black newspapers and were unaware of their militancy, although in the 1950s as racial tensions increased and segregationists spoke out in letters to the editor in daily newspapers it became clear that some, at least, were well aware of black newspaper advocacy and blamed it for a large part of the assault on segregation. Perhaps, Myrdal mused, the black press was tolerated because of a "certain abstract feeling among all Americans for the freedom of the press which, even in the South, covers the Negro newspapers" (1962, 910).

Whatever the reason, it is sobering that black newspapers in the segregationist South in the 1930s and 1940s were freer from disruption, harassment, and seizure than some campus newspapers have been in the 1990s.

In 1993, student newspapers and other campus publications were seized and destroyed in a wave that swept over at least twenty campuses and then, ultimately by some counts, to as many as one hundred. Here are some news items:

University of Pennsylvania, April 15, 1993—About 60 black students organized by the black student league on the U. Penn campus destroyed 14,000 copies of the *Daily Pennsylvanian* (nearly the entire press run). The black students said they were protesting the racist slant of the newspaper; in particular, they cited a conservative columnist who had attacked Martin Luther King Jr. and what he saw as the University's preferential treatment of blacks in admissions and disciplinary procedures.

University of Maryland, Nov 2, 1993—Ten thousand copies of the *Diamondback* [the student newspaper] were stolen from campus distribution points. . . . The thieves . . . left behind fliers that said "due to its racist nature, the Diamondback will not be available today—read a book."

Black students had criticized the newspaper's coverage as racially insensitive after at least two incidents: a fashion supplement that featured mostly white models and a report on a speech that misspelled Frederick Douglass as "Franklin Douglas" and misidentified W. E. B. DuBois's book *The Souls of Black Folk* as *The Sales of Black Folk*.

This event took place five years ago, and since then the destruction of campus newspapers has abated but not ceased. For example, on election day, November 5, 1996, 23,000 copies of the *Daily Californian*, the student newspaper at the University of California at Berkeley, were seized and later burned by students angry over an editorial supporting Proposition 209, a proposition to ban affirmative action.

Well, you might ask, isn't it justifiable to halt the distribution of a publication when it contains clear and provable errors? But consider this: at a critical point in the civil rights movement, white segregationists in Alabama made a concerted effort to silence civil rights leaders and the press. They sued for libel, charging they had been slandered in an advertisement in the *New York Times*. The ad appealed for money to support Dr. Martin Luther King. And, let it be noted, it contained at least five errors of fact.

An all-white jury ruled against the *Times* for printing the ad and four black ministers whose names were on the ad. They were ordered to pay $500,000, and a judge ordered the seizure of all the ministers' assets, including banking and savings accounts. The Reverend Ralph Abernathy's five-year-old Buick was seized, as was a small plot of land he owned. A shiver of fear went through the civil rights movement. Would the price of protest be the loss of everything the leaders owned?

Emboldened by the verdict, Alabama officials filed more suits against the *Times* and other media companies. They asked for millions. Quite clearly, the aim was to halt the civil rights movement in its tracks by preventing news coverage of it.

Finally, the Supreme Court ruled in the case, which was called *Times v. Sullivan.* It said that civil rights leaders and the press had a right to discuss public issues such as segregation, even if they made errors in the process. In its decision, the Court cited "a profound national commitment to the principle that debate on public issues should be uninhibited, robust, and wide-open." It also declared that erroneous statement is inevitable in free debate and that it must be protected if the freedoms of expression are to have the "breathing space" that they "need . . . to survive."

If this is indeed the national commitment, why should it, how could it, be any less on the college campus? And yet it has been less. All too often it has been forgotten that black freedom owes much to press freedom and the right to protest and dissent. And the freeness of American society as a whole owes much to black Americans' determination to exercise freedom of expression in the press and in militantly nonviolent protest in the streets.

Much the same can be said of the women's movement. Even the right to vote might never have been granted to women had they not insisted on their right to full and unfettered expression. As a result, they expanded free expression for all of us.

Consider this: In recent decades millions of Americans have marched around the White House, many of them to protest war, racial segregation, the death penalty, capital punishment, and on and on.

Many of these protesters marched without knowing that they owe this right to the persistence of women suffragists little more than eighty years ago. Let us take a look in detail and perspective at suffragist protest at the White House and just how much it pushed freedom forward in our nation.

The nation was shocked on January 9, 1917, when women suffragists announced they were weary of waiting for their just rights and would picket the White House gates. They wanted to persuade President Wilson to back a constitutional amendment guaranteeing women the right to vote. They called themselves "silent sentinels." They were determined to avoid the rock throwing and raucous disturbances employed by women suffragists in England. "Mr. President, What Will You Do for Woman Suffrage?" asked one picket sign. "How Long Must Women Wait for Liberty?" queried another. Although the methods were modest by today's standards, rage erupted across the country. The suffragists were accused of being lawless, pernicious, impudent, ill-mannered, disrespectful, dangerously radical, invaders of the president's privacy, and, in general, a threat to the American way of life and to an orderly democratic process.

Listen to what was said on editorial pages at the time: "No one can imagine the socialists, prohibitionists, or any other party conceiving of a performance at once so petty and so monstrous," the *New York Times* declared. "One could not imagine even the I.W.W. [a radical labor organization known as "the Wobblies"] attempting it." "Picketing the White House," huffed the *Philadelphia Inquirer*, "is a piece of impudence that would not be tolerated for a moment if it were done by men." The *Richmond Times Dispatch* pronounced it to be a "breach of good manners." "If everyone who wanted some particular measure or legislation undertook to picket the White House," the *New York World* said, "it would be besieged by a mob reaching from Baltimore to Richmond."

"There must be sufficient law to deal with their pernicious activities," added the *Public Ledger* of Philadelphia. "If there is not, a law should be passed forbidding them. The nation, not the President, is shamed by the acts of these deluded campaigners."

The *Washington Evening Star* suggested the pickets might want to change the scene of their protest—to the Capitol. "If picketing has any value whatever it should be undertaken to the Capitol, the scene of legislation, the place to which the suffragists must look for action," the *Star* said.

It seems clear that much of the nation and the press opposed the picketing, at least in part because they looked on the White House as a private home rather than as an official residence that doubled as a government nerve center.

Considering the foreboding on editorial pages, the first few months of demonstrations were surprisingly anticlimactic. Wilson and his staff initially reacted good-spiritedly. When the president's car drove past the pickets, he sometimes acknowledged them with a smile, a wave, or a salute. When what the *Star* described as a "cold, piercing wind" blew across the White House grounds on the second day of picketing, presidential aides invited the pickets into the mansion to warm themselves. The pickets said they could not accept without the permission of their leaders. The leaders responded by shortening the tours of duty for the pickets and supplying them with hot chocolate.

Despite their efforts, the suffragists struggled to keep interest in the picketing alive. They held State Days, on which delegations from Maryland, Pennsylvania, New York, Virginia, and New Jersey came in turn. The White House remained calm. So did the public. Picketing dropped from the front pages. Then inside-the-paper coverage became sporadic.

The mood began to swing in April, when the United States entered World War I, and the suffragists continued their picketing, despite criticism that it was unpatriotic. Suffragists recalled that Susan B. Anthony had reluctantly cut down on her prosuffrage activities during the Civil War, only to see the vote granted at war's end to black men but not to women of any color or creed.

When world leaders showed up at the White House to meet with President Wilson about war plans, the suffragists greeted them with picket signs. Arthur Balfour, leader of the British mission, called at the White House and saw suffragist banners inscribed with the precise words Wilson had used in his war message: "We shall fight for the things which we have always held nearest our hearts—for democracy, for the right of those who submit to authority to have a voice in their own governments."

On June 22 the signs greeting a delegation from the new Russian Republic (the Kerensky government) were more pointed. A huge banner said: "President Wilson and Envoy [Elihu] Root are deceiving Russia when they say 'We are a Democracy, help us win the world war so that democracy may survive.' We the women of America tell you that

America is not a democracy. Twenty million American Women are denied the right to vote. President Wilson is the chief opponent of their national enfranchisement. Help us make this nation really free. Tell our Government it must liberate its people before it can claim Free Russia as an ally." Anger spread through the White House, the government, and the streets. Within twenty-four hours, hecklers pulled down the banner three times—once with police looking on.

As tensions grew, officials of the District of Columbia police informed the pickets they would be arrested if they returned. Rows of policemen formed outside the pickets' headquarters the next day and, within minutes, arrested two pickets who marched to the White House. The first pickets were released without charges. But, ultimately, ninety-seven women spent up to six months in the Occoquan Workhouse. When they refused to eat, they were wrestled to the floor or their beds, and tubes were shoved down their throats. Thirty women resisted so persistently that the Wilson administration worried that some might die. A shift in public opinion to the women's cause added to the worry. It was the beginning of the end.

On November 27 and 29, all of the pickets were released unconditionally from prison. On January 9, 1918, President Wilson reversed his position on suffrage and announced he was now in favor of a constitutional amendment. The amendment cleared Congress in the summer of 1919 and, with three-quarters of the states approving, was adopted on August 26, 1920.

In winning the right for women to vote, the suffragists also established the right to picket the White House for future generations of both sexes. More than three months after the pickets were released from prison, the U.S. Court of Appeals for the District of Columbia ruled that their arrests and sentences were invalid: they had been breaking no law in picketing the White House, even in wartime. Over the decades, protest at the White House grew steadily, thanks to the suffragists, and today it is accepted as a basic right.

In 1991, during the demonstrations against the Gulf War, the protesters in Lafayette Park chanted, waved signs, and beat a drum so loudly and so incessantly that President Bush complained it kept him awake at night. U.S. Park Service police arrested a drummer and charged her with violating the decibel levels regulation aimed at preserving the tranquillity of federal parks. A three-judge panel of the U.S. Court of Appeals overturned the conviction. In a ruling that would have delighted the suffragist pickets, the court said the Park Service could not expect to regulate the area around the White House like a normal park. The reason was simple. The area, the court said, has become "a primary assembly point for First Amendment activity." In short, even our president must put up with protest and opposing views—even at the cost of sleep.

The suffragists made a point that we should be mindful of today and all the days that follow. We protect ourselves and our causes when we express ourselves and our convictions, not when we suppress the opinions of others. If others can be suppressed, so in the end may we be suppressed. We must learn this lesson on our campuses or risk unraveling our heritage on our campuses. And the campus is a place for learning.

Thank you for inviting me here today. It is always a delight to come to Ann Arbor. It is a special privilege to give a lecture that honors, and attempts to redress the wrong done to, three courageous university professors who asserted their rights in the McCarthy era and paid a heavy price. I salute Professors Chandler Davis, Clement Markert, and the late Mark Nickerson, whose life was remarkable and inspiring. I salute the University of Michigan for a greatness that includes trying to right its wrongs. I thank you, the audience, for listening. Thank you.

WORK CITED

Myrdal, Gunnar. *An American Dilemma, Twentieth Anniversary Edition*, 910. New York: Harper & Row, 1962.

Money and Academic Freedom
a Half-Century after McCarthyism:
Universities amid the Force Fields of Capital
David A. Hollinger

In 1971 Lewis Powell, then a prominent lawyer in Richmond, Virginia, not yet nominated by President Nixon for the Supreme Court, outlined a plan for neutralizing liberal and radical professors without running afoul of the academic freedom of individual faculty. The plan involved the use of money and corporate connections. Powell's memorandum of 1971, to the details of which I will turn in a moment, is of interest today as an emblem for how the location of the issue of the political autonomy of universities has changed during the half-century since the McCarthy era. Back then, the issue was highly visible in the domain of public doctrine, where political ideas are policed by state power. Faculty were purged for holding the wrong views, for being unwilling to declare their opinions, and for refusing to sign loyalty oaths. Now, the question of the political autonomy of universities is the most visible elsewhere: in the force fields of capital, where profit functions like gravity, where knowledge takes the form of property, where human energy is converted into money, and where values dance to the sound of markets. It is in that dynamic and multilayered space that we may lose what political autonomy universities have managed to achieve and maintain.

Before I turn to the instructive details of the Powell memorandum, I want briefly to remind us of a combination of circumstances that render the political autonomy of universities worth worrying about and why it is thus necessary for us to locate the question as precisely as we can. Universities have become more and more central to the social, cultural, and economic life of the United States, yielding increased pressures to reduce universities to inventories of instruments for this or that interest. Faculties, in the meantime, have become less able to agree on what ethos identifies the university, yielding a diminished capacity to justify to the public the rights and privileges of faculties. Each of these two circumstances—an institution expected to do more and more for society, and a faculty less and less confident about any common purpose—has its own sources. But the two are caught up with each other dialectically. The more tasks that the society persuades or forces universities to accept, the more of a challenge it is for faculties to constitute themselves as a distinctive solidarity. The less able professors are to act together, the more they tend to identify themselves with the constituencies beyond campus—professional, ethnoracial, economic, and political—eager to exploit the university as a tool. This dialectic facilitates the parceling out of the university into a series of relationships between specific segments of the university on the one hand and congruent, specific segments of society on the other.

This dialectic is not new. But it is now intensifying. And it may be unstoppable. It is not clear how many people care about stopping it. Universities with the structure and functions we take for granted are the products of a particular historical moment long since gone. They came into being during the forty years after the Civil War and were adapted gradually over the course of the century just ended. These institutions may be replaced in our new century by a series of new institutions carrying out this or that function currently assigned to universities. Among the apparent harbingers of this future are the transfer of more and more undergraduate instruction into the hands of temporary and part-time faculty, the rise of "virtual universities," the increasing quality and quantity of research carried out in industrial laboratories, the legal and technical capacity of private corporations to create knowledge that belongs only to them, the willingness of some university leaders to undercut the peer review process by lobbying directly with Congress for research grants, and the pressures for profiteering placed on campus administrators by the terms of the Bayh-Dole Act. The whole problem of the political autonomy of universities may disappear, because there will be nothing to be autonomous about.

Perhaps a suspicion to this effect explains a certain timidity in today's efforts to defend universities? Perhaps a sense of inevitability is behind the fact that today's critical discussion of higher education includes no book remotely comparable to Clark Kerr's *The Uses of the*

University, which thirty-seven years ago, amid the era of the American university's most prodigious growth, tried to explain in a spirit of confidence and hope what a knowledge-centered institution could do for a democratic society. Whatever one may think of this book, it was not timid. And it really did defend, in terms that made sense at the time, quality higher education for a large public.

Yet universities have virtues that are not yet apparent in the institutions poised to take their place. The effective defense of universities requires political will and a certain amount of solidarity across disciplines and schools. That will and that solidarity seem to me to be in shorter supply now than fifty years ago. Faculty senates were not united in opposition to McCarthyism, but they displayed a degree of unity and an extent of common purpose that is hard to find today. But the challenges of the McCarthy era were radically different from those of our own time. Just how different we can begin to see when we examine the Powell memorandum and its aftermath.

The Powell memorandum originated when a Richmond neighbor and friend of Powell's, an officer of the National Chamber of Commerce, asked Powell's advice on what might be an appropriate agenda for the educational committee of the Chamber.[1] Powell's response was entitled "Attack on American Free Enterprise System," and it summarized this "attack" as including the activities of Ralph Nader and of the people who were bombing banks, all of whom Powell linked to the teachings of such university professors as the University of California at San Diego philosopher Herbert Marcuse. In dealing with this "attack," Powell suggested that *big business*—a term he used in a matter-of-fact way, without irony—finance and direct a comprehensive program of cultural reform designed especially to diminish the influence of liberal and radical university professors. The "imbalance" toward the left found within college and university faculties was, Powell asserted, "the most fundamental problem" facing defenders of the free enterprise system. That Powell believed this—that he believed in the enormous cultural authority of universities and that it was on the political orientation of these institutions that the future of the nation might turn—is itself an interesting feature of his memorandum.

I sometimes wish one of Powell's more sophisticated billionaire friends would have explained to him a basic deal that the journalist Joe Queenan has described. Queenan points out that the way the world works is this:

Leftist intellectuals with hare-brained Marxist ideas get to control Stanford, MIT, Yale, and the American Studies department at the University of Vermont. In return, the right gets IBM, Honeywell, Disney World, and the New York Stock Exchange. Leftist academics get to try out their stupid ideas on impressionable youths between 17 and 21 who don't have any money or power. The right gets to try out its ideas on North America, South America, Europe, Asia, Australia, and parts of Africa, most of which take Mastercard. The left gets Harvard, Oberlin, Twyla Tharp's dance company, and Madison, Wisconsin. The right gets NASDAQ, Boeing, General Motors, Apple, McDonnell Douglas, Washington D.C., Citicorp, Texas, Coca-Cola, General Electric, Japan, and outer space.

This, adds Queenen, "seems like a fair arrangement."[2] But Powell, being unaware that this deal had been struck, proceeded to outline for the chamber a number of specific measures. All of these measures involved the calculated use of the money and connections of leading corporations. Among Powell's proposals were the following, although Powell does not present them in quite the same order: First, big business should find ways to provide sustained financial support outside the academy for social science and humanities scholars with sound views. This was a crucial initiative, because these scholars would then enjoy a base independent from the committees that controlled hiring and promotion in the universities and from the academically dominated review panels that greatly influenced the dispensing of grant money in the then-existing public and private agencies. Second, big business should establish a network of popular speakers and media personalities who could effectively popularize the ideas developed by the scholars. These publicists would write for newspapers and magazines, and, above all, would appear on television, keeping before the public the National Chamber's perspective on issues of public policy. Third, big business should lobby trustees and administrators at colleges and universities concerning the political "imbalance" of their faculties, hoping gradually to see more and more conservative intellectuals integrated into these faculties. Fourth, big business should urge campus schools of business administration to broaden their curriculum and their role in campus life. Business schools might even offer their own range of courses to compete with those offered by departments of political science, sociology, and history. This initiative would counteract the exclusive claims to academic expertise made by the liberal-dominated social science departments.

Powell's program included several additional features, beyond these four. It called for the careful supervision of the writing of textbooks and of the processes of their adoption by school boards and administrators. It called for the strict monitoring by the National Chamber of the political content of television programs and urged that a steady drum beat of complaints be sent to the television networks and to the Federal Communications Commission objecting to the liberal bias of most television programs. It called for an ideological repositioning of popular magazines, including specifically *Atlantic Monthly, Life,* and *Reader's Digest,* so that editors would publish more articles supportive of the "American way of life." Powell said something should be done about the selection of books on display in corner newsstands and in airports and in drugstores. Too many of the books easily found there were written by such authors as the Black Panther Eldridge Cleaver and the radical Yale law professor Charles Reich, whose *The Greening of America,* long since forgotten, was extravagantly admired and worried about in 1971. In place of such nefarious books, Powell wanted to see prominently on display books written by defenders of the system. But the core of Powell's program related to universities.

Powell's program differed instructively from the best known of earlier efforts to bring under control the apparently subversive influence of professors. Powell was not advocating a ferreting-out campaign, by which any individuals would be targeted for investigation or firing, no matter how repugnant the National Chamber might find their views. Powell did refer to Communists, and he still accepted at face value, and with sincere alarm, the Federal Bureau of Investigation's (FBI's) annual list of what it termed Communist speakers on American campuses. But Powell sketched an approach altogether different from that of red hunters back in the 1940s and 1950s. At no time, even when ranting against the hated and notorious Marcuse, did Powell perpetuate the McCarthyite tradition of calling for the termination of faculty whose ideas Powell found subversive. Even when linking the teachings of campus social scientists and philosophers to the bombings of banks—thirty-nine violent attacks on branches of the Bank of America had been made in the last year and half, Powell reminded the

Chamber—Powell never suggested that any action be taken against Marcuse and his kind personally.

Powell's goals, strategy, and tactics were all more sophisticated than those of the McCarthyites. Powell proposed to work through private rather than public channels. And it was no quick fix; it would take many years, Powell said, and it required discipline and patience. It was not a project for "the fainthearted," he warned explicitly. Powell advocated quiet, long-term, carefully planned—dare I use the word *conspiracy?*—to bring about the neutralization of the academic forces he opposed. And, although Powell's program depended on money and position, it was still a strategy more of persuasion than of brute force. To use language Powell did not employ but that I believe captures the relevant distinction, Powell proposed to operate more in the realm of discursive power than in that of juridical power. The goal was to shift the intellectual center of gravity in the social sciences and the humanities, where the curriculum and the content of knowledge had potential relevance to politics. That is where the money and the connections were to be deployed. A crucial aspect of the Powell memorandum, then, is that it assumes that what really matters about professors is their professional intellectual work, not their personal political activities. At no time does Powell even mention the physical or biological sciences or engineering. Back in the McCarthy era, at issue were generally the activities and rights of individual professors, whether their fields had obvious political relevance or not. The Board of Regents of the University of California imposed the loyalty oath on everyone. Powell was not worried about the mechanical engineering professor who had been slow to leave the Communist Party, or the physicist who was friendly with Soviet colleagues, or the chemist who refused on principle to declare his loyalty to the United States.

Powell had a take on academic freedom very different from that of the un-American activities committees of old. Those committees often sneered at the very idea of academic freedom and implied or even asserted that the chief function of academic freedom was to protect scoundrels from justice. In a famous session of the House Un-American Activities Committee (HUAC) in 1953, the counsel for HUAC badgered the University of Chicago historian Daniel J. Boorstin, later destined to become librarian of Congress, into a humiliating reassurance that the academic freedom of Boorstin and other witnesses had been infringed in no way by HUAC's investigations of communism on campuses. Powell, by contrast, warned that for big business to attack the principle of academic freedom would be "fatal" to the program of action Powell was advocating. "Few things are more sanctified in American life than academic freedom," he warned. The chamber could act to advance greater "openness," "fairness," and "balance," ideals that were, he observed, fully consistent with academic freedom.

Indeed, Powell was so concerned about the matter of academic freedom that, even within the presumed privacy of this communication to members of his own tribe, he returned to it repeatedly. When talking about the textbook aspect of his program he said that what he had in mind was "not an intrusion upon" academic freedom but "an aide to it." He took a frankly interest-group approach to academic freedom, asserting that "civil rights" organizations had "insisted" on "rewriting many . . . textbooks" and that labor unions, too, had lobbied for textbooks fair to organized labor. It was time for big business to do the same, Powell said. Again, when asking that university trustees and presidents be lobbied to change the political orientation of faculties, Powell told his confidants that this was a delicate project that would backfire if done crudely; he asked that big business work discreetly through alumni groups and trustees to "strengthen" academic freedom by ensuring balance on faculties.

It is important to note that Powell was not asking universities to be disinterested or objective. Powell saw professors as advocates. The problem was that they were advocating the wrong things. Powell's talk about "balance" aimed to put strong conservative voices up against liberal and radical advocates. Powell's objection to Marcuse was not that Marcuse was unprofessional but that Marcuse was advocating the wrong cause.

A few minutes ago I applied to Powell's analysis of the political function of scholarship the Foucaultian distinction between discursive and juridical power, thereby inviting us to see how we might assimilate Powell's thinking into our own conversation about power/knowledge. I want now to call attention to a silence within Powell's memorandum that invites a similar translation. The silence to which I refer is the absence, anywhere in his document, of any sense that universities might have a function other than to support or to undermine a given regime. Powell takes for granted that the university is a set of instruments for interests outside the university. Powell does not employ the terms *oppositional* or *hegemonic* and *counter-*

hegemonic, but his memo treats the university purely and simply as an instrument of what many people would colloquially call hegemonic or counterhegemonic forces. Powell seems to have achieved this view of the world without the help of Marx or Gramsci or Foucault. Powell's silence is far from peculiar to him. I do not want to make Powell sound more like "one of us" than he truly was, but I believe it is fair to say that within the academy during the past few decades there has been a widespread reluctance to assign to universities a positive cultural function unique to them rather than merely in the service of one set or another of economic, ethnoracial, technological, or political interests. This reluctance is often covered by a certain toughness of posture, an unwillingness to appear too idealistic about higher education, a worldly acceptance of the status of the university as a bundle of outcomes rather than as an agent in its own right.

Such studied realism is easy to understand and has much to recommend it. The truths that support this realism are accessible even to the simplest of minds. But the people who built modern universities in the late nineteenth and early twentieth centuries saw beyond these obvious truths. Had those academic pioneers succumbed to this easy realism, had they been incapable of a robust, risk-taking idealism, had they been unwilling to proclaim the university to be an independent cultural agent, they would not have been able to put in place the chief ideological defenses of universities on which we still rely. Universities would not then have achieved the measure of autonomy that they did manage to achieve. One need not romanticize the past or ignore the political and economic matrix of the early growth of American higher education to recognize that a signal accomplishment of the generation of Daniel Coit Gilman, Charles W. Eliot, Andrew Dickson White, and William Rainey Harper is the enormous amount of unrestricted money they obtained for building universities.

Private donors and state legislators were to be persuaded that universities knew what they were doing and could be trusted with money. The builders of American universities, whether public or private, made a great production of the distinctive character of their institutions and of the necessity of letting them chart much of their own future in relation to notions of the society's interests that these academic leaders worked hard to formulate in their own terms. We now find naive and fatuous many of their formulations, and we hasten to distance ourselves from their cloying, Victorian conceits. But their project of maximum autonomy was perpetuated and critically revised by the somewhat less embarrassing Arthur O. Lovejoy and John Dewey and the other professors who founded the American Association of University Professors (AAUP) in 1915, rendering universities yet more autonomous by limiting the discretion through the exercise of which administrators could capitulate to outside political pressures. Without all this, universities would not have come into possession of a tradition of academic freedom strong enough to affect the strategies of people such as Lewis Powell.

Powell outlined a program to which academic freedom's defense of individual faculty rights spoke hardly at all. Money did pour in to conservative think tanks. Television punditry has changed; we have moved from the solitary and ostensibly consensual Eric Sevareid to a pluralistic screen on which we can always expect to see either William Bennett or William Kristol. Some business schools have pursued joint appointments, yielding more and more professors of political science and economics and law and sociology who are also fractionally appointed in schools of business and thus protected by the system of remuneration and peer review maintained by schools of business. Complaints that social scientific and humanities faculties were skewed to the left, that these faculties were not genuinely open to conservative ideas and were unfair in their assessment of conservative job candidates? Such complaints became routine, culminating in the furor over "political correctness." Centers and institutes designed to circumvent if not to discredit the university-based disciplinary establishments? The Olin Foundation, the Manhattan Institute, the Heritage Foundation, the Witherspoon Foundation, and the Free Press are among the organizations often associated with such efforts. None of this just happened. A merit of the Powell memorandum is that it constitutes evidence of how clear and calculating was some of the thought behind this campaign.

But it would be absurd to attribute this campaign to Powell personally. He was not the only one thinking along these lines. The columnist Jack Anderson soon made Powell's memorandum public, in any case, after Nixon nominated Powell for the Supreme Court. The National Chamber itself then published the document in its own house organ. It would be equally absurd, and I now enter a second disclaimer made necessary by my breezy use of the Powell memorandum, to imply that everything in universities that Powell disliked should be defended just because Powell disliked it. Some would even insist that the real threat to academia's autonomy has not been big business but faculty colleagues whose persistent foolishness rendered universities more vulnerable in a political environment to which these colleagues were irresponsibly oblivious. Another disclaimer: the social science and humanities departments of our universities have not exactly folded under the pressure of the program outlined by Powell. Although the charges of political correctness have done some real damage to the standing of universities with the public, I do not see much evidence that hiring committees have compromised their judgments about what counts as excellent scholarship to bring more conservatives into departments of English, philosophy, and sociology. Whatever the lobbyists of big business may have accomplished through their pressure on universities, one goal that seems to have eluded them is diminishing the power of disciplinary peer review in the hiring process.

Yet the Powell memorandum is at least an artifact of the migration of the question of the political autonomy of universities. Once visible chiefly in the juridical space where the political ideas and conduct of individuals are policed by the state but are protected by classical academic freedom doctrine, the question is now the most importantly located where Powell was more comfortable with it: in the company of money, in relatively unregulated economic space, where classical academic freedom doctrine is less relevant. There, economic incentives and disincentives for certain kinds of work are presented to individual faculty, to research groups, to departments, to entire schools, and to whole campuses. And anyone who has had the slightest contact with the fund-raising aspects of universities today knows that plenty of people with money are thinking about just what can be done with these incentives and disincentives.

Academic priorities have always been set in economic contexts and no doubt always will be. When I invoke the generation of Daniel Coit Gilman and Andrew Dickson White and William Rainey Harper and refer to the relative lack of restrictions on the funds they obtained from Johns Hopkins and Ezra Cornell and John D. Rockefeller and other industrialists, I certainly do not mean that all that went on in an economic vacuum. It is a matter of degree. At issue is the authority exercised by universities as corporate entities in responding to economic contingencies and the principles that govern the exercise of that authority. Can universities maintain a value system in some tension with the value system of the commercial marketplace? How much tension? I do not know exactly how this tension should be managed, and I will not pretend to have worked out much of a program to deal with the challenges to which I am here calling attention. But I am convinced of at least two things: I am convinced that the bulk of today's academic leadership is not thinking systematically about this issue and is going with the flow. And I am convinced that one place to observe this tension between academia's value system and that of the commercial marketplace of the surrounding society is the salary policy of universities.

I focus on salary policy because this happens to be an arena in which we can view, relatively unobstructed, the operation of academic corporate authority in relation to the commercial marketplace. And in salary policy we find compelling evidence that the gap is closing between what universities value and what is valued in the commercial marketplace.

Faculty salaries in the United States have never been as uniform as they remain even today in many of the European universities, where the government often sets a flat rate for everyone. Modest salary differentials are part of the tradition in the United States. But the tradition also includes what we might call "medical school exceptionalism." Medical school salaries have been much higher on the grounds of "opportunity costs." Higher salaries were needed to attract men and women who could be out there healing the sick and billing for their services. Certain other highly paid professions created similar conditions. Exceptionalism spread to law schools. Yet the University of California long resisted law school exceptionalism in the name of cross-campus equity and did not formally adopt a special scale for law until 1969. Engineering and business followed suit. The University of California's special scale for Schools of Engineering and Business was phased in during the early 1980s, giving de jure status to salary differentials by school that had long since been de facto.

In our present historical moment, as confidence in the university as a distinctive workplace declines and as the university increasingly appears to be merely a site for careers defined in other arenas, the argument for salary equity across departments and school loses the force it once had. If some biologists in science departments are doing work similar to that done in medical schools, some ask, why not extend medical school exceptionalism to biology? A vivid index of the decline of faculty solidarity is the willingness of universities nationally to tolerate increasing salary differentials by field for faculty of equal merit as judged by peer review within each field. I am not talking about the pros and cons of the star system. I am talking about institutional decisions to take entire fields and pay a lot more money to people in those fields than to colleagues of comparable stature in other fields.

I am going to cite some figures from a survey of salaries in effect during the 1998–99 academic year at Harvard, Yale, Princeton, Columbia, Massachusetts Institute of Technology, Stanford, and California Institute of Technology. I selected these seven because I found that they were the ones with whom my own campus, Berkeley, was most often forced to compete for our best faculty. The average salary for full professors of economics at those universities—taken together—was revealed to be $122,000. This figure does not count summer ninths and research accounts. Nor, of course, does this figure include consulting fees and other forms of private remuneration that depend to some extent on the standing one enjoys as a result of holding a professorship at a prestigious university. The average full professor's salary in the same institutions for faculty of the same age and career stage was $104,000 in the basic science disciplines and $98,000 in the humanities.

Part of the significance of these last two figures is that humanities professors, generally paid the lowest salaries, have remained fairly close to their comparably distinguished colleagues in mathematics and physics and chemistry at the most prestigious of the research universities. The gap is considerably greater at universities of lesser prestige. The general rule is that the less stature the institution has by prevailing indicators, the greater the gap between the sciences and the humanities in basic salary. Also, the summer ninths common in the sciences and rare in the humanities render the comparison somewhat misleading. But the gap between scientists and humanists on the one hand and economics on the other is enormous. A greater gap separates business administration from everyone else in the same survey: business professors logged in at $144,000. At the level of an entering assistant professor, moreover, it is not uncommon for a recruit in business administration to be offered a salary of $100,000, while a comparably qualified recruit in mathematics or history will be offered a salary of $45,000 or even less. New assistant professors of economics, too, are often hired at salaries twice that of comparably qualified entry-level colleagues in English, psychology, philosophy, or anthropology. The same pattern applies to the salaries of deans. Those heading commercially relevant professional schools, such as law and business, are paid much more than deans of arts and sciences.

A consistent pattern is that faculty whose academic skills are of the sort that enable them to make the most money on the side, without resigning their professorships, are also the people to whom universities are willing to pay the highest salaries. This tendency is becoming more pronounced each year. It is seen in the remarkable escalation of salaries in the fields of economics, business administration, law, biotechnology, and computer science. At the same time, those faculty whose careers are the most fully centered in universities, and who have the least opportunity to generate private income through consulting and other outside activities, are the ones to whom universities pay the least. A young economist only a few years beyond the Ph.D. who has published but a handful of papers may be awarded a higher annual salary than a distinguished midcareer mathematician who has won the Field Medal or than a senior humanist who has served as poet laureate of the United States. A garden-variety professor in several of the professional schools can expect to receive two summer ninths every year as a matter of course, whereas some of the most accomplished professors of German literature or of art history may go twenty years with only an occasional summer ninth, and then usually for performing a time-consuming service. The same pattern extends even to staff support. Campuses frequently tolerate extraordinary variations, yielding much higher levels of staff support in certain professional schools able to raise the money and in grant-oriented science units. Overhead is not distributed equally but tends to go to those who, as they say, "earn" it. The pattern is rendered all the more problematic when student enrollment figures are taken into account. The faculty groups paid the most have the smallest number of students. Schools of business and law are dramatic examples of the combination of low faculty-student ratios and exceptionally high salaries.

What happens, then, is this: *universities pay the most money to faculty whose careers are the least defined by the research and teaching mission of universities and pay the least money to those faculty whose careers are the most fully defined by the universities' research and teaching missions.* This is the reality that I wish more of our academic leaders would confront and address. What presidents and provosts generally prefer to do is to fall into old routines about the differences between the sciences and the humanities, which is not at issue. By diverting us into that old science-versus-humanities conversation what solidarity faculties may retain gets diminished all the more. Presidents and provosts need to be forthright about the centrality of basic science, humanities, and social science to universities and to guard against the further fragmentation of this arts-and-science core.

To be sure, no single campus, no matter how fearless its president and its deans, can fight this battle alone. The pattern is national. Any individual university that tries to go against the trend will lose out to universities willing to revise their salary policies in the direction of the nonacademic marketplace. But national academic leaders find this matter beyond their control, too. I have talked with a number of university presidents about this problem, and I see little evidence that anything is being done about it.

"Opportunity costs" are instantly cited, and to "ignore" them is to be "naive." Yet it is interesting to contemplate what might happen if our leaders formed a cabal. Perhaps Lee Bollinger and Harold Shapiro and Robert Berdahl and Neil Rudenstine and a number of other presidents could come to a friendly agreement. Sherman Anti-Trust Act be damned! If the airlines can do it, why not our Lee and Harold? Our captains of the academic industry might promise each other that none of their institutions would pay economists more than a certain dollar amount. If Texas Tech University will not join in the agreement, some of our leading economists can ponder the prospects of a move to Lubbock.

I hope our colleagues in economics and at Texas Tech can forgive this bit of levity, but it remains to be seen whether universities will prove able to define themselves as a sufficiently corporate entity to defend more than a shred of the old tradition of salary equity. According to that tradition, being on a faculty, rather than being part of a transacademic profession, is the primary context in which merit judgments are translated into dollars. Faculties themselves are honestly divided about salary policy. Some regard as anachronistic the very idea that academia is so distinctive a realm. These colleagues doubt that a university is marked off sufficiently from Dow Chemical or Bell Laboratories or Price Waterhouse or Cravath Swain or the *Washington Post* to justify the reluctance of campuses to move yet further toward matching industrial salary offers. I have heard more than one professional school dean at Berkeley observe that academic salaries are not high enough to bring on to our faculty those experienced practitioners whose ability to instruct students in the workaday profession makes their hiring a priority for their school. The students want to learn not from someone who "has only studied it," these deans report, but from someone who has "really done it." The striking implication here is that the line between the professional school and the profession should be even less sharp than it now is and that location in a university is only a minor part of professional training.

If salary policy affords a relatively unobstructed view of the gradual acceptance by universities of the values of the commercial marketplace, we at least know, as a result of what we see there, what to look for when we scrutinize research policy. I am not going to say much about research policy because this topic is already generating a reasonable amount of critical discussion. The *Atlantic* recently carried an extensive discussion of it. I recommend "The Kept University," by Eyal Press and Jennifer Washburn,[3] but I find it significant that the lead for discussing these matters publicly is more often taken by journalists than by academic administrators. This supports my sense that the people with the most institutionalized responsibility for identifying and dealing with major crises in academia are not as engaged as they should be.[4]

Yet when dealing with research policy, as opposed to salary policy, it is not always easy to agree on what counts as evidence of our autonomy. This difficulty is seen even in so well studied an aspect of recent academic history as federal funding of academic research during the cold war. Universities accepted billions upon billions of federal dollars given in the name of national defense, but universities were far from passive. Rebecca S. Lowen's *Creating the Cold War University,* a recent book about Stanford, shows that university officials acted consciously and systematically to take advantage of federal dollars.[5] One cannot say that Stanford failed to exercise authority as a corporate entity. Although Lowen argues that defense money turned Stanford in certain directions and away from others, some observers would insist that provosts and deans at Stanford, Harvard, Berkeley, and elsewhere took wise advantage of the National Defense Education Act and other opportunities to build programs in science and in foreign languages that were academically warranted and demand no apology. Had academic leaders not made such skillful use of federal defense dollars, the argument might proceed, universities would not have been powerful enough to worry Powell in 1971.

For all the similarities between private and federal funding of university research, there is one important difference, however, that, at the risk of belaboring the obvious, can be underscored here. The aims behind federally funded research, and the various guidelines that attend upon federal grants, have been decided on through a political process that has at least some connection to democracy and to the public interest. Insofar as universities are operating in the public interest, as I believe they should, and insofar as universities must respect the decisions of democratically elected representatives of the public, as I believe they must, the priorities embedded in federal dollars are *in principle* less at odds with the mission of universities than are the priorities embedded in dollars provided by profit-seeking corporations. This is not to deny that massive federal support of certain kinds of research and not others may have greater overall influence on the direction of universities than private funding, nor is it to deny that federal funding is often guided by the priorities of powerful private interests in the society. It is only to call attention to a principle that renders vigilance about private funding all the more important on the grounds of basic democratic theory. Hence a ratcheting up of vigilance on behalf of free inquiry and the public interest is justified at this historical moment, when private capital is positioned to play a greater role than ever in determining the future of universities. Public universities, especially, are at risk of being significantly transformed by the combination of diminished state support for "elite" academic programs and increased dependence on private donors.

The vigilance to which I refer is potentially divisive. Indeed, any effort to confront directly the question of the political autonomy of universities at this time will take place within the dialectic to which I referred at the outset. The more extensive, dispersed, and particularistic become the interests to which we are asked to respond, the more problematic becomes our inability to state clearly to ourselves and to the public what we are; the less able we are to act in concert and to defend ourselves as a corporate entity, the more we risk falling into random and ad hoc responses to the economic incentives and disincentives that surround us.

The development of a coherent and compelling vindication of universities will not go very far toward meeting the challenge of political autonomy in our time. It is only a start. Yet this modest step is not being taken. I am not persuaded that universities are being defended as well as they might be. Most administrative leadership, by focusing narrowly on the economic contributions universities make to localities, regions, states, and the nation, gives away too much. We thus invite the narrowing of the criteria by which universities are held accountable and we encourage the economic beneficiaries of universities to exercise greater control over their shape and orientation. This problem is especially acute in public universities.

While most university presidents run on about the contributions universities make to the economy, the modest project of clarifying the character and role of the university for the public has been inhibited by the humanities parochialism that dominates public discussion of higher education by professors. Professors are doing very little to right the balance. Indeed, one savant after another taking stock of academia turns out to pay no attention whatsoever to the physical and biological sciences, to say nothing of the professional schools. This makes it all the easier for presidents and provosts to ignore the ranting of humanists as the naive effusion of people who have no understanding of the political economy of science. David Damrosch's *We Scholars,* Zachary Karabell's *What Is College For?*, Bill Readings's *The University in Ruins,* and a steady stream of essays in *Critical Inquiry* and other learned quarterlies all treat universities as if they consisted mainly of English departments.[6] Even when the role of literary studies is indicated as the specific topic of discussion, the argument is usually expressed in terms of a diagnosis of and prescription for the university as a whole. What's good for English is assumed to be good for all. If English professors doubt something, then no one in the world has any business taking it seriously. The ignorance of American humanists about the circumstances under which their colleagues in molecular biology and chemical engineering work is appalling and makes it exceedingly difficult to expect that colleagues in the natural sciences will make common cause with humanists in defense of their shared interests in the autonomy of the universities.

This humanities parochialism is manifest in the current enthusiasm for a university "based on dissensus." Eschewing "the search for consensus" as impossible in the wake of multicultural insights into the world's diversity and postmodern insights into the relativity of knowledge, some of our humanists call for a "community of dissensus" devoted to the presentation of "irreconcilable" and "mutually opaque goods." The very ideal of knowledge would be downplayed in favor of the ideal of respect, declares J. Hillis Miller, arguing, ostensibly, on the basis of a global outlook critical of American nationalism and Western imperialism. The mission of the new university would be to respect difference and to use the reality of difference to resist the "totalizing forces" of technology and the global capitalist economy. There appears to be nothing frivolous in Miller's abandonment of the whole idea that better knowledge about the world might enable us to cope with it more effectively. Yet there is something suspect, if not downright phony, about a call for a new consensus around the ideal of dissensus. The shared understanding of the evidence and reasoning by which dissensus should be preferred constitutes a consensus as demanding as any other. And I wonder how much attention we owe to discussants who betray no interest in what the ideal of dissensus would do to science departments, or even social science departments, and who, while urging us to build a university of dissensus, are capable of offering such bland and complacent afterthoughts as the following: "It is difficult to imagine," allows a pensive J. Hillis Miller, "how such a university would or should be organized, how it would be administered, who would decide how funds should be allotted, and how its accomplishments in teaching and research would be measured."[7]

Miller underestimates our capacity for agreeing on what counts as good scholarship and science, even in the social scientific and humanistic fields, where agreement is inevitably more elusive. By underestimating this capacity, Miller and his kind diminish a credibility with the public and with each other that we have a right to claim, and they ignore a basis for internal academic solidarity that we very much need. We often hear it said that disciplines and subdisciplines in the social sciences and the humanities have no effective standards for evaluating scholarship, that "anything goes," that internal intellectual conflicts mock as fraudulent the whole idea of scholarly consensus. These complaints miss the mark.

Three years of scrutinizing the reports of search committees and tenure committees and stacks of letters solicited for merit reviews at Berkeley[8] have led me to the conclusion that the old peer review system still works remarkably well for identifying intellectual excellence, even in disciplines and subdisciplines in which conflicts over basic theoretical questions are genuine and deep. This capacity for agreement about intellectual merit is masked, however, by real disagreements, and more often by uncertainties, about two other things: first, the intellectual direction in which a particular program should go, and, second, the extent to which academic decisions should respond to this or that social interest. Many of the most severely split votes in appointment and tenure cases, and many of the dossiers of outside letters displaying the greatest disparities in merit assessment, turn out on close scrutiny to reflect disagreements about these other questions.

Does a given scholar's direction suit a particular unit's current needs as well as those needs might be served by a scholar of equal merit who worked on something else? To what extent should the university use its hiring and promotion actions to help remedy the social prejudices that have resulted in the historic underrepresentation in the academy of certain groups of people? Given the severity of this or that social pathology, especially within one's state or region, how important is it that we have on our faculty people who study that pathology? Given the value to the campus of a certain private foundation's support, how important is it that this foundation's nonbinding expectations about a given faculty position or program be honored? Such questions, I am saying, are matters of frequent uncertainty and disagreement. Pretending to assess intellectual merit while actually responding to one or more of these other issues generates the impression that disciplines and subdisciplines are less functional than they are.

I do not want to exaggerate the distinction between questions about scholarly merit and questions about program direction and social responsibility. Being committed to the exploration of what the salient research community regards as "the right questions" is of course part of a merit evaluation. And I certainly do not want to present too positive a picture of the capacity of scholars to behave professionally. Accusing ourselves of collective bad faith, as Terry Eagleton recently observed, has become a mark of good character.[9] I would not want to be thought seriously deficient in that regard.

But distinguishing these two sorts of issues—the one about the intellectual merit of a scholar's work and the other about the role that universities should play in society—may even help us to engage more productively our disagreements about issues of the second variety. The most helpful engagement with these issues known to me is a book of 1996 entitled *The Future of Academic Freedom*, edited by Louis Menand. Most contributors to this book take for granted that the political autonomy of universities is the central foundation for academic freedom and that political autonomy depends on the credibility with which universities can represent themselves as something more than a set of instruments in the service of regimes and counterregimes defined outside academia. Edward Said, Thomas Haskell, Joan Scott, and other contributors predicate the political autonomy of universities on a distinctive ethical practice they attribute to scientists and scholars. This book may not be to our own time what Kerr's *The Uses of the University* was to its time, but so far as I am concerned it is the best thing going. I want to call attention to the essay of Edward Said because it is driven by a cosmopolitan preoccupation with the same diversities in modern life that led Reading, Miller, Francois Lyotard, and others to the ideal of "dissensus." Said, himself a professor of English, offers a bracing repudiation of humanities parochialism.

What defines the academic "calling," as Said describes it with unabashed idealism, is "the unending search for truth," which entails "a particular process of inquiry, discussion, and exchange" not exclusive to colleges and universities but not "encountered as regularly outside as inside the academy."[10] Said believes in plain talk about truth and knowledge. Now, Said does not need to be instructed that "truth" is a contested concept and that inquiry takes place within a matrix of power, but he will not yield the vocabulary of *veritas* to his enemies. Said is one of the anglophone world's most conspicuous and accomplished critics of the epistemic arrogance and cultural imperialism sometimes said to be indissoluably bound up with truth talk. Said, the scourge of "Orientalism" and of a host of Eurocentric conceits, and a formidable critic of models of knowledge that presuppose an eternally existing truth to which we can gain unmediated access, is determined to salvage from the discourse wars *a vocabulary with which the academy can communicate honestly with the public.*

But Said is less worried about the hermeneutic preciousness of his colleagues—always putting the word *truth* in quotation marks—than about the danger that some of them will relinquish valuable ideals, including academic freedom itself, because these ideals have been tainted when used to protect right wingers and racists and because these ideals have been invoked by Alan Bloom and by those who have lambasted the liberal arts academy for political correctness. Said, who can scarcely contain his contempt for Bloom, worries that defenders of diversity who share his disgust with Bloom will be so shortsighted as to yield the ideal of academic freedom to Bloom and his kind rather than to claim it for their own and be willing to struggle over its meaning.

And struggle Said is prepared to do, not only against the Alan Blooms of this world but also against other apostles of what he sees as narrowness, including, especially, those who make a production in an academic setting of their ethnoracial and national identities. "We should think of academic freedom," Said insists in the climactic passage of his essay, not as invitation to develop and indulge particularistic identities but "as an invitation to give up on" the identities that claim us outside the academy. Central to the culture of universities for Said is a commitment to truth as one's primary client and to a community of inquiry just as deep and wide as we can make it. Knowledge, insists Said, is not a function of the identities we bring to inquiry but is something for which we put such identities at *"risk."*[11] For Said, universities are agents of cosmopolitanism, and the foundation for faculty solidarity is a commitment to cosmopolitan ideals.

Now, Said is far from the first to associate universities with cosmopolitanism. Indeed, one of the arresting features of his formulation of cosmopolitanism is the ease with which it can be mapped on top of the classical ideology of science as developed by Charles Peirce during the era of the development of modern universities. Peirce emphasized the dependence of knowledge on imperfect communities of human knowers rather than on the properties of the world itself. Although Pierce was inspired by the physical sciences, the ethic of inquiry he proposed applied throughout the realm of belief, including what we now call the social sciences and humanities.[12]

Hence the intellectual viability and strategic appeal of Saidian cosmopolitanism as an academic ideology are enhanced by the ease with which it can be assimilated into a set of dispositions sanctioned by tradition within the academic world and across the lines that separate scientists from humanists. And cosmopolitanism is an ideal for universities that a substantial portion of the public—even, perhaps, a suspicious public—might actually understand and appreciate.[13] This hope may be vain, but Lewis Powell himself gives us at least slight reason to entertain it.

I invoke Powell near the end of this lecture because there is another incident in his career that involves academic freedom and the question of the political autonomy of universities and that even involves a hint of cosmopolitanism. In the *Bakke* case of 1978, Pow-

ell wrote an opinion that is generally credited with providing the constitutional foundation for affirmative action. Universities could take
ethnoracial categories into account among other considerations, wrote
Powell, in the interests of cultural diversity. It was the cosmopoli-
tanizing, deprovincializing functions of universities on which Powell's reasoning in the *Bakke* case was founded.

I want to call attention not only to the incipient cosmopolitanism
of Powell's call for campuses that displayed and explored a great range
of "ideas and mores" but also to Powell's simultaneous defense of the
political autonomy of universities. It is because of the principle of academic freedom, argued Powell, that universities must be left great lati-
tude to decide their own admissions policies. And if, in the context of
that autonomy, universities choose to promote cultural diversity, there
is no constitutional prohibition on their doing just that.

It may be ironic that the man who saved affirmative action in universities—for twenty years, at least—was the same Virginia lawyer
who seven years before had plotted for the political neutralization and
transformation of faculties. But Powell's two engagements with universities and academic freedom, whatever else we may learn from considering them together, can remind us of the complexity of our relationship with those who are skeptical about us and can remind us that
searching for common ground is not always a mistake.

NOTES

This lecture was first presented as the 1999 Davis, Markert, Nickerson Lec-
ture at the University of Michigan. The text published here is a revised version presented as part of my Merle Curti Lectures at the University of Wisconsin, March 2000, under the general title "Cosmopolitanism and
Solidarity." For helpful, critical suggestions I want to thank Steven N. Brint,
Carol J. Clover, John D'Arms, Catherine Gallagher, Carla Hesse, Joan Heifetz
Hollinger, Bruce Kuklick, J. W. Peltason, Mark Schwehn, and Harold T.
Shapiro. Some of these will be disappointed that I did not follow their advice
more fully than I have.

1. "The Powell Memorandum," *Washington Report* 11, no. 23 (October
23, 1972). This document is printed without page numbers. All of my quotations from the document are taken from this published version in *Washington Report*, which is a publication of the National Chamber of Commerce.
Powell's memorandum is dated August 23, 1971. I want to acknowledge that
I first learned of this document when it was called to my attention by
Michael Wald of the Stanford Law School.

2. Joe Queenan, *The Imperial Caddy: The Rise of Dan Quayle and the Decline and Fall of Practically Everything Else* (New York: Hyperion, 1992), 132–33.

3. Eyal Press and Jennifer Washburn, "The Kept University," *Atlantic,* March 2000, 39–54.

4. I am struck with the ruefully expressed concern of Robert M. Rosenzweig, recently retired after a distinguished tenure as president of the American Association of Universities (the organization of leading research universities in the United States) that many universities in the new rush for dollars may not be able to distinguish between what is central to their mission and what is marginal; see Rosenzweig, "What's for Sale These Days in Higher Education?" distributed by the Center for Studies in Higher Education, University of California, Berkeley, 1999.

5. Rebecca S. Lowen, *Creating the Cold War University: The Transformation of Stanford* (Berkeley and Los Angeles: University of California Press, 1997).

6. A refreshing exception, which appeared after this lecture had been revised for publication, is Masao Miyoshi, "Ivory Tower in Escrow," *boundary 2* 27 (spring 2000): 7–50. Miyoshi, a professor of literature, treats several of the salient issues in the political economy of higher education today differently than I do, but his article is one of the most comprehensive and honest confrontations of the salient issues written by a humanist. It deserves extensive discussion.

7. J. Hillis Miller, "Literary and Cultural Studies in the Transnational University," in *"Culture" and the Problem of the Disciplines,* edited by John Carlos Rowe (New York: Columbia University Press, 1998), 64–65.

8. I refer here to my service (1996–99) on the Berkeley campus's Committee on Budget and Interdepartmental Relations. The Berkeley Budget Committee, as it has been known informally since its creation in 1919, is unusual among American academia's personnel review committees for the extent to which it brings rank-and-file faculty into the routine governance of the university. The committee's nine members, who are appointed by the Academic Senate to rotating terms of three years each, advise the campus's administration not only on promotions and outside appointments but on all personnel actions, including salary raises, at all ranks in all schools and colleges. The committee meets regularly with the campus's senior administrative officers, with whom it generally maintains cordial and collegial working relations. The experience of chairing this committee 1998–99 made me aware of the challenges to American higher education today that I address in this lecture.

9. Terry Eagleton, "In the Gaudy Supermarket," *London Review of Books* 21 (May 13, 1999): 3. "Nothing is more voguish in the guilt-ridden US academia than to point to the bad faith of one's position. It is the nearest a Post-Modernist can come to authenticity."

10. Edward Said, "Identity, Authority, and Freedom: The Potentate and the Traveler," in *The Future of Academic Freedom,* edited by Louis Menand (Chicago: University of Chicago Press, 1996), 215.

11. Said, "Identity," 227.

12. *The Future of Academic Freedom* includes a helpful discussion of Peirce's relevant ideas; see Thomas L. Haskell, "Justifying the Rights of Academic Freedom in the Era of Power/Knowledge," 43–90.

13. The growth of the New Cosmopolitanism as a movement in American academia during the 1990s is an encouraging sign. For an excellent collection of essays representative of the movement, see Pheng Cheah and Bruce Robbins, eds., *Cosmopolitics: Thinking and Feeling beyond the Nation* (Minneapolis: University of Minnesota Press, 1998). This volume offers a much richer sense of the movement than the more widely noticed book revolving around a manifesto of the philosopher Martha Nussbaum, Joshua Cohen, ed., *For Love of Country: Debating the Limits of Patriotism* (Boston: Beacon Press, 1996). For an overview of this movement, see David A. Hollinger, "Reflections on the New Cosmopolitanism," *Constellations* (forthcoming).

Contributors

David Halberstam

David Halberstam is one of America's best-known authors. He graduated from Harvard in 1955 and spent the early days of the civil rights movement covering events for newspapers in Mississippi and Tennessee. During the 1960s he was a foreign correspondent for the *New York Times*. As a young reporter assigned to Saigon in 1962, he was part of a small group of journalists who refused to accept the official optimism of the American government. For that reporting he won the Pulitzer Prize for international reporting in 1964. His other awards include the Page One Award, Newspaper Guild of New York, 1962; the George Polk Memorial Award, Long Island University, 1963; the Louis M. Lyons Award, 1964; and the Overseas Press Club Award, 1973. Subjects he has tackled range from the Japanese auto industry to rowers competing to enter the Olympic Games. In 1986 he received the Political Book Award for *The Reckoning*. That book and two of his other books, *The Best and the Brightest* and *The Powers That Be*, have been described collectively as a trilogy on power in America.

He is the author of sixteen books of fiction and nonfiction and has contributed articles to magazines such as *Atlantic Monthly, Esquire, Harper's Bazaar,* and *McCall's*. He is the recipient of numerous honorary degrees including one from the University of Michigan in 2000. He is just completing his latest book, in which he uses Bosnia and Kosovo as a mirror of American policy and politics.

Peggie J. Hollingsworth

Since 1992 Peggie J. Hollingsworth has been president of the Academic Freedom Lecture Fund and was chairperson of the University of Michigan Senate and of the Senate Advisory Committee on University Affairs, the executive committee of the University Senate, during the 1990–91 academic year, when the Senate's Davis, Markert, Nickerson Lecture on Academic and Intellectual Freedom was established. She is a former member of the Primary Research Faculty at the University of Michigan. She received a B.S. in biology and chemistry from the University of Toledo, an M.A. in molecular biology from Bowling Green State University, and a Ph.D. in toxicology from the University of Michigan. She is the author of numerous articles in peer-reviewed journals, chapters in books, and abstracts in the proceedings of various national and international meetings and is coeditor of a series of monographs, including Lectures on Science Education, 1991–92, Lectures on Ethics and Science, 1992–93, and Science Education for the 21st Century. In 1992 and in 1994 she was a visiting scholar in the First Department of Pharmacology of the Hokkaido University Medical School.

In 1999–2000 Hollingsworth served as president of Sigma Xi, the Scientific Research Society, an international honor society composed of over 80,000 scientists and engineers. She is also a past president of the University of Michigan Chapter of Sigma Xi. She is a former member of the Alumni Society Board of Governors of the University of Michigan School of Public Health and of the Executive Committee of the Alumni Association Board of Trustees of Bowling Green State University. She is a founding member of the Coalition for the Advancement of Blacks in the Biomedical Sciences. In 1990 she was the recipient of the prestigious Academic Women's Caucus Sarah Goddard Power Award, given to women who have made outstanding contributions to better the status of women at the University of Michigan. She also received the University of Michigan President's Medallion in 1991, the University of Michigan Association of Black Professionals and Administrators High Achievement Award and the University of Michigan Alumni Association Special Appreciation Award in 1992, and the University of Michigan Distinguished Faculty Governance Award in 1994. For five years she served as a member of the Minority Programs Review Committee of the National Institute of General Medical Sciences.

Robert M. O'Neil

Robert M. O'Neil became founding director of the Thomas Jefferson Center for the Protection of Free Expression in August 1990, after serving five years as president of the University of Virginia. He continues as a member of the university's law faculty, teaching courses in constitutional law of free speech and church and state, First Amendment and the arts, and a new course entitled Free Speech in Cyberspace.

After serving as law clerk to U.S. Supreme Court Justice William J. Brennan Jr., O'Neil began his teaching career in 1963 at the University of California Law School at Berkeley, where he chaired the Academic Senate Committee on Academic Freedom.

His administrative career began as provost of the University of Cincinnati in the early 1970s. He was vice president of Indiana University for the Bloomington campus and later president of the statewide University of Wisconsin system before coming to Virginia. He taught law at each institution.

In 1990 he chaired the National Association of State Universities and Land-Grant Colleges, serving also on the executive committee of the Association of American Universities and the boards of the Carnegie Foundation for the Advancement of Teaching, the Educational Testing Service, and the Johnson Foundation.

He now serves as a trustee or director of the Commonwealth Fund, the Fort James Corporation, the Teachers Insurance and Annuity Association (TIAA), and the Media Institute. He is a member of the American Bar Association Conference Group of Lawyers and Media Representatives and the editorial board of the American Bar Association's *Human Rights Journal.*

In Virginia he serves as president of the Virginia Coalition for Open Government and as chairman of WVPT Public Television.

Until June 1999, he chaired Committee A (Academic Freedom and Tenure) of the American Association of University Professors, of which he was general counsel in 1970–72 and again in 1990–92.

He is the author of several books, including *Free Speech: Responsible Communication Under Law, The Rights of Public Employees* (2nd edition, 1993), *Classrooms in the Crossfire* (1981), and *Free Speech in the College Community* (1997), as well as many articles in law reviews and other journals.

A native of Boston, O'Neil holds three degrees from Harvard and honorary degrees from Beloit College and Indiana University. His wife, the former Karen Elson, is a secondary school English teacher and department chair at the St. Anne's Belfield School in Charlottesville. Their children are Elizabeth, a graduate of Duke and Stanford; Peter, a graduate of Berkeley; David, a graduate of Princeton and third-year student at Harvard Law School; and Benjamin, a fourth-year undergraduate at the University of Virginia.

Lee C. Bollinger

Lee C. Bollinger is president of the University of Michigan and a member of the faculty of the Law School. He is a graduate of the University of Oregon and Columbia Law School, where he was an articles editor of the *Law Review.* After serving as law clerk for Judge Wilfred Feinberg on the U.S. Court of Appeals for the Second Circuit and for Chief Justice Warren Burger on the U.S. Supreme Court, he joined the faculty of the University of Michigan Law School in 1973. In 1987 he was named the dean of the University of Michigan Law School, a position he held for seven years. He became provost of Dartmouth College and professor of government in July 1994 and was named the twelfth president of the University of Michigan in November 1996. His primary teaching and scholarly interests are focused on free speech and First Amendment issues, and he has published numerous books, articles, and essays in scholarly journals on these and other subjects. Two highly acclaimed contributions to First Amendment literature include *Images of a Free Press,* (1991), and *The Tolerant Society: Freedom of Speech and Extremist Speech in America,* (1986). He is a fellow of the American Academy of Arts and Sciences.

President Bollinger was born in Santa Rosa, California, and raised there and in Baker, Oregon. He is married to Jean Magnano Bollinger, who graduated from the University of Oregon and received a master's degree from Columbia University. She is an artist with studios in Vermont and Dexter, Michigan. They have two children—a son, Lee, a graduate of the University of California at Berkeley and the University of Michigan Law School; and a daughter, Carey, a graduate of Harvard University and presently a student at Columbia Law School.

Catharine R. Stimpson

Catharine R. Stimpson is university professor and dean of the Graduate School of Arts and Science at New York University. From January 1994 to October 1997 she served as director of the Fellows Program at the MacArthur Foundation in Chicago. Simultaneously, she was on leave from her position as university professor at Rutgers, the State University of New Jersey–New Brunswick, where, from 1986 to 1992, she was also dean of the Graduate School and vice provost for graduate education. Before going to Rutgers, she taught at Barnard College, where she was also the first director of its Women's Center. Now the editor of a book series for the University of Chicago Press, she was the founding editor of *Signs: Journal of Women in Culture and Society* from 1974 to 1980. The author of a novel, *Class Notes* (1979, 1980), and the editor of seven books, she has also published over 150 monographs, essays, stories, and reviews in such places as *Transatlantic Review, Nation, New York Times Book Review, Critical Inquiry,* and *boundary 2.* A selection of essays, *Where the Meanings Are,* appeared in 1988. Her book on Gertrude Stein is under contract to the University of Chicago Press. Professor Stimpson has lectured at approximately 350 institutions and events in the United States and abroad. Her public service has included the chairpersonships of the New York State Council for the Humanities, the National Council for Research on Women, and the *Ms. Magazine* Board of Scholars. In 1990, she was the president of the Modern Language Association. She is now the chair of the National Advisory Committee of the Woodrow Wilson National Fellowship Foundation and a member of the board of PBS and several educational institutions. As a member of the Editorial Group of *Change* magazine from 1992 to 1994, she wrote a regular column about education and culture.

Born in Bellingham, Washington, she was educated at Bryn Mawr College, Cambridge University, and Columbia University. She holds honorary degrees from Upsala College, Monmouth College, Bates College, Florida International University, the State University of New York at Albany, Hamilton College, the University of Arizona, Wheaton College, Hood College,

Union College, Holy Cross College, and Santa Clara University. She has also won Fulbright and Rockefeller Humanities Fellowships.

Walter P. Metzger

Walter P. Metzger has been a member of the Department of History of Columbia University since 1950 and is now an emeritus professor. He is the author of *Academic Freedom in the Age of the University*, the second in the two-volume *Development of Academic Freedom in the United States* (with Richard Hofstadter); "History of Academic Tenure in America" in *Faculty Tenure* (Commission on Academic Tenure); "The Academic Profession in the United States" in *The Academic Profession: National Settings* (Burton R. Clark, editor); coauthor of *Freedom and Order in the University* (with Paul Goodman and John Searle); and editor of a forty-volume Arno series on the academic profession in the West. He has also written extensively on the sociology of professions, academic freedom and tenure in the law, and a variety of topics on American intellectual and social history.

At various times, Professor Metzger has been a fellow at the Center for Advanced Study in the Behavioral Sciences, Palo Alto, California; a visiting scholar at Nuffield College, Oxford; and a director of or consultant to many foundations and public agencies, including the National Academy of Sciences, the Danforth Foundation, the Meyerson Commission, the National Endowment for the Humanities, and the National Institute for Mental Health.

He was elected fellow of the American Academy of Arts and Sciences in 1971, has served as a member of Committee A of the American Association of University Professors since 1957, and is currently at work on a history of the American academic profession.

Linda Ray Pratt

Linda Ray Pratt is a professor of English at the University of Nebraska–Lincoln and past president of the American Association of University Professors (AAUP). She received her B.A. from Florida Southern College and her M.A. and Ph.D. from Emory University. She joined the faculty of the University of Nebraska as an instructor in 1968 and became a professor of English in 1977. She has served as chair of the Department of English at Nebraska and is currently interim dean of the College of Arts and Sciences.

Professor Pratt has served as the chair of the Women's Caucus of the Midwest Modern Language Association (1986), chair of Committee G on the Status of Part-Time Faculty of the AAUP (1990–94), vice president of the AAUP (1990–92), president of the AAUP (1992–94), and member of the Executive Committee of Associations of Departments of English (ADE).

Her fields of expertise are Victorian and modern poetry and higher education. She is the recipient of a Distinguished Teaching Award from the University of Nebraska (1988), the Maud Hammond Fling Fellowship (1988), and the Faculty Development Fellowship (1980 and 1988). She has published numerous articles in *Academe* on topics of concern to the professoriat, including "Liberal Education and the Postmodern University" (1994).

She is the author of "Going Public: Political Discourse and the Faculty Voice," in *Critical Issues in Higher Education:* "On the Status of Non-Tenure Track Faculty," in *Academe;* "Disposable Faculty: Part-Time Exploitation as Management Strategy," in *Will Teach For Food: Academic Labor in Crisis;* and *Matthew Arnold Revisited.*

Avern Cohn

Judge Avern Cohn was born July 23, 1924, to Irwin I. and Sadie Levin Cohn. He attended the University of Michigan, John Tarleton Agricultural College, Stanford University, and Loyola School of Medicine. He served in the U.S Army from 1943 to 1946. He received his J.D. from the University of Michigan Law School in 1949. He was admitted to the Michigan State Bar in December 1949.

Judge Cohn engaged in private practice in the law office of Irwin I. Cohn from 1949 to 1961 and at Honigman, Miller, Schwartz and Cohn from 1961 to 1979. Judge Cohn held the following public positions: Michigan Social Welfare Commission, 1963; Michigan Civil Rights Commission, 1972–75 (chair 1974–75); and Detroit Board of Police Commissioners, 1975–79 (chair 1979).

Judge Cohn is a member of several bar associations, including the Detroit Bar Association, the State Bar of Michigan, the Federal Circuit Bar Association, the Federal Bar Association, and the American Bar Association. He was chairperson, Special Committee on Court Congestion, State Bar of Michigan, 1977–78; representative assembly, State Bar of Michigan, 1973–79; past trustee, Detroit Bar Association Foundation; past director, Detroit Bar Association; member, American Law Institute; and director, American Judicature Society.

Judge Cohn has been active in numerous organizations in political, secular, and Jewish life. He is a past president of the Jewish Welfare Federation of Metropolitan Detroit. He has three children and six grandchildren.

Judge Cohn was appointed Judge, U.S. District Court, Eastern District of Michigan, on October 9, 1979, by President Jimmy Carter.

Roger W. Wilkins

Roger W. Wilkins, since 1988 the Clarence J. Robinson Professor of History and American Culture at George Mason University in Fairfax, Virginia, and, since 1990 a network commentator for National Public Radio, is a distinguished author, scholar, and public servant.

During the Kennedy administration he served as assistant director of the U.S. Community Relations Service in the Department of Commerce (1964–66) and as a special assistant to the administrator of the Agency for International Development in the State Department (1962–64). In the Johnson administration, he served as an assistant attorney general (1966–69).

In a distinguished journalism career, he has written for the *New York Times* as a member of the editorial board and a columnist (1974–79), the *Washington Post* as a member of the editorial page staff (1972–74), and the *Washington Star* as associate editor (1980–81). He also has been a network radio commentator for CBS News (1980–83) and for the Mutual Broadcasting System (1983–88). While on the editorial staff of the *Washington Post*, he earned a Pulitzer Prize in 1972, which he shared with Woodward, Bernstein, and Herblock, for Watergate coverage. He is the author of numerous articles in scholarly journals and of a highly acclaimed autobiography, *A Man's Life* (1982); and with former U.S. Senator Fred R. Harris he edited *Quiet Riots: Race and Poverty in the United States.* His most recent book is *Jefferson's Pillow* (2000). In 1997 he delivered the seventh annual University of Michigan Senate's Davis, Markert, Nickerson Lecture on Academic and Intellectual Freedom.

Professor Wilkins received his A.B. in 1953 and his J.D. in 1956 from the University of Michigan. As president of the student chapter of the National Association for the Advancement of Colored People (NAACP) at the University of Michigan in the early 1950s, he personally petitioned the regents on behalf of the three professors who are honored by the University of Michigan Senate's Lecture on Academic and Intellectual Freedom. A past chairman of the Pulitzer Prize Board, he currently serves as chairman of the Board of Trustees of the African American Institute, chairman and publisher of the NAACP journal *Crisis,* and member of the board of the NAACP Legal Defense Fund.

Eugene L. Roberts Jr.

When he received an honorary doctor of laws degree from the University of Michigan at its 1997 spring commencement, Eugene L. Roberts Jr. was described as the "legendary dean of American newspaper editors, the recognized voice of journalism's universal core values: accuracy, balance, and courage." A 1954 graduate of the University of North Carolina, Eugene Roberts began his long and distinguished career in journalism as a farm reporter for the *Goldsboro New-Argus* and then as the city hall reporter for the *Norfolk Virginian-Pilot.* After several years as a labor writer and then the metropolitan editor for the *Detroit Free Press,* in 1965 he joined the staff of the *New York Times,* where he first headed that paper's coverage of the civil rights movement in the South and then served as its chief war correspondent in Vietnam.

In 1972 Roberts became the executive editor of the *Philadelphia Inquirer,* and in the subsequent eighteen years led that newspaper to national prominence and its staff to seventeen Pulitzer Prizes. In 1991 he became professor of journalism at the University of Maryland–College Park but took a leave of absence in 1994 to return to the *New York Times* as its managing editor. In 1998 he retired from the *New York Times* and returned to his professorship at Maryland. In 1998 he delivered the eighth annual University of Michigan Senate's Davis, Markert, Nickerson Lecture on Academic and Intellectual Freedom.

Eugene Roberts has received numerous awards, has delivered many named lectures, and has held many university-related appointments, professional appointments, and elected positions. He has edited or authored two books and has had his journalistic writings anthologized in six others. Among the awards he has received are the Columbia Journalism Award (1996), the Fourth Estate Award for Distinguished Contributions to Journalism (1993) from the National Press Club, the Distinguished Contributions to Journalism Award (1989), the Elijah Parish Lovejoy Award (1989), John Peter Zenger Award (1987), John S. Knight Award (1987), and William Allen White Award (1985), to name only a few. Among the many boards on which he serves or has served are the Advisory Board of the Academic Freedom Lecture Fund (1997 to present), the Board of Visitors for Nieman Fellowships at Harvard University (1996 to present), and the Executive Board (1986–91) and the Board of Visitors (1980 to present) of the University of Michigan Fellowships in Journalism.

David A. Hollinger

David A. Hollinger is Chancellor's Professor of History at the University of California at Berkeley. Prior to moving to Berkeley he was a professor of history at the University of Michigan (1977–92) and before that taught at the State University of New York at Buffalo (1969–77). Throughout his career he has been active in faculty governance. His most recent book is *Science, Jews, and Secular Culture: Studies in Mid-Twentieth Century American Intellectual History* (1996). His other books include *Postethnic America: Beyond Multiculturalism* (1995) and *In the American Province* (1985). During the past five years his articles have appeared in *Representations, Daedalus, Journal of American History, Public Historian, Diacritics, The Cambridge Companion to William James,* and *Constellations.* He has been a Guggenheim Fellow, Fellow of the Center for Advanced Study in the Behavioral Sciences, and a member of the Institute for Advanced Study. He has been elected Merle Curti Lecturer at the University of Wisconsin and Harmsworth Professor at the University of Oxford. He serves as a trustee of the National Humanities Center. In 1997 he was elected to the American Academy of Arts and Sciences.